Needle Nausea

Coping with Trypanophobia

Riley Miller

ISBN: 978-1-998557-75-2
Imprint: darkside.exe

Contents

Introduction **1**
The Fear of Needles 1

Chapter One: A Brief History of Needles **21**
The Ancient Origins of the Needle 21

Chapter Two: Understanding Trypanophobia **47**
The Anatomy and Physiology of Fear 47

Chapter Three: Early Childhood Experiences and Trypanophobia **67**
The Impact of Early Medical Experiences 67

Chapter Four: Coping Strategies for Trypanophobics **93**
Cognitive Behavioral Therapy 93

Chapter Five: Overcoming Trypanophobia in Adulthood **125**
Traumatic Experiences and Long-Term Impact 125
Chapter Six: Supporting Loved Ones with Trypanophobia 148

Chapter Six: Supporting Loved Ones with Trypanophobia **151**
Empathy and Understanding 151

Chapter Seven: The Future of Trypanophobia Research **181**
Neuroscience and Brain Imaging Studies 181

Index **207**

Introduction

The Fear of Needles

Overview of Trypanophobia

Trypanophobia, also known as needle phobia, is a specific phobia characterized by an intense and irrational fear of needles or medical procedures involving needles. It is estimated that up to 10

The fear of needles can manifest in various ways. Some individuals may experience a rapid heartbeat, sweating, dizziness, or even fainting at the sight or anticipation of a needle. Others may avoid medical procedures altogether, putting their health at risk. The fear of needles can also lead to increased anxiety and avoidance behaviors, which can interfere with routine medical check-ups or necessary treatments.

1.1.1.1 The Fear Response and Its Effects on the Body

When confronted with a phobic object or situation, the body responds with a natural stress response known as the fight-or-flight response. In the case of trypanophobia, the fear response is triggered by the sight, thought, or anticipation of needles. The amygdala, a small almond-shaped structure in the brain responsible for processing fear, becomes hyperactive, sending distress signals to the rest of the body.

The physiological effects of the fear response can be debilitating for individuals with needle phobia. Increased heart rate, elevated blood pressure, rapid breathing, and trembling are common symptoms. Some individuals may also experience nausea, sweating, and even gastrointestinal distress. These physical sensations can exacerbate the fear response, creating a vicious cycle of anxiety and panic.

1.1.1.2 The Impact of Trypanophobia on Daily Life

Trypanophobia can have a significant impact on an individual's daily life, as they may go to great lengths to avoid situations involving needles. Simple tasks like getting a flu shot, giving blood, or receiving necessary medical treatments can become overwhelming and distressing. Individuals with trypanophobia may suffer from health consequences due to their avoidance behavior, as they may delay or skip necessary medical interventions.

The fear of needles can also impact a person's mental well-being. Anxiety, depression, and feelings of shame or embarrassment are common among those with trypanophobia. The constant fear and avoidance of needles can lead to a diminished quality of life, as individuals may restrict their activities or avoid healthcare altogether.

1.1.1.3 Seeking Support and Treatment for Trypanophobia

Acknowledging and seeking help for needle phobia is an important step towards managing and overcoming the fear. The journey to recovery is unique for each individual, but there are several treatment options available that have shown promising results.

Cognitive-behavioral therapy (CBT) is a widely used and effective approach for treating phobias, including trypanophobia. CBT helps individuals identify and challenge irrational thoughts and beliefs about needles, gradually exposing them to needle-related situations in a controlled and supportive environment. This exposure therapy allows individuals to develop healthier coping mechanisms and reduces their fear response over time.

In severe cases of trypanophobia, medication may be prescribed to manage anxiety symptoms. Anti-anxiety medications or beta-blockers can help individuals cope with their fear during medical procedures. However, it is crucial to consult with a qualified healthcare professional to determine the most appropriate treatment approach.

1.1.1.4 Overcoming Trypanophobia: A Journey of Resilience

Overcoming trypanophobia requires patience, determination, and a supportive network. The process often involves gradually exposing oneself to needles in a controlled and safe environment, with the guidance of a therapist or healthcare provider. Support groups and online communities can also be valuable sources of encouragement and understanding.

It is important to recognize that trypanophobia is not a sign of weakness or irrationality. This phobia can stem from various factors, including past traumatic experiences or a genetic predisposition to anxiety. By understanding the underlying causes and working towards building resilience, individuals can regain control over their fear and lead healthier, more fulfilling lives.

While the path to overcoming needle phobia may be challenging, it is not insurmountable. With the right support, resources, and treatment, individuals can conquer their fear of needles and achieve a sense of empowerment over their own health. In the following chapters, we will delve deeper into the history, causes, and treatment options for trypanophobia, providing you with a comprehensive guide to coping with and overcoming this debilitating phobia.

Prevalence and Impact

Trypanophobia, the fear of needles, is a common and debilitating phobia that affects a significant portion of the population. While it is difficult to determine the exact prevalence of trypanophobia, studies suggest that it affects approximately 20

The impact of trypanophobia extends beyond the individual level and has wider societal implications. For instance, individuals with trypanophobia may avoid routine vaccinations, leading to decreased immunization rates and increased risk of outbreaks of preventable diseases. Moreover, the fear of needles can interfere with necessary medical procedures, such as blood tests and injections, making it challenging for healthcare providers to deliver appropriate care.

The fear and anxiety associated with needles can have a cascading effect on individuals' mental and physical well-being. It can cause individuals to delay or avoid seeking medical treatment, resulting in undiagnosed or untreated medical conditions. This can lead to complications, worsening symptoms, and reduced quality of life.

In addition to the fear and avoidance of medical procedures, trypanophobia can also impact an individual's daily life. Jobs that require regular exposure to needles, such as healthcare professionals or laboratory technicians, may be out of reach for those with trypanophobia. Furthermore, the fear can lead to social isolation, as individuals may avoid social situations or activities that they perceive as potentially exposing them to needles, such as concerts or sporting events.

The impact of trypanophobia goes beyond the immediate fear and avoidance. It can result in long-term mental health issues, such as anxiety disorders and depression. Additionally, the fear can lead to profound feelings of shame and embarrassment, as individuals may perceive their fear as irrational or weak. This can further exacerbate the negative impact of the phobia on their overall well-being.

It is important to recognize that the prevalence and impact of trypanophobia can vary across different populations and cultures. Cultural factors, including past experiences, beliefs, and societal attitudes towards medical procedures, can influence the development and manifestation of the phobia. Therefore, a comprehensive understanding of trypanophobia should consider not only the individual's fear but also the broader cultural context in which it exists.

Addressing the prevalence and impact of trypanophobia requires a multi-dimensional approach. This includes raising awareness about the phobia, reducing stigma, and providing support and resources for individuals who experience it. By understanding and addressing the prevalence and impact of trypanophobia, we can work towards a more inclusive and compassionate healthcare system that meets the needs of all individuals, regardless of their fear of needles.

Personal Stories of Trypanophobia

Personal stories provide a powerful insight into the lived experiences of those who suffer from trypanophobia, shedding light on the profound impact this fear can have on individuals. Their narratives not only help us understand the complexity of this phobia, but also offer hope and inspiration for those seeking to cope with and overcome it.

Meet Rachel, a 32-year-old woman, who has been living with trypanophobia since childhood. Rachel vividly recalls her first encounter with a needle at the age of six when she needed a vaccination. The sight of the needle sent her into a state of panic, resulting in a full-blown meltdown. Ever since that traumatic experience, Rachel has developed an overwhelming fear of needles, avoiding any medical procedures involving injections at all costs. She shares how this fear has limited her ability to seek appropriate medical care, causing significant distress and anxiety whenever she comes into contact with medical professionals.

Similarly, we are introduced to Mark, a 40-year-old man who has never outgrown his needle phobia. Mark vividly remembers a traumatic incident during his teenage years when he needed dental work that required injections. The fear and distress he experienced during the procedure left a lasting impact on him, making it extremely challenging for him to undergo any medical or dental procedures involving needles. Mark's fear has not only affected his own health but has also caused strain in his personal relationships, as his loved ones struggle to understand and support him.

Then there's Sarah, a 25-year-old college student who developed trypanophobia after a series of traumatic encounters with needles during hospitalization due to a serious illness. Sarah speaks about the terror she felt as she watched medical professionals approach her with needles, triggering intense panic attacks and a loss of control. She describes the profound impact this fear has had on her daily life, avoiding routine medical check-ups and preventive treatments.

These stories provide a glimpse into the challenges faced by individuals with trypanophobia. They depict the profound impact this phobia can have on one's physical well-being, mental health, and overall quality of life. From avoiding necessary medical procedures to experiencing excessive anxiety and panic attacks, trypanophobia can become a constant source of distress, limiting individuals' ability to lead a healthy and fulfilling life.

However, personal stories like those of Rachel, Mark, and Sarah also demonstrate the resilience and determination individuals have shown in their journey to overcome trypanophobia. Through therapy, support groups, and exposure techniques, these individuals have made significant progress in managing their fear. They offer hope to others facing similar challenges, inspiring them to seek help, explore coping strategies, and ultimately overcome trypanophobia.

While personal stories serve as a powerful tool to raise awareness and foster empathy, it is important to remember that everyone's experience with trypanophobia is unique. The severity of fear, triggers, and coping mechanisms may vary from person to person. By listening to these stories and appreciating the diversity of experiences, we can gain a deeper understanding of trypanophobia and work towards creating a more supportive and inclusive environment for individuals living with this phobia.

Conclusion

Personal stories are windows into the complex world of trypanophobia, offering valuable insights into the challenges faced by individuals and the potential for recovery. By acknowledging and understanding the impact of trypanophobia, we can work towards developing effective strategies to support and empower those living with this phobia. Through empathy, education, and a commitment to destigmatization, we can create a world where individuals with trypanophobia feel heard, understood, and confident in seeking the help they need.

Historical Perspectives on Needle Phobia

Throughout history, the fear of needles, known as trypanophobia, has been a subject of fascination and concern. This chapter explores the historical context of needle phobia, shedding light on its origins and the societal impact it has had over the years.

The Ancient Origins of Needle Phobia

The roots of needle phobia can be traced back to ancient times, where the use of needles was prevalent in various cultures. Needles were initially created for practical purposes, such as sewing and clothing construction. However, they soon found their way into medical practices, creating a new source of fear and anxiety for individuals.

In ancient Egypt, needles were utilized for mummification procedures. The practice involved puncturing the body to extract organs and later preserve the body using salt. It is believed that the association of needles with pain and death during this time may have contributed to the development of needle phobia in later generations.

Similarly, ancient Chinese medicinal practices involved the use of acupuncture, which utilized thin needles to stimulate specific points in the body. Though acupuncture is widely accepted today, the insertion of needles into the skin was undoubtedly a source of fear and trepidation for many individuals.

Symbolism and Rituals

Alongside their practical purposes, needles have also held symbolic meaning in various cultures throughout history. In some societies, needles were associated with witchcraft and sorcery, believed to be tools of evil or manipulation.

The fear of needles in these contexts can be attributed to a combination of superstition and cultural beliefs. The idea that a needle could be used to harm or control an individual may have contributed to the development of needle phobia as a means of self-preservation and protection.

Additionally, needles have been utilized in various rituals and ceremonies. In many cultures, body piercings and tattoos have served as rites of passage or religious symbols. While these practices hold significant cultural meaning, the act of puncturing the skin with a needle can naturally evoke fear and discomfort in individuals.

The Role of Needles in Traditional Medicine

Traditional medicine practices across different cultures have employed the use of needles for therapeutic purposes. For example, traditional Chinese medicine utilizes acupuncture to balance the flow of energy in the body, addressing various health conditions.

Similarly, Ayurvedic medicine, a traditional healing system in India, utilizes the practice of Pricking (Siddha) to stimulate healing and promote wellness. These historical uses of needles in medicine reflect the belief in the body's innate ability to heal itself through the appropriate application of needles.

The Evolution of Needles in Modern Healthcare

With the advancement of medical science, the role of needles in healthcare has evolved significantly. The development of hypodermic needles revolutionized the field of medicine, allowing for the safe and efficient administration of medications and vaccinations.

However, this progress also brought about a surge in needle-related anxiety and phobias. The sharp and invasive nature of hypodermic needles, along with their association with medical procedures and potential pain, have led to an increase in individuals developing trypanophobia.

Controversies and Ethical Dilemmas Surrounding Needles

Despite the crucial role needles play in modern healthcare, controversies and ethical dilemmas have accompanied their use. One of the most notable controversies is the transmission of bloodborne diseases, such as HIV and hepatitis, through contaminated needles.

This revelation further fueled the fear and anxiety surrounding needles, as individuals became aware of the potential risks associated with their use. The development of safety precautions, such as needle sterilization and the use of disposable needles, has been paramount in addressing these concerns and minimizing the spread of infections.

Needle Safety and Regulations

In response to the aforementioned controversies, needle safety and regulations have become a vital component of healthcare systems worldwide. Organizations like the World Health Organization (WHO) and the Centers for Disease Control and Prevention (CDC) have established guidelines and protocols to ensure the safe handling and disposal of needles.

Furthermore, advancements in needle design, such as retractable needles and needleless injections, have been introduced to minimize the risk of accidental needlestick injuries for healthcare professionals. These developments aim to alleviate anxiety associated with needle-related procedures and enhance patient and healthcare provider safety.

The Future of Needles

As healthcare technology continues to advance, the future of needles is rapidly changing. Needle phobia is a catalyst for the exploration of alternative methods for drug delivery and blood sampling.

Scientists and researchers are actively developing innovative technologies, such as microneedles and transdermal patches, to replace traditional hypodermic needles. These advancements aim to enhance patient comfort and reduce the fear and anxiety associated with needle-related procedures.

Moreover, the integration of robotics and automation in healthcare settings shows promise in improving the precision and efficiency of needle-related procedures. Robotic assistance in needle placement and intravenous catheter insertion may alleviate anxiety by minimizing the risk of human error.

In conclusion, understanding the historical perspectives of needle phobia provides valuable insights into the development and impact of this specific fear. From ancient rituals to modern medical practices, needles have left a profound mark on human history. By exploring historical roots, society can continue to progress in addressing and supporting individuals affected by trypanophobia.

The Psychological Mechanisms Behind Trypanophobia

Trypanophobia, the fear of needles, is a complex psychological condition that manifests in various ways. To understand the underlying mechanisms, we must explore the psychological factors that contribute to the development and maintenance of this phobia. In this section, we will delve into the cognitive, emotional, and behavioral aspects of trypanophobia, as well as the theories that help explain its origin and persistence.

Cognitive Factors

Cognitive factors play a significant role in the development and perpetuation of trypanophobia. One of the key cognitive mechanisms involved is selective attention. People with trypanophobia tend to focus their attention on the perceived negative aspects of needles, such as pain, discomfort, or potential harm. They may also ruminate on past negative experiences, reinforcing their fear and anxiety.

Another cognitive aspect is catastrophic thinking. Trypanophobics often engage in catastrophic thinking, imagining the worst-case scenarios associated with needle-related procedures. They may create vivid mental images of fainting, contracting infections, or experiencing severe pain, which intensify their fears. These cognitive distortions contribute to the maintenance of the phobia by reinforcing negative beliefs associated with needles.

Moreover, cognitive biases, such as confirmation bias and memory biases, contribute to the reinforcement of trypanophobic beliefs. Confirmation bias leads individuals to seek information that confirms their existing beliefs, while memory biases contribute to the distortion of past experiences, enhancing negative memories and downplaying positive ones related to needle procedures.

Emotional Factors

Emotional factors also play a crucial role in the experience of trypanophobia. The intensity of fear and anxiety associated with needles varies among individuals and can be influenced by several emotional processes.

Classical conditioning is a significant aspect of the emotional experience of trypanophobia. Negative experiences, such as painful injections or traumatic medical procedures, can lead to the association of needles with fear and distress. Over time, this conditioned fear response becomes automatic, triggering anxiety and avoidance behaviors.

Furthermore, the fear of needles also elicits a physiological response in trypanophobics. The activation of the sympathetic nervous system results in increased heart rate, sweating, and trembling. These bodily sensations intensify the experience of fear, creating a vicious cycle of anticipation, anxiety, and avoidance.

Behavioral Factors

Behavioral factors play a crucial role in the maintenance of trypanophobia. Avoidance behaviors are a primary characteristic of this phobia. Individuals with trypanophobia tend to avoid any situations, medical or otherwise, that involve needles. This avoidance can lead to detrimental consequences, such as forgoing necessary medical treatments, vaccinations, or blood tests.

Avoidance behaviors are often reinforced through negative reinforcement. When trypanophobics avoid needle-related situations, they experience immediate relief from anxiety, reinforcing the idea that avoidance is an effective coping mechanism. This negative reinforcement strengthens the association between needles and fear, perpetuating the phobia.

Theories of Trypanophobia

To understand trypanophobia more comprehensively, psychologists have proposed several theories to explain its origin and persistence.

The two-factor theory of fear proposes that trypanophobia involves both classical conditioning and operant conditioning. Classical conditioning establishes an association between needles and fear, while operant conditioning reinforces avoidance behaviors through negative reinforcement.

The expectancy theory posits that trypanophobics anticipate the experience of intense fear and discomfort during needle-related procedures. This expectation contributes to the development and maintenance of the phobia. The theory suggests that altering these expectations through cognitive restructuring techniques could help reduce trypanophobia symptoms.

The social learning theory emphasizes the role of observational learning in the development and maintenance of trypanophobia. Individuals may acquire fear and anxiety through observing others experiencing distress during needle-related procedures. This vicarious learning process can shape negative beliefs and amplify fear responses.

Addressing Psychological Mechanisms

Understanding the psychological mechanisms behind trypanophobia is crucial for developing effective treatment approaches. By targeting the cognitive, emotional, and behavioral factors, individuals can learn to manage their fear and reduce avoidance behaviors.

Cognitive-behavioral therapy (CBT) is a widely used treatment approach for trypanophobia. This therapeutic approach aims to identify and modify dysfunctional thoughts and beliefs associated with needles. By challenging catastrophic thinking and encouraging realistic reinterpretation of needle-related experiences, CBT can help individuals develop healthier perceptions of needles.

Exposure therapy, another evidence-based treatment for trypanophobia, involves gradual and systematic exposure to needle-related situations in a safe and controlled environment. Through repeated and prolonged contact with needles, individuals can learn to confront their fears and develop new, non-threatening associations with these objects.

In conclusion, trypanophobia is influenced by various psychological mechanisms, including cognitive biases, emotional conditioning, and avoidance behaviors. The understanding of these mechanisms is essential for developing effective interventions and improving the quality of life for individuals living with this phobia. By addressing cognitive distortions, modifying fear responses, and gradually exposing individuals to needle-related situations, we can help them overcome their fears and regain control over their lives.

Further Reading

- Antony, M. M., & Stein, M. B. (2020). Oxford handbook of phobia and anxiety. Oxford University Press.

- Wolitzky-Taylor, K. B., Horowitz, J. D., Powers, M. B., & Telch, M. J. (2008). Psychological approaches in the treatment of specific phobias: A meta-analysis. Clinical Psychology Review, 28(6), 1021-1037.

- Ougrin, D. (2011). Efficacy of exposure versus cognitive therapy for anxiety disorders: Systematic review and meta-analysis. BMC Psychiatry, 11(1), 200.

Exercises

1. Recall a personal experience related to needles and try to identify any cognitive biases or cognitive distortions present in your thought processes during that time. How did these thought patterns contribute to your fear or anxiety?

2. Imagine you are designing an exposure therapy program for someone with trypanophobia. Outline the steps involved in the hierarchy of exposures, starting from the least anxiety-provoking situation to the most anxiety-provoking one.

3. Research and find a success story or testimonial of someone who has overcome their trypanophobia. What strategies or treatments did they find most effective in their journey towards recovery? Share the story with a friend or family member, emphasizing the importance of understanding and supporting individuals with trypanophobia.

Misconceptions and Stereotypes

Misconceptions and stereotypes surrounding trypanophobia often contribute to the lack of understanding and empathy towards individuals with this fear. Educating ourselves and debunking these misconceptions is crucial in creating a supportive and inclusive environment for trypanophobics. In this section, we will explore some common misconceptions and stereotypes associated with trypanophobia and provide the necessary context to challenge them.

Misconception 1: Trypanophobia is a Sign of Weakness

One common misconception surrounding trypanophobia is the belief that it is a sign of weakness or cowardice. This stereotype undermines the complexity of this fear and trivializes its impact on individuals' lives. Trypanophobia is not a choice or a personal flaw; it is a psychological response triggered by the fear of needles or injections. It is important to understand that fears and phobias are not indicative of weakness but rather a natural part of the human experience.

Misconception 2: Trypanophobia is Irrational

Another misconception is that trypanophobia is entirely irrational and unfounded. While it may seem irrational to someone who does not experience this fear, it is essential to recognize that fear responses are often rooted in personal experiences, trauma, or conditioning. Trypanophobia can emerge from past traumatic experiences with needles, witnessing painful procedures, or even stories or portrayals of medical procedures in the media. Understanding the underlying reasons for trypanophobia helps in fostering empathy and compassionate support.

Misconception 3: Trypanophobics are Overreacting or Attention-Seeking

A common stereotype associated with trypanophobia is that individuals who experience this fear are overreacting or seeking attention. This misunderstanding stems from a lack of awareness about the intensity of the fear response and its impact on daily life. Trypanophobics may experience heightened anxiety, panic attacks, or even avoidance behaviors when faced with needles or medical procedures. It is essential to recognize the validity of these experiences and provide understanding and support rather than dismissing them.

Misconception 4: Trypanophobics Can Simply "Get Over It"

There is a misconception that trypanophobics can easily overcome their fear by merely facing needles repeatedly. While exposure therapy can be an effective treatment approach, it is essential to acknowledge that each individual's journey with trypanophobia is unique. Overcoming this fear requires personalized strategies and professional guidance. Blanket statements suggesting that trypanophobics can simply "get over it" do not take into account the complexity and individuality of fear responses.

Misconception 5: Trypanophobia is Rare or Insignificant

Trypanophobia is often overlooked, as it may seem relatively uncommon compared to other fears or phobias. However, research suggests that trypanophobia affects a significant number of individuals worldwide. Additionally, the impact of this fear on quality of life, healthcare access, and overall well-being should not be underestimated. By raising awareness and providing support, we can create a more inclusive society that recognizes the significance of trypanophobia.

Misconception 6: Trypanophobia Always Results in Avoidance

While avoidance behaviors are common among trypanophobics, it is incorrect to assume that all individuals with trypanophobia will consistently avoid medical procedures or vaccinations. The severity of fear and the individual's coping mechanisms can vary greatly. Some trypanophobics may find ways to tolerate or manage their fear, especially when confronted with the potential benefits or necessity of medical interventions. Understanding the diverse range of responses can help challenge the misconception that trypanophobics always avoid medical care.

Misconception 7: Trypanophobia Can Be Easily Overcome with Distractions

A common misconception is that providing distractions, such as music or engaging activities, can alleviate the fear experienced by trypanophobics. While distractions can be helpful for some individuals, they are not a one-size-fits-all solution. Trypanophobia requires a holistic and personalized approach that addresses the underlying fears and anxieties. Distractions alone may not address the core issues associated with the fear of needles.

Misconception 8: Trypanophobia Only Affects Children

Trypanophobia is often misconceived as a fear that predominantly affects children. While it is true that early medical experiences can contribute to the development of trypanophobia, this fear can persist into adulthood and impact individuals of all ages. Understanding that trypanophobia is not limited to childhood experiences is crucial for providing appropriate support and interventions for individuals across the lifespan.

Challenging Misconceptions: Creating Empathy and Support

Challenging and debunking these misconceptions is a vital step towards creating a more compassionate and supportive environment for trypanophobics. By fostering empathy, understanding, and awareness, we can contribute to reducing the stigma and barriers faced by individuals with trypanophobia. It is important to educate ourselves and others, promote open dialogue, and encourage the use of inclusive strategies that consider the diverse experiences and needs of trypanophobics.

Remember, overcoming stereotypes and misconceptions is a collective effort that requires continuous learning, empathy, and compassion to create a more understanding and supportive society.

Challenges and Stigmas Faced by Trypanophobics

Living with trypanophobia, the fear of needles, brings forth numerous challenges and stigmas that can greatly impact the daily lives of those affected. Understanding and addressing these challenges is crucial for providing the necessary support and care to individuals experiencing this phobia.

The Fear of Medical Procedures

One of the primary challenges faced by trypanophobics is the fear of medical procedures involving needles. This fear can result in avoidance behaviors and a reluctance to seek necessary medical care. Routine vaccinations, blood tests, and even essential medical procedures may trigger severe anxiety and panic attacks in trypanophobics, making it difficult for them to take proactive steps in managing their health.

Example: Sarah, a trypanophobic individual, avoids visiting the dentist due to her fear of injections. Consequently, she suffers from dental decay, which could have been prevented with regular check-ups and treatments.

Stigmatization and Misunderstanding

Another significant challenge faced by trypanophobics is stigmatization and misunderstanding from others who fail to comprehend the severity of their phobia. Friends, family members, and even healthcare professionals may dismiss their fear, leading to feelings of isolation, shame, and anxiety about seeking support.

Example: John, a trypanophobic individual, is often labelled as "overreacting" or "being dramatic" when expressing his fear of needles. This constant invalidation further fuels his anxiety and makes it difficult for him to open up about his phobia.

Barriers to Treatment

Trypanophobics often encounter barriers when seeking treatment, exacerbating their challenges. Limited access to specialized healthcare providers who understand and have experience in managing needle phobia can hinder their progress in overcoming their fear. Additionally, the fear itself acts as a barrier, making it difficult for individuals to attend therapy or face their fear in controlled environments.

Example: Emma, a trypanophobic individual, lives in a remote area with limited mental health resources. This lack of access to a specialized therapist further prolongs her struggle with her phobia, as she is unable to receive the professional help she needs.

Impaired Quality of Life

The fear of needles can significantly impact various aspects of a trypanophobic individual's life, leading to a diminished quality of life. Simple tasks, such as receiving a vaccination, donating blood, or even watching medical-related scenes in movies or TV shows, may trigger intense fear and anxiety. This fear can restrict social activities, limit career choices, and create a barrier to enjoying everyday experiences.

Example: James, a trypanophobic individual, declines invitations to social events at hospitals or medical institutions, missing out on opportunities to connect with friends and engage in meaningful experiences.

Self-Stigmatization and Internalized Shame

Trypanophobics often internalize the stigma associated with their phobia, leading to self-stigmatization and feelings of shame. They may question their own strength and resilience, feeling embarrassed about their fear and perceiving themselves as weak or abnormal. This internalized shame can worsen anxiety symptoms, creating a vicious cycle that hinders personal growth and recovery.

Example: Rebecca, a trypanophobic individual, constantly berates herself for her fear of needles, believing that she should be able to overcome it on her own. This self-criticism perpetuates her anxiety and prevents her from seeking the help she needs.

Impact on Relationships

The challenges faced by trypanophobics can extend to their relationships with others. Friends and family members who do not understand the phobia may become frustrated or dismissive, straining these relationships. The fear of needles may also affect intimate relationships, as the phobia can interfere with sexual health discussions, family planning, and even fertility treatments.

Example: Michael, a trypanophobic individual, faces difficulties discussing plans for starting a family with his partner due to the fear of medical procedures and potential injections during fertility treatments. This strain on their relationship adds to his emotional burden.

Educational and Professional Setbacks

Trypanophobia can also cause educational and professional setbacks. Fear of needles may lead to missed school or work days due to necessary medical appointments or the avoidance of certain career paths that involve medical procedures. This fear can hinder educational and career advancement, limiting opportunities and impacting self-esteem.

Example: Emily, a trypanophobic individual, drops out of nursing school due to her fear of needles, feeling unable to overcome the required medical injections. This decision significantly impacts her educational and career aspirations.

Addressing these challenges and stigmas faced by trypanophobics requires a comprehensive approach that includes education, awareness, specialized support, and destigmatization efforts. By fostering empathy, providing access to resources, and creating fear-free environments, we can support individuals in overcoming their fears and improving their overall well-being.

Importance of Understanding and Addressing Trypanophobia

Understanding and addressing trypanophobia is of utmost importance due to its widespread impact on individuals and society as a whole. This section explores the significance of recognizing and addressing this phobia, highlighting the personal, societal, and healthcare-related implications it entails.

Trypanophobia, the fear of needles, is a deeply rooted and prevalent phobia that affects a significant portion of the population. It is estimated that approximately 20

Failure to address trypanophobia can result in delayed medical interventions, missed vaccinations, and skipped necessary blood tests. This can lead to worsened health conditions, increased mortality rates, and the spread of preventable diseases. Additionally, individuals with trypanophobia often experience heightened stress and anxiety, which can further negatively impact their overall well-being.

On a societal level, understanding and addressing trypanophobia can help reduce the economic burden associated with delayed and avoidable medical treatments. It can also contribute to the prevention of outbreaks of contagious diseases by ensuring vaccination rates remain high. By addressing this fear, we can create a healthier and more resilient society.

Addressing trypanophobia is equally important from a healthcare perspective. Healthcare providers must be aware of the prevalence and impact of this phobia to provide appropriate care for patients. Building trust and open communication with trypanophobic individuals is crucial to ensure their needs are met and to minimize potential harm caused by avoidable medical procedures. By recognizing and addressing trypanophobia, healthcare providers can enhance patient-centered care and improve overall healthcare outcomes.

Moreover, understanding trypanophobia can help debunk misconceptions and stereotypes associated with needle fear. Society often dismisses this phobia as insignificant or irrational, leading to stigmatization and lack of support for affected individuals. By shedding light on the psychological mechanisms behind this fear, we can challenge these misconceptions and promote empathy and understanding.

In order to address trypanophobia effectively, it is important to adopt a multidimensional approach. This involves educating healthcare providers, policymakers, and the general public about the nature and impact of trypanophobia. By increasing awareness, we can establish a supportive environment that fosters early intervention and appropriate management strategies.

Research plays a vital role in understanding the underlying causes of trypanophobia and developing effective treatment approaches. By investing in research and creating interdisciplinary collaborations, we can explore innovative techniques and therapies, such as virtual reality and neuroscientific interventions, to alleviate the fear of needles.

To ensure the successful understanding and addressing of trypanophobia, it is crucial to involve all relevant stakeholders, including healthcare professionals, researchers, educators, patients, and their families. By working together, we can develop tailored interventions and support systems that address the unique needs of individuals coping with needle fear.

In conclusion, understanding and addressing trypanophobia is of paramount importance. By acknowledging the impact of this phobia on individuals and society, promoting empathy and awareness, and investing in research and collaborative efforts, we can pave the way for effective management strategies and support systems. Through our collective commitment, we can empower individuals with trypanophobia to overcome their fears and lead healthier lives.

Organization of the Book

In this book, we will explore the fascinating details, history, and real-life cases of Trypanophobia, also known as the fear of needles. Let's take a brief look at how the book is organized and what each chapter will cover.

Chapter 1: Introduction ———————————————- We will begin by introducing the concept of Trypanophobia and its impact on individuals' lives. We will discuss the prevalence of this phobia and share personal stories of those who have experienced it. Furthermore, we will examine the historical perspectives on needle phobia, including ancient beliefs and superstitions surrounding needles. This chapter will also delve into the psychological mechanisms behind Trypanophobia and address common misconceptions and stereotypes associated with this phobia. Finally, we will shed light on the challenges and stigmas faced by Trypanophobics and emphasize the importance of understanding and addressing this fear.

Chapter 2: A Brief History of Needles ————————————————— This chapter will take a deeper dive into the origins and evolution of needles. We will explore how needles have been used in traditional medicine, rituals, and symbolism throughout history. Additionally, we will examine the role of needles in early medical practices and their influence on society. Controversies and ethical dilemmas surrounding needles will also be discussed, along with safety regulations. Lastly, we will explore the future of needles and potential advancements in needle technologies.

Chapter 3: Understanding Trypanophobia ———————————————————- In this chapter, we will explore the anatomy and physiology of fear, providing an in-depth understanding of how fear manifests in individuals with Trypanophobia. We will discuss the fight or flight response, the role of the amygdala, and the impact of neurotransmitters on fear conditioning. Brain imaging studies specific to Trypanophobia will be examined, along with genetic and environmental factors that contribute to the development of this phobia. We will also debunk common misconceptions about fear and explore the spectrum of needle-related phobias.

Chapter 4: Early Childhood Experiences and Trypanophobia ——————————————————————- This chapter will focus on the impact of early medical experiences on the development of Trypanophobia. We will explore the role of painful injections and traumatic memories in shaping a fear of needles. Additionally, we will discuss parental influence, emotional regulation, and coping strategies for children with Trypanophobia. Play therapy, exposure techniques, and therapeutic approaches will be explored, along with ways in which parents and healthcare providers can collaborate to empower children and provide support both at home and in school. Case studies will be shared to demonstrate successful outcomes in overcoming Trypanophobia during childhood.

Chapter 5: Coping Strategies for Trypanophobics ———————————————————- In this chapter, we will explore various coping strategies for individuals with Trypanophobia. Cognitive-behavioral therapy techniques, such as gradual exposure and cognitive restructuring, will be discussed in detail. Relaxation techniques, mindfulness, and meditation practices will also be explored. We will delve into the emerging use of virtual reality therapy for needle phobia and the potential role of art therapy and creative expressions in coping with this fear. Furthermore, we will discuss the use of support groups, peer counselors, and pharmacological interventions for severe cases. Finally, we will emphasize the importance of adopting a holistic approach by integrating multiple coping strategies.

Chapter 6: Overcoming Trypanophobia in Adulthood ———————————————— This chapter will focus on adults who continue to grapple with Trypanophobia. We will explore the long-term impact of traumatic experiences and the fear of medical procedures and interventions. Overcoming barriers and addressing shame will be addressed, along with therapeutic techniques specifically tailored for adults with Trypanophobia. The role of hypnotherapy, neuro-linguistic programming techniques, personal growth, and empowerment will be explored in-depth. Success stories and testimonials from individuals who have successfully overcome this fear will provide inspiration and motivation. Finally, we will discuss advocacy efforts and the importance of raising awareness about Trypanophobia.

Chapter 7: Supporting Loved Ones with Trypanophobia ———————————————— This chapter will provide guidance for friends and family members of individuals with Trypanophobia. We will emphasize the importance of empathy and understanding and provide effective communication strategies. Education and creating a fear-free environment will be addressed, along with accommodations in healthcare settings. We will discuss how loved ones can support accessible treatment options and collaborate with healthcare providers to ensure the best possible care for their trypanophobic family member. Additionally, we will explore the importance of seeking professional help together and the necessity of self-care to avoid caregiver burnout.

Chapter 8: The Future of Trypanophobia Research ————————————————- In this concluding chapter, we will discuss the cutting-edge research on Trypanophobia and explore various areas for future exploration. Neuroscience and brain imaging studies will provide insights into the neural mechanisms underlying this phobia. We will also delve into the genetic and epigenetic factors that contribute to Trypanophobia. Additionally, we will explore the role of developmental trauma and the importance of early intervention. Technological innovations like virtual reality therapy and novel pharmacological treatments will be discussed. We will also examine how cultural perspectives and societal implications influence Trypanophobia. Lastly, we will emphasize the need for collaborative efforts between researchers and practitioners by addressing funding and resources for Trypanophobia research and encouraging a transdisciplinary approach to understanding this fascinating phobia.

By structuring the book in this manner, we aim to provide a comprehensive exploration of Trypanophobia that covers its historical context, the psychology behind fear, developmental influences, coping strategies, and the importance of support from loved ones. Additionally, we will delve into cutting-edge research and shed light on the future of Trypanophobia research. Throughout the book, real-life stories and case studies will be incorporated to make the content relatable and engaging for readers. With this organization, readers will gain a deep understanding of Trypanophobia and be equipped with the knowledge and tools necessary to cope with and overcome this fear.

Chapter One: A Brief History of Needles

The Ancient Origins of the Needle

Early Medical Uses of Needles

The history of needles dates back to ancient times, where they were initially used for various purposes beyond medical applications. Needles, in their simplest form, were crafted from bones, antlers, or thorns and served as tools for sewing clothes, creating decorative patterns, and even as weapons in early civilizations. However, it wasn't until the development of metalworking techniques that needles began to play a significant role in medicine.

The Birth of Acupuncture

One of the earliest recorded medical uses of needles can be traced back to ancient China, around 6000 BCE. The practice of acupuncture emerged during the Neolithic period, where long, thin needles made from sharpened stones or bone were used to stimulate specific points on the body to promote healing. These points, known as meridians, were believed to be interconnected pathways through which energy, called "qi" (pronounced "chee"), flowed.

Ancient Chinese medical texts, such as the Huangdi Neijing (Yellow Emperor's Inner Canon), provided detailed descriptions and instructions on the use of acupuncture needles. The skilled practitioners of acupuncture would carefully insert the needles into specific acupuncture points along the meridians to restore the balance of qi and promote the body's natural healing processes.

Acupuncture needles were initially made from materials like bamboo, stone, and bronze. Over time, advancements in metalworking techniques led to the production of finer, more precise needles made from copper, gold, and silver. These metal needles not only increased the accuracy of acupuncture treatments but also allowed for the sterilization of needles, reducing the risk of infection.

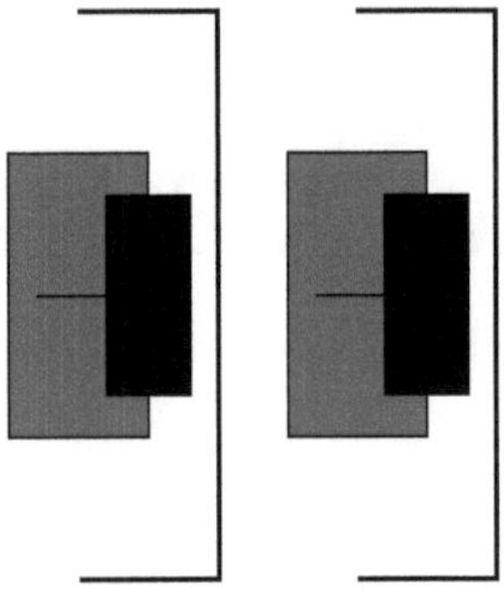

Figure 0.1: Comparison of early stone needle (left) and metal needle (right) used in acupuncture.

Bloodletting and Early Surgical Procedures

In ancient Greece and Rome, needles were utilized for bloodletting, a common medical practice aimed at restoring the balance of the bodily humors. In accordance with the humor theory, it was believed that illnesses were caused by an imbalance of blood, phlegm, yellow bile, and black bile. By using specialized instruments such as lancets or fleams, physicians would puncture veins or arteries to drain excess blood from the body, with the aim of restoring health.

Over time, the medical applications of needles expanded beyond bloodletting. In ancient India, surgeons known as the Sushruta Samhita developed techniques for surgical procedures such as cataract removal, hernia repair, and even rhinoplasty. Needles played a crucial role in these surgeries, as they were used for suturing wounds and closing incisions.

Ancient Medical Needle Manufacturing

The manufacturing process of early medical needles was a labor-intensive task. Metalworkers carefully crafted these needles by hand, using primitive tools and techniques. They would heat the metal and then hammer, file, and polish it to create a thin, pointed needle.

During this period, needle making was often a family trade, passed down through generations. The skill and craftsmanship required to produce high-quality medical needles were highly valued.

Safety Concerns and Advancements

While the use of needles in medical practices showed promising results, there were concerns regarding cleanliness and the potential for infection. In ancient times, sterilization techniques were limited, and the reuse of needles without proper cleaning posed significant risks to patients.

Figure 0.2: Advancements in needle manufacturing from ancient times to the present day.

As medical knowledge and understanding evolved, so too did the advancements in needle manufacturing and safety practices. With the discovery of microorganisms and the development of germ theory in the 19th century, sterilization techniques became more refined and effective. The introduction of disposable needles in the 20th century further reduced the risk of cross-contamination.

Today, medical needles are manufactured using sophisticated machinery and precise techniques. They are made from high-quality materials such as stainless steel, which allow for sharp, durable, and sterile needles. Needle sizes and designs have also evolved to cater to specific medical procedures, ensuring optimal patient comfort and safety.

Unconventional Example: Bee Venom Therapy

While not a widespread medical practice, bee venom therapy deserves mention due to its historical relevance and unconventional nature. Dating back to ancient Egypt and Greece, this therapy involves the controlled administration of bee venom through a needle sting.

The belief behind this therapy lies in the unique properties of bee venom, which contains various active compounds that have anti-inflammatory, analgesic, and immune-modulating effects. Advocates of this therapy claim that bee venom can alleviate symptoms of rheumatoid arthritis, multiple sclerosis, and other inflammatory conditions.

Despite its controversial nature and limited scientific evidence, some individuals still seek bee venom therapy as an alternative treatment option. However, it is crucial to note that this therapy should only be administered by trained professionals, as bee venom can cause allergic reactions and other adverse effects.

Conclusion

The early medical uses of needles encompassed a fascinating array of practices, from acupuncture in ancient China to bloodletting and surgical procedures in ancient Greece and Rome. These ancient techniques paved the way for the development of modern medical procedures involving needles.

Advancements in both needle manufacturing and safety protocols have significantly improved patient well-being and reduced the risk of infection or cross-contamination. However, it is essential to approach unconventional therapies like bee venom therapy with caution, seeking guidance from trained healthcare professionals.

Understanding the historical context and evolution of early medical needle usage provides valuable insights into the nature of medicine and the continuous pursuit of effective treatments. By appreciating the progress made in needle technology, we can further enhance medical practices and continue to improve patient care.

Symbolism and Rituals

Symbolism and rituals associated with needles have a long and rich history that spans across various cultures and time periods. From ancient civilizations to modern societies, needles have held significant meanings and have been used in various rituals and ceremonies. In this section, we will explore some of the fascinating symbolism and rituals associated with needles.

Needles as Symbols of Healing

In many cultures, needles are seen as symbols of healing and restoration. The use of needles in medical treatments and therapies can be traced back to ancient civilizations such as Egypt, China, and Greece. These cultures believed that the insertion of needles at specific points on the body could restore balance and harmony, leading to improved physical and mental well-being.

For example, in Traditional Chinese Medicine (TCM), acupuncture is a well-known practice that involves the insertion of thin needles into specific points on the body to stimulate the flow of energy, known as Qi, and restore the body's balance. This ancient healing technique is still widely practiced today and is recognized for its effectiveness in treating various health conditions.

Similarly, in Ayurvedic medicine, a traditional system of healing in India, needles are used in a technique called Marma therapy. Marma points are specific points on the body where the vital energy, or Prana, is believed to be concentrated. By applying pressure or inserting needles into these points, energy flow is regulated, leading to physical and emotional healing.

The symbolism of needles as tools for healing is also prevalent in modern medical practices. Injections and vaccinations, although feared by many, are crucial for preventing and treating diseases. Needles, in this context, are seen as instruments of health and deliverers of life-saving medications.

Needles in Rituals and Ceremonies

Needles have also been used in various rituals and ceremonies across different cultures throughout history. These rituals often carry symbolic meanings and serve as a way to connect with the spiritual realm or mark significant life events.

In some Native American cultures, needle-like objects, such as bone awls or cactus spines, were used in rituals related to vision quests or rites of passage. These needles were used to create small punctures in the skin, symbolizing the opening of a spiritual portal or a connection between the individual and the divine. The rituals were believed to facilitate personal growth, self-discovery, and spiritual enlightenment.

In traditional Japanese culture, needles have been used in the art of Kintsugi, which involves the repair of broken pottery using powdered gold or silver mixed with lacquer. The process of repairing the broken pieces with the golden seams symbolizes the beauty of imperfection and the acceptance of change and transformation.

In some African cultures, needles and sewing play a significant role in rituals related to birth and marriage. For example, in Swahili culture, during a wedding ceremony, the bride and groom have their wrists joined together with a single strand of thread, symbolizing their union and commitment to each other.

Cultural Beliefs and Superstitions

Beyond symbolism and rituals, needles have also been associated with cultural beliefs and superstitions in various societies. Some cultures believe that needles have protective properties and can ward off evil spirits or negative energy when worn as jewelry or carried in pockets.

In Chinese culture, it is believed that needles can bring good luck. Traditionally, it was common for people to insert needles into the seams of their clothes or pin them to their hats to attract fortune and protect against misfortune.

On the other hand, many cultures also associate needles with pain and discomfort, leading to various superstitions and taboos. For instance, some believe that it is unlucky to drop a needle or to step on one, as it may bring bad luck or cause illness.

Contemporary Symbolism and Meanings

In contemporary society, needles have acquired new symbolism and meanings, particularly in the context of tattooing and body modification. Many individuals choose to decorate their bodies with intricate needlework in the form of tattoos to express their personal stories, beliefs, or cultural identities.

The act of getting a tattoo itself can also be seen as a symbolic ritual. It often involves a personal journey, introspection, and the marking of a significant event or transformation in a person's life.

Furthermore, needles have taken on symbolic meanings in various art forms and literature. Writers and artists often use needles as metaphors for pain, vulnerability, or the complexity of human emotions. This symbolism can be seen in literature, poetry, visual arts, and even in contemporary music.

Overall, the symbolism and rituals associated with needles reflect the deep cultural, spiritual, and psychological significance that these objects hold. Whether it is their association with healing, rites of passage, or artistic expressions, needles have seamlessly woven themselves into the fabric of human history, leaving behind a trail of captivating stories and beliefs that continue to intrigue and inspire us today.

References

- Taylor, K. J. (2018). TCM: A Natural Guide to Traditional Chinese Medicine. Penguin. - Sreejith, B. N., & Ashtamurthy, H. S. (2016). Marma therapy in Ayurveda: A critical review. Journal of Ayurveda and Integrative Medicine, 7(2), 115-119. - Denetdale, J. (2012). Reclaiming Diné History: The Legacies of

Navajo Chief Manuelito and Juanita. University of Arizona Press. - Yellin, E. (2007). Tattoos: The Ancient and Mysterious History. Smithsonian Magazine. Retrieved from https://www.smithsonianmag.com/history/tattoos-144038580/ - Rouska, E., Koidou, E., & Zidianakis, E. (Eds.). (2021). Bodily Undoing: Somatic Thoughts in Performance Art. Amsterdam: Valiz. - Poe, E. A. (1845). The Tell-Tale Heart. The Pioneer.

The Role of Needles in Traditional Medicine

Throughout history, needles have played a significant role in various traditional medical practices across cultures. The use of needles for therapeutic purposes can be traced back thousands of years, highlighting the enduring belief in their healing power. This section will explore the cultural and historical significance of needles in traditional medicine, shedding light on the diverse ways they have been utilized.

Acupuncture: A Holistic Healing Practice

One of the most well-known applications of needles in traditional medicine is acupuncture. Originating in ancient China over 3,000 years ago, acupuncture is based on the concept of qi, the life force that flows through the body along meridian pathways. In this practice, thin needles are inserted at specific points along these meridians to restore the balance of qi and promote health.

Acupuncture is commonly used to alleviate pain, treat various ailments, and promote overall well-being. Traditional Chinese medicine practitioners believe that the insertion of needles stimulates the body's energy flow, facilitating self-healing processes. These needles are typically made of stainless steel and vary in length depending on the area being treated.

The effectiveness of acupuncture has been a topic of debate in the scientific community. However, numerous studies have validated its therapeutic benefits, particularly in pain management and stress reduction. Modern research has shown that acupuncture stimulates the release of endorphins, neurotransmitters that relieve pain and promote a sense of well-being. Furthermore, studies using functional magnetic resonance imaging (fMRI) have revealed the brain's response to acupuncture, providing a neurological basis for its effects.

Ayurvedic Medicine: The Science of Life

In India, the ancient healing system of Ayurveda employs various techniques, including the use of needles, to restore balance and harmony within the body. Ayurvedic medicine is based on the belief that each individual possesses a unique constitution, or dosha, comprising three elements: Vata (air and ether), Pitta (fire and water), and Kapha (earth and water). When there is an imbalance in these elements, illness ensues.

A specific Ayurvedic technique known as Marma therapy utilizes the precise application of pressure on specific points on the body, similar to acupuncture. These points are considered vital energy centers where physical, emotional, and spiritual elements intersect. Needles may be used in Marma therapy to stimulate these points, promote energy flow, and restore balance.

The needles used in Ayurvedic medicine are typically thinner than those used in acupuncture and are often made of gold, silver, or steel. The choice of material is believed to have therapeutic properties, enhancing the healing effects of the treatment. While scientific research on Marma therapy is limited, there is growing interest in investigating its potential benefits and understanding the mechanisms behind its effectiveness.

Japanese Acupuncture: A Unique Technique

In Japan, acupuncture has its own distinct approach, known as Kampo or Manaka acupuncture. This technique incorporates the use of specialized needles and diagnostic methods, focusing on individualized treatment based on meridian imbalances and pulse diagnosis.

In Japanese acupuncture, the needles used are often thinner and shorter than those used in other traditions. They are finely crafted from high-quality stainless steel, which allows for precise and gentle insertion. The unique aspect of Japanese acupuncture lies in its emphasis on palpation and pulse diagnosis. Practitioners assess the pulse in various positions to identify imbalances and select the appropriate points for treatment.

Japanese acupuncture places particular importance on the interconnectedness of the body's systems. Needles are inserted not only at the site of discomfort but also in distant locations along corresponding meridians to address the root cause of the imbalance. The aim is to restore harmony and promote overall well-being.

Other Traditional Practices

Needles have also been employed in other traditional medicine practices around the world. In the ancient Indian practice of Ayurvedic Ksharasutra, specially treated medicated threads are used to treat various anal and rectal conditions. These threads, which contain herbal extracts, are inserted into fistulas, hemorrhoids, or other affected areas to promote healing.

In traditional Korean medicine, known as Hanbang, needles are used for a technique called acupoint embedding therapy. Thin needles are inserted into specific points on the body and fixed in place with adhesive tape, allowing for a continuous stimulation of the acupoints over time. This method is believed to restore energy balance and treat various conditions.

Traditional medicine systems in other cultures, such as Tibetan medicine and Native American healing practices, also incorporate the use of needles in therapies and rituals. These diverse practices demonstrate the universal recognition of the therapeutic potential of needles in promoting health and well-being.

Conclusion

The historical and cultural significance of needles in traditional medicine is undeniable. From acupuncture in ancient China to Ayurvedic Marma therapy in India and Japanese acupuncture techniques, various cultures have recognized the healing power of needles. These practices not only highlight the holistic approach to healthcare but also provide valuable insights into the potential benefits of needle-based therapies.

While scientific research on traditional needle-based practices is ongoing, their effectiveness in promoting health and well-being has been acknowledged by countless individuals throughout history. Understanding the role of needles in traditional medicine not only enriches our knowledge but also opens the door to exploring new possibilities for integrative approaches to healthcare. By embracing the wisdom of ancient healing traditions, we can gain a deeper understanding of the therapeutic potential of needles and further enhance our well-being.

The Evolution of Needles in Modern Healthcare

In order to understand the evolution of needles in modern healthcare, we must first delve into the early origins of these medical instruments. Needles have been used for medical purposes for thousands of years, with evidence dating back to ancient civilizations such as the Egyptians, Greeks, and Romans.

Early Medical Uses of Needles

Early medical uses of needles were primarily focused on bloodletting and acupuncture. Bloodletting, the practice of removing blood from a patient's body, was believed to restore the balance of fluids and alleviate various illnesses. Ancient physicians used sharpened stone or metal tools, which eventually evolved into the needle-like instruments we use today.

Acupuncture, originating in ancient China, involves the insertion of thin needles into specific points on the body to promote healing and relieve pain. The ancient Chinese used needles made from stone, bone, or bamboo, which were gradually replaced with metal needles over time.

Symbolism and Rituals

Needles have also played significant roles in religious and cultural rituals throughout history. In many ancient cultures, needles were associated with spiritual or supernatural powers. They were used by shamans, priestesses, and healers in divination practices, rituals, and ceremonies.

For example, in ancient Egyptian mythology, the goddess Sekhmet was believed to mend the wounds of the sick and injured using a magical needle. In Norse mythology, the Norns, the goddesses of fate, wove the destinies of mortals using needles and threads. These ancient beliefs reflect the significance and symbolism associated with needles in early civilizations.

The Role of Needles in Traditional Medicine

Traditional systems of medicine, such as Traditional Chinese Medicine (TCM) and Ayurveda, have long utilized needles for therapeutic purposes. In TCM, acupuncture is believed to balance the flow of vital energy or "qi" in the body, promoting health and well-being. Similarly, Ayurvedic medicine utilizes needle-like instruments known as "shringa" for various therapeutic techniques.

The use of needles in traditional medicine demonstrates the early recognition of their potential healing properties and their ability to stimulate specific points on the body to achieve therapeutic effects.

The Evolution of Needles in Modern Healthcare

With the advancements in medical science and technology, needles have undergone significant transformations to meet the evolving needs of healthcare practices. Here are some key milestones in the evolution of needles in modern healthcare:

Metal Needles and Improvements in Design: During the 19th century, metal needles became widely used in medical procedures. The invention of the hypodermic needle by Francis Rynd in 1844 revolutionized drug delivery and allowed for the direct injection of medications into the bloodstream.

Subsequent improvements in needle design, such as the introduction of the beveled tip by Alexander Wood in the mid-19th century, enhanced the ease and precision of needle insertion. The development of disposable needles in the 20th century improved safety and helped prevent the spread of infections.

Needle Size and Gauge: The size and gauge of needles have been standardized to ensure consistent and reliable performance. The gauge refers to the thickness or diameter of the needle, with smaller gauge numbers indicating larger needle diameters. For example, a 20-gauge needle is thicker than a 25-gauge needle.

Advancements in manufacturing techniques have allowed for the production of needles with smaller diameters, reducing patient discomfort and the risk of tissue damage. Ultra-thin needles, such as those used in insulin pens, have made the administration of medications less invasive for individuals with chronic conditions.

Safety Features: In response to concerns about needlestick injuries and the transmission of bloodborne pathogens, safety features have been incorporated into modern needles. These include retractable needles, which retract into a protective sheath after use, and needleless systems that eliminate the risk of accidental needlesticks.

The introduction of safety-engineered devices has significantly improved the safety of healthcare workers and patients, reducing the risk of needlestick injuries and the potential transmission of infections, such as HIV and hepatitis.

Alternative Needle Delivery Systems: In addition to traditional needles, alternative needle delivery systems have emerged to cater to specific medical needs and patient preferences. For example, transdermal patches and inhalable devices provide a non-invasive route for drug administration, eliminating the need for needle insertion.

Microneedles, tiny needles less than 1mm in length, have gained attention for their potential use in painless drug delivery and minimally invasive diagnostic tests. These microneedles penetrate the outer layer of the skin without reaching the nerve endings, making them virtually painless.

Needle-free Injection Systems: Needle-free injection systems are another innovative development that aims to reduce needle anxiety and improve patient comfort. These systems use high-pressure or air-powered technology to deliver medications through the skin without a needle.

These needle-free injection systems are particularly beneficial for individuals with needle phobia or those who require frequent injections. They offer a less invasive option and can also enhance medication absorption for certain drugs.

Controversies and Ethical Dilemmas Surrounding Needles

While needles have revolutionized healthcare and saved countless lives, they have also been a subject of controversy and ethical dilemmas.

One contentious issue is the use of needles in capital punishment, specifically in lethal injection procedures. Critics argue that the use of lethal injections, which involve administering drugs through needles, can lead to prolonged and agonizing deaths, violating the Eighth Amendment of the United States Constitution.

Another ethical concern is the use of needles in biomedical research involving animals. Organizations advocating for animal welfare argue that the use of needles for procedures and blood sampling can cause unnecessary pain and distress to animals. This has prompted the development of alternative techniques and technologies to reduce the reliance on needles in animal research.

Needle Safety and Regulations

The safety and regulation of needles in healthcare settings have become paramount over the years. Regulatory agencies, such as the Food and Drug Administration (FDA) in the United States, have established guidelines and standards for the development, manufacturing, and use of needles.

These regulations ensure proper sterilization techniques, labeling requirements, and quality control measures are in place to minimize the risk of infections and ensure patient safety. Furthermore, healthcare facilities have implemented stringent protocols for safe needle disposal to prevent injuries and the improper reuse of needles.

The Future of Needles

As technology continues to advance, the future of needles in healthcare holds exciting possibilities. Researchers are exploring new materials and manufacturing techniques to develop even thinner and more flexible needles, further reducing patient discomfort.

Needle-free technologies are expected to gain popularity, offering patients a more convenient and painless alternative to traditional needles. The development of biodegradable needles and microneedle patches could also revolutionize drug delivery by providing controlled release and targeted therapies.

In conclusion, the evolution of needles in modern healthcare encompasses a rich history, scientific advancements, and ethical considerations. From their ancient origins in bloodletting and acupuncture to their current use in innovative drug delivery systems, needles have transformed the field of medicine. While challenges and controversies persist, ongoing research and development promise a future where needles are safer, more efficient, and less invasive in promoting health and well-being.

Advances in Needle Manufacturing

The manufacturing of needles has come a long way throughout history, with advancements in technology and materials greatly improving their quality and functionality. These advancements have not only enhanced the safety and effectiveness of medical procedures but have also played a pivotal role in reducing the fear and anxiety associated with needle phobia. In this section, we will explore some of the notable advances in needle manufacturing that have transformed the field of healthcare.

Introduction to Needle Manufacturing

To fully appreciate the advancements in needle manufacturing, it is essential to understand the basic process involved in producing these tiny yet significant medical instruments. Needle manufacturing typically involves several stages, including material selection, wire drawing, needle grinding, and tip sharpening.

Material Selection

The choice of material for needles depends on their intended use and the specific requirements of medical procedures. Historically, needles were predominantly made of stainless steel due to its durability and resistance to corrosion. While stainless steel needles are still widely used today, advances in materials science have introduced alternative options that offer unique advantages.

One significant advancement is the utilization of ultrafine and superelastic alloys, such as Nitinol (nickel-titanium). Nitinol needles possess shape memory characteristics, allowing them to return to their original shape after being deformed. This property is particularly useful in applications such as chronic pain management and minimally invasive surgeries where flexible and resilient needles are required.

Furthermore, the development of biocompatible polymers, such as polyethylene and polypropylene, has revolutionized needle manufacturing. These materials offer excellent compatibility with the human body, reducing the risk of adverse reactions and enabling the production of disposable, single-use needles that enhance patient safety.

Wire Drawing

Wire drawing is a critical step in needle manufacturing that involves reducing the diameter of the chosen material to achieve the desired size for the needle. Traditionally, this process required multiple passes through various dies to gradually decrease the wire's diameter. However, advancements in microfabrication techniques have introduced innovative methods such as laser cutting and electrochemical machining. These processes allow for precise and rapid production of needles with high dimensional accuracy, minimizing the risk of discomfort or tissue damage during medical procedures.

Needle Grinding and Tip Sharpening

The grinding and sharpening of needle tips are crucial for ensuring optimal functionality and minimizing patient discomfort. Traditional methods involved manual grinding and sharpening, which had limitations in terms of precision and consistency. However, modern needle manufacturing techniques have leveraged computer numerical control (CNC) technology to automate and streamline this process.

CNC-based needle grinding machines utilize highly precise robotic systems, diamond grinding wheels, and advanced algorithms to shape and sharpen needle tips with unparalleled accuracy. Additionally, computer-aided design (CAD) software enables the customization of needle tips to suit specific medical applications. This innovation has opened up new possibilities in the field of needle design, allowing for the creation of needles with unique geometries optimized for specialized procedures.

Advancements in Coating Technologies

Needle coatings play a vital role in enhancing patient comfort, reducing friction during insertion, and minimizing tissue damage. Recent developments in coating technologies have significantly improved the performance and usability of needles.

One notable advancement is the introduction of lubricious coatings. These coatings, typically made of hydrophilic polymers, reduce the surface friction of needles, making them smoother and more comfortable during insertion. Lubricious coatings also enable easier penetration into tissues, reducing the force required for needle insertion and minimizing the potential for patient discomfort.

Furthermore, antimicrobial coatings have gained prominence in recent years. These coatings, often composed of silver nanoparticles, inhibit the growth of bacteria on the needle surface, reducing the risk of infection during medical procedures. The integration of antimicrobial coatings into needle manufacturing has played a crucial role in reducing the incidence of needle-related infections and improving patient outcomes.

Quality Control and Standards

In the field of needle manufacturing, adherence to strict quality control standards is essential to ensure the safety and reliability of these medical instruments. Regulations and standards set by organizations such as the International Organization for Standardization (ISO) and the U.S. Food and Drug Administration (FDA) govern various aspects of needle manufacturing, including dimensional specifications, material properties, and sterility requirements.

Advancements in technological capabilities have enabled more stringent quality control measures. Automated inspection systems utilizing computer vision and machine learning algorithms can detect defects, deviations, and irregularities in needles with high precision, ensuring that only needles meeting the required standards are released for medical use.

Conclusion

Advances in needle manufacturing have undoubtedly transformed the field of healthcare, revolutionizing medical procedures and patient experiences. From the development of new materials to the integration of cutting-edge fabrication techniques, every aspect of needle manufacturing has witnessed significant improvements. These advancements have not only enhanced the safety and efficacy of medical interventions but have also contributed to alleviating the anxiety and fear associated with needles. As research continues to push the boundaries of needle manufacturing, future innovations hold the potential to further optimize these crucial medical instruments and improve patient care.

The Impact of Needles on Society

The use of needles has had a profound impact on society throughout history. From ancient medical practices to modern healthcare systems, the needle has played a crucial role in various aspects of our lives. In this section, we will explore the different ways in which needles have influenced and shaped society.

Medical Advancements

One of the most significant impacts of needles on society can be seen in the field of medicine. Needles have revolutionized the way we administer medication, perform surgeries, and diagnose diseases. The invention of the hypodermic needle in the mid-19th century marked a turning point in medical practices. It allowed for the direct delivery of medications and vaccines into the bloodstream, bypassing the digestive system and rapidly providing relief to patients.

The use of needles in medical procedures has made it possible to perform complex surgeries with precision and minimize the invasiveness of treatments. For instance, needles are used to inject local anesthesia, making surgeries less painful and more manageable for patients. Moreover, the development of needle-based diagnostic techniques, such as fine-needle aspiration, has enabled the early detection of diseases like cancer, greatly improving patient outcomes.

Disease Prevention and Control

Needles have also played a critical role in disease prevention and control. The widespread use of vaccines, delivered through needle injections, has helped eradicate and control numerous infectious diseases. Diseases like polio, measles, and rubella have been significantly reduced or eliminated due to global vaccination programs.

In addition to vaccines, the use of needles for blood testing has been crucial in identifying and monitoring the spread of various diseases. Blood samples obtained through needle pricks are analyzed in laboratories to detect infections, monitor chronic conditions, and diagnose diseases. This allows healthcare professionals to intervene timely and implement necessary measures to prevent further transmission.

Safety and Health Regulations

The impact of needles on society is not solely limited to medical advancements but also extends to safety and health regulations. In recent times, there has been a growing concern about the safe disposal of needles to prevent accidental injuries and the spread of infectious diseases.

Sharps containers, specifically designed for the disposal of needles and other sharp medical instruments, have become a standard practice in healthcare settings. These containers ensure the safe containment and disposal of used needles, minimizing the risk of needlestick injuries for both healthcare workers and the general public.

Moreover, stringent regulations and guidelines governing the manufacturing, usage, and disposal of needles have been implemented to ensure their quality and safety. These regulations ensure that needles are sterile, reduce the risk of contamination, and meet specific standards for various medical procedures. Compliance with these regulations has significantly improved patient safety and reduced the incidence of needle-related complications.

Ethical and Social Considerations

The impact of needles on society also raises ethical and social considerations. The fear of needles, known as trypanophobia, affects a significant portion of the population and can pose challenges in healthcare settings. Medical professionals must be sensitive to the needs and fears of individuals with trypanophobia and work towards creating a supportive and anxiety-free environment.

The proliferation of needle-related procedures has also contributed to the development of bioethical debates. Issues such as informed consent, the overuse of injections versus alternative administration methods, and the potential for misuse and abuse of needles have sparked discussions within the medical community and beyond. Balancing the benefits and risks associated with needle procedures requires careful consideration of ethical principles and societal values.

Environmental Impact

Another aspect of the impact of needles on society lies in their environmental implications. The disposal of needles, especially in large quantities, poses a challenge in terms of waste management. Improper disposal can lead to environmental contamination and pose risks to waste handlers and the general public.

To minimize environmental impact, needle disposal programs have been implemented in many healthcare facilities, promoting the safe and proper disposal of used needles. In addition, efforts are being made to develop environmentally-friendly alternatives to traditional needles, such as needle-free injections or biodegradable materials, which could help mitigate the environmental footprint of needle usage.

Public Perception and Cultural Symbolism

Needles also hold cultural and symbolic significance in various societies. In some cultures, needles have been associated with healing and spiritual rituals. Acupuncture, a traditional Chinese medical practice that involves the insertion of thin needles into specific points on the body, is one such example. Acupuncture has gained recognition and popularity worldwide, highlighting the cultural impact and perception of needles beyond medical procedures.

Furthermore, needles have been used as symbols of resilience, strength, and bravery in different contexts. Tattoos, for instance, often involve the use of needles to inject ink into the skin, allowing individuals to express their identities and stories. The symbolism associated with needles reflects the diverse interpretations and meanings attached to these objects across different cultures and societies.

In conclusion, needles have had a multifaceted impact on society, ranging from medical advancements and disease prevention to safety regulations and cultural symbolism. The continuous evolution of needle-based technologies and practices will undoubtedly shape our future, as we strive to ensure better healthcare, safety, and quality of life. It is essential to consider both the benefits and the ethical implications associated with needles, as we navigate the complex relationship between technology, society, and human well-being.

Controversies and Ethical Dilemmas Surrounding Needles

The use of needles in various domains, especially in healthcare, has led to numerous controversies and ethical dilemmas over the years. These issues arise from concerns about safety, autonomy, consent, and the balance between the benefits and risks associated with needle-related procedures. In this section, we will explore some of the common controversies and ethical dilemmas surrounding needles.

Safety of Needle Procedures

One of the primary concerns related to needles is safety. While advances in needle manufacturing and regulations have significantly improved safety standards, there have been instances of needle-related injuries and transmission of infections.

Needlestick injuries, which occur when a healthcare worker accidentally pierces their skin with a contaminated needle, pose a considerable risk for transmitting bloodborne pathogens such as HIV, hepatitis B, and hepatitis C. These incidents raise ethical questions about the responsibility of healthcare institutions and professionals to ensure the safety of their employees.

Another safety concern arises from the reuse of needles. In resource-limited settings, where access to new, sterile needles is limited, practitioners may resort to reusing needles, significantly increasing the risk of infection transmission. This practice is particularly common in settings where injection drug use is prevalent.

Balancing the need for sterile equipment with the limited resources available becomes an ethical dilemma in such contexts.

Informed Consent and Autonomy

Informed consent is a fundamental ethical principle that underpins medical procedures involving needles. Patients have the right to be fully informed of the risks, benefits, and alternative options related to any procedure requiring needle insertion. However, obtaining informed consent for needle-related procedures can be challenging, especially when the patient has an excessive fear of needles or when the procedure is urgent.

Patients with needle phobia, such as trypanophobics, may be unable to provide valid consent due to their heightened anxiety and fear. Balancing the need for informed consent with the urgency of the procedure poses an ethical dilemma for healthcare providers. In such cases, healthcare professionals must assess the patient's capacity to provide consent and consider alternative approaches, such as involving a support person or considering sedation.

Additionally, the autonomy of certain populations might be compromised when it comes to needle procedures. For example, children or individuals with cognitive impairments may not fully understand the implications of the procedure or may lack the capacity to provide informed consent. Encouraging shared decision-making and ensuring the involvement of caregivers or family members in decision-making processes become crucial in such scenarios.

Needle-Related Procedures and Pain Management

The experience of pain during needle-related procedures is a well-known ethical concern. For some individuals, the fear of pain associated with needles can be debilitating and may lead to avoidance of necessary medical interventions. Healthcare providers must balance the necessity of the procedure with the minimization of pain and distress.

Ethical dilemmas arise when healthcare professionals have to make decisions regarding pain management during needle-related procedures. The use of topical anesthetics, distraction techniques, and other pain management interventions can help alleviate the fear and discomfort associated with needle procedures. However, these interventions may not always be feasible or appropriate in every situation.

Furthermore, balancing the need for pain management with potential risks, such as adverse reactions to anesthetics or delayed diagnosis due to sedation, further complicates the ethical landscape surrounding needle-related procedures.

Needle Disposal and Environmental Impact

Ethical concerns related to needles are not limited to the healthcare setting but also extend to the proper disposal of used needles and their environmental impact. Improper disposal of needles can lead to injuries, especially among waste handlers.

Additionally, the environmental impact of discarded needles poses a significant ethical dilemma. Needles and other medical waste can pose a risk to public health when they end up in landfills, water bodies, or public spaces. Proper disposal methods, including the use of sharps containers, are crucial to mitigate these risks.

Finding sustainable solutions for the disposal of needles, such as needle exchange programs, safe injection sites, and recycling initiatives, becomes imperative to ensure the safety of both individuals and the environment.

Equitable Access to Needle-Related Interventions

Equitable access to needle-related interventions is an ongoing ethical issue, particularly in low-income and marginalized communities. Disparities in healthcare resources and infrastructure can lead to unequal access to sterile needles, vaccination programs, and other needle procedures.

Lack of access to clean needles can contribute to the transmission of infectious diseases, particularly among individuals who engage in injection drug use. Providing equitable access to harm reduction programs, such as needle exchange programs, can help address this issue and prevent the spread of bloodborne infections.

Furthermore, ensuring equitable access to needle-related interventions goes beyond physical access. Factors such as cultural beliefs, stigma, and discrimination may affect an individual's willingness to seek necessary needle procedures. Addressing these social determinants of health becomes crucial in promoting equitable access and reducing health disparities.

Ethical Considerations in Research and Innovation

As needle-related technologies continue to advance, ethical considerations in research and innovation become vital. Investigational studies involving needle procedures must adhere to rigorous ethical standards, including ensuring the voluntary participation and informed consent of participants, as well as balancing potential benefits with risks.

The development of new needle-based technologies and techniques raises ethical questions about potential conflicts of interest, industry influence, and equitable distribution of resources. Ensuring transparency, accountability, and independent evaluation of new innovations is essential to maintain ethical standards.

Additionally, incorporating patient perspectives and experiences in research and innovation processes can help address ethical concerns and guide the development of more patient-centered needle-related interventions.

Conclusion

Controversies and ethical dilemmas surrounding needles arise in various contexts, including healthcare, research, and environmental impact. Balancing safety, informed consent, pain management, equitable access, and ethical research practices becomes crucial in addressing these issues. By recognizing and ethically navigating these dilemmas, we can strive for a safer and more patient-centered approach to needle-related procedures.

Needle Safety and Regulations

When it comes to needles, ensuring safety is of utmost importance. The medical community is well aware of the risks associated with needle practices and has implemented various regulations and guidelines to mitigate these risks. In this section, we will delve into the world of needle safety and explore the regulations aimed at protecting both healthcare providers and patients.

The Importance of Needle Safety

Needle-related injuries pose a significant risk to healthcare workers, patients, and the general public. Accidental needlestick injuries can result in the transmission of bloodborne pathogens such as hepatitis B, hepatitis C, and human immunodeficiency virus (HIV). According to the World Health Organization (WHO), millions of healthcare workers are exposed to the risk of needlestick injuries each year.

Aside from the transmission of infections, poorly designed or improperly handled needles can also lead to a range of complications. These include pain, bruising, nerve damage, and the formation of granulomas or abscesses at the injection site. In some cases, needle-related injuries may even result in long-term disability or death.

Regulatory Bodies and Guidelines

To address the issue of needle safety, regulatory bodies around the world have developed guidelines and standards for the proper handling and disposal of needles. These guidelines aim to minimize the risk of needlestick injuries and ensure the safe use of needles across various healthcare settings.

One key organization in this regard is the Occupational Safety and Health Administration (OSHA) in the United States. OSHA's Bloodborne Pathogens Standard outlines specific requirements for the safe management of sharps, which includes needles, in healthcare facilities. The standard mandates the implementation of safety devices, such as retractable needles, to reduce the risk of needlestick injuries.

Similarly, the International Organization for Standardization (ISO) has developed several standards related to needle safety. ISO 7864 specifies requirements for sterile hypodermic needles for single use, including quality control, marking, and packaging. ISO 23908 provides guidelines for the design and testing of sharps injury protection devices (SIPDs) to prevent needlestick injuries.

Other regulatory bodies and organizations, such as the Centers for Disease Control and Prevention (CDC) and the World Health Organization (WHO), also contribute to the development of guidelines and best practices for needle safety. These guidelines cover a wide range of topics, including safe injection practices, needle disposal, and personal protective equipment (PPE) requirements.

Advances in Needle Safety Technology

In recent years, there have been significant advancements in needle safety technology aimed at further reducing the risk of needlestick injuries. One notable development is the introduction of safety-engineered devices (SEDs) or needlestick prevention devices.

SEDs are designed to minimize the risk of accidental needlestick injuries by incorporating built-in safety features or mechanisms. These features may include retractable needles, shielding mechanisms, or needle encapsulation systems. By activating these safety mechanisms after use, healthcare providers can minimize the risk of accidental needlestick injuries during needle removal and disposal.

Additionally, advancements in needle manufacturing have resulted in the production of ultra-sharp, high-quality needles. These needles are designed to minimize tissue trauma, reduce pain during injections, and improve overall patient comfort.

It is worth noting that while technologically advanced safety devices are available, their adoption and usage in healthcare settings can vary. This may be due to cost considerations, training requirements, or resistance to change. However, efforts are being made to educate healthcare providers about the importance of needle safety and encourage the widespread implementation of safety devices.

Patient Education and Empowerment

Needle safety is not just the responsibility of healthcare providers; patients also need to be informed and empowered to ensure their own safety. Understanding safe injection practices and being proactive in asking healthcare providers about their needle safety protocols can go a long way in reducing the risk of needle-related complications.

Patients should also be aware of their rights when it comes to needle safety. They have the right to ask whether safety devices are being used during procedures and to request the use of a safety device if one is not initially provided. Open communication between patients and healthcare providers is crucial in creating a safe environment for all.

Unconventional Solution: Needle Exchange Programs

While not directly related to needle safety in healthcare settings, needle exchange programs have emerged as an unconventional yet effective solution in reducing the risk of needle-related infections. Needle exchange programs provide sterile needles to intravenous drug users in exchange for used syringes, thus preventing the sharing of contaminated needles and the transmission of bloodborne diseases.

These programs not only protect individuals who use drugs but also contribute to community health by reducing the overall prevalence of bloodborne infections. They serve as a harm reduction strategy, offering resources and support for individuals struggling with addiction while also minimizing the risk of needle-related complications.

Conclusion

Needle safety and regulations play a vital role in minimizing the risks associated with needle practices. Compliance with guidelines and standards ensures the safety of healthcare providers and patients alike. As technology advances, the development and implementation of safety devices continue to evolve, further reducing the risk of needlestick injuries.

By staying informed, advocating for safe practices, and fostering open communication, both healthcare providers and patients can contribute to a culture of needle safety. Together, we can strive for a future where the fear and risks associated with needles are minimized, empowering individuals to seek the medical care they need without unnecessary apprehension.

The Future of Needles

In this chapter, we will explore the exciting possibilities and advancements in the field of needles. As technology continues to evolve, so too does the design and function of needles. From innovations in materials to improve patient comfort, to the development of smart needles that can monitor vital signs, the future of needles holds great potential for revolutionizing healthcare and addressing the challenges faced by needle phobics.

Nanotechnology and Biocompatible Materials

One of the most promising areas of research in needle development lies in the field of nanotechnology. Scientists are exploring the use of nanomaterials to create ultra-fine needles that are virtually painless and cause minimal tissue damage. These needles, often referred to as "nanoneedles," have the potential to revolutionize medical procedures by reducing patient discomfort and improving precision.

Additionally, advances in biocompatible materials are making needles safer and more efficient. Traditional needles are typically made of stainless steel, which can be sharp but may cause discomfort and pain during insertion. Researchers are now exploring alternative materials, such as biodegradable polymers and ceramic composites, that are both sharp and biocompatible. These materials minimize tissue damage and reduce the risk of infection.

Microtechnology and Miniaturization

The future of needles is closely intertwined with microtechnology and miniaturization. As electronic components become smaller and more powerful, the potential for integrating technology into needles becomes increasingly feasible. Miniaturized sensors, for example, can be embedded into the tip of a needle to provide real-time feedback on tissue characteristics, blood chemistry, and drug delivery effectiveness. These smart needles have the potential to revolutionize procedures by precisely targeting specific areas and minimizing the risk of complications.

Furthermore, advancements in microfabrication techniques enable the creation of hollow needles with complex internal structures. This allows for improved fluid management, such as controlled drug release and sampling, which can enhance the effectiveness of treatments and diagnostics.

Needle-free Technologies

While needles have been the primary tool for medical interventions for centuries, needle-free technologies are emerging as an alternative for various applications. Needle-free injections, for instance, use high-velocity jets of medication to deliver drugs through the skin without the need for traditional needles. This approach eliminates the fear and pain associated with injections, making it particularly beneficial for individuals with trypanophobia.

Moreover, advancements in transdermal drug delivery systems offer a non-invasive alternative to injections. These systems use patches or devices that deliver medications through the skin, bypassing the need for needles altogether. Although not suitable for all types of medications, transdermal delivery provides a convenient and painless alternative for certain treatments.

Artificial Intelligence and Robotics

Artificial intelligence (AI) and robotics play a significant role in the future of needles. Robotics-assisted procedures have gained popularity in surgical interventions for their precision and control. By integrating AI algorithms and robotics, procedures that require needle insertion can be performed with improved accuracy, reducing the risk of complications and shortening recovery times.

Additionally, AI can be utilized to create personalized needle insertion paths based on patient-specific anatomical data. This approach ensures that needles are placed optimally, minimizing tissue damage and improving patient comfort.

Barriers and Ethical Considerations

While the future of needles presents exciting possibilities, there are several barriers and ethical considerations that need to be addressed. For instance, the cost of developing and implementing advanced needle technologies can be prohibitive, limiting accessibility, particularly in resource-limited settings. Ensuring equitable access to these innovations should be a priority to maximize their potential benefits.

Moreover, ethical concerns arise when discussing invasive procedures and the impact on patient autonomy. While advancements in needle technology aim to minimize pain and discomfort, it is crucial to respect patients' preferences and provide them with the choice of alternative methods when appropriate.

Conclusion

The future of needles holds immense potential for improving the healthcare experience for patients and addressing the challenges faced by those with needle phobia. With advancements in nanotechnology, microtechnology, needle-free technologies, artificial intelligence, and robotics, the landscape of medical interventions involving needles is undergoing a transformative shift. However, it is crucial to address barriers, ensure equitable access, and prioritize patient autonomy to achieve the full potential of these innovations. By continuing to push the boundaries of needle technology, we can create a future where medical interventions are not only effective but also more comfortable and less intimidating for all individuals.

Chapter Two: Understanding Trypanophobia

The Anatomy and Physiology of Fear

The Fight or Flight Response

The fight or flight response is a primal, automatic physiological reaction that occurs in response to perceived threats or danger. It is a built-in survival mechanism that prepares the body to either confront the threat head-on or escape from it. This response is deeply rooted in our evolutionary history and is controlled by a complex interplay between the nervous system and the endocrine system.

When faced with a threat, whether it be physical or psychological, a cascade of changes takes place within the body. The sympathetic branch of the autonomic nervous system becomes activated, leading to a series of physiological changes that enable us to respond effectively in the face of danger. The parasympathetic branch, on the other hand, helps to restore the body to its normal state once the threat has passed.

One of the key components of the fight or flight response is the release of stress hormones, particularly adrenaline (epinephrine) and norepinephrine. These hormones are released by the adrenal glands and have a widespread effect on different organs and systems in the body.

The release of adrenaline triggers a number of immediate physiological changes. For instance, the heart rate and blood pressure increase, allowing more blood to flow to the muscles. This enhances physical strength and agility, preparing the body for physical confrontation or escape. At the same time, blood vessels in non-essential organs, such as the digestive system, constrict, redirecting blood flow to the muscles and vital organs.

Alongside these cardiovascular changes, the fight or flight response also affects respiration. Breathing becomes faster and shallower, which helps to oxygenate the blood and provide a burst of energy. The bronchial tubes in the lungs dilate, allowing for increased airflow and better oxygen exchange.

Moreover, the fight or flight response impacts glucose metabolism. The release of stress hormones triggers the liver to release glucose into the bloodstream, providing an immediate source of energy to fuel physical exertion. This increase in blood glucose levels ensures that the body has the necessary resources to either fight or flee.

In addition to these physiological changes, the fight or flight response also affects various other bodily systems. For instance, the pupils dilate to enhance visual acuity, helping to spot potential threats. The digestive system slows down, as energy is diverted away from non-essential functions like digestion towards survival-related activities. The immune system may also experience temporary suppression, as resources are allocated towards more immediate threats.

It is important to note that the fight or flight response is not only triggered by acute physical threats but also by psychological stressors. For instance, an upcoming exam or public speaking engagement can elicit a similar response, even though there may not be any immediate physical danger. The body reacts as if it were facing a physical threat, leading to increased heart rate, sweating, and other physiological symptoms.

Understanding the fight or flight response is crucial in the context of trypanophobia, as this fear triggers the same physiological reactions. Trypanophobics often experience intense anxiety and panic symptoms, such as increased heart rate, sweating, and shortness of breath, when faced with the prospect of needle-related procedures. These reactions are a direct result of the fight or flight response and underscore the profound impact that fear can have on the body.

To effectively cope with trypanophobia, it is important to recognize the underlying fight or flight response and develop strategies to manage it. Techniques such as deep breathing, relaxation exercises, and cognitive restructuring can help individuals regain control over their physiological reactions and reduce anxiety levels.

It is also worth noting that prolonged exposure to stress or chronic activation of the fight or flight response can have negative health consequences. High levels of stress hormones, such as prolonged elevation of adrenaline, can contribute to the development of health problems like hypertension, cardiovascular disease, and immune dysfunction. Therefore, managing stress and finding healthy coping mechanisms is essential for overall well-being.

In conclusion, the fight or flight response is an innate survival mechanism that prepares the body for action in the face of perceived threats. Understanding this physiological response is crucial in addressing trypanophobia and developing effective coping strategies. By acknowledging the power of the fight or flight response and implementing techniques to manage it, individuals can regain control over their fear and minimize its impact on their lives.

The Role of the Amygdala

The amygdala, a small almond-shaped structure located deep within the brain's temporal lobe, plays a crucial role in the experience and processing of fear. It is an ancient and evolutionarily conserved structure that has been implicated in various emotional and behavioral responses, particularly those related to threat detection and fear conditioning. Understanding the role of the amygdala is essential for comprehending the mechanisms underlying trypanophobia.

One of the amygdala's primary functions is to process and interpret sensory information, especially stimuli that may pose a potential threat to an individual's safety. When confronted with a fearful or potentially dangerous situation, the amygdala acts as an alarm system, rapidly assessing the situation and triggering a cascade of physiological and behavioral responses.

The amygdala receives sensory inputs from various regions of the brain, including the thalamus, hippocampus, and cortex. These inputs carry information about the external environment, such as visual, auditory, and tactile cues associated with threat or danger. Upon receiving these inputs, the amygdala evaluates the sensory information and determines whether it poses a threat or not.

Neurons in the amygdala are specialized in recognizing and responding to fear-related stimuli. Studies have shown that specific subregions within the amygdala, such as the basolateral complex (BLA) and the central nucleus (CeA), are particularly involved in fear processing. The BLA is responsible for the acquisition and storage of fear memories, while the CeA mediates the expression of fear responses.

The amygdala's role in fear processing becomes particularly relevant in the context of trypanophobia. Individuals with trypanophobia often exhibit an exaggerated fear response to needles, even in situations where the threat is minimal or non-existent. This heightened fear response can be attributed, at least in part, to an overactive amygdala.

Functional neuroimaging studies have consistently shown increased activation in the amygdala in individuals with trypanophobia when exposed to needle-related stimuli. This hyperactivity reflects an exaggerated fear response and may contribute to the intense anxiety and avoidance behaviors commonly observed in these individuals.

Furthermore, studies have demonstrated that amygdala activation is robustly connected to other brain regions involved in fear processing, such as the prefrontal cortex and the hypothalamus. These connections enable the amygdala to influence cognitive processes, emotional regulation, and the coordination of physiological responses associated with fear.

The amygdala's interaction with the prefrontal cortex is particularly relevant in the context of trypanophobia. The prefrontal cortex plays a crucial role in cognitive appraisal, decision-making, and emotion regulation. In individuals with trypanophobia, the amygdala's heightened activity can disrupt the prefrontal cortex's ability to modulate the fear response effectively.

Understanding the neural circuitry involving the amygdala and its connections to other brain regions offers insights into potential therapeutic interventions for trypanophobia. Techniques such as cognitive-behavioral therapy (CBT) and exposure therapy aim to modulate amygdala activation and rewire the fear response by engaging the prefrontal cortex in reappraisal and regulation of fear.

In summary, the amygdala serves as a key component of the brain's fear circuitry and plays a critical role in the experience and processing of fear. In the context of trypanophobia, an overactive amygdala contributes to the heightened fear response to needles. By understanding the complex interplay between the amygdala and other brain regions involved in fear processing, researchers and clinicians can develop effective therapeutic strategies to help individuals cope with and overcome trypanophobia.

Neurotransmitters and Fear Conditioning

Fear conditioning is a process by which an individual learns to associate a neutral stimulus with a fear-inducing event, resulting in the development of a fear response to that stimulus. This process involves the neurotransmitters in the brain, which are chemical messengers that allow communication between neurons. In this section, we will explore the role of neurotransmitters in fear conditioning and how they contribute to the development and regulation of fear.

The Role of Neurotransmitters in Fear Conditioning

Several neurotransmitters play key roles in fear conditioning, including serotonin, dopamine, norepinephrine, glutamate, and gamma-aminobutyric acid (GABA).

Each neurotransmitter acts on specific receptor sites in the brain, influencing the processing and modulation of fear-related information.

1. **Serotonin:** Serotonin is a neurotransmitter that is involved in regulating mood, emotions, and anxiety. It is released by neurons in the brainstem and projects to various brain regions, including the amygdala, which plays a crucial role in fear conditioning. Studies have shown that serotonin can inhibit fear and reduce anxiety by binding to specific serotonin receptors, such as 5-HT1A and 5-HT2A receptors, in the amygdala.

2. **Dopamine:** Dopamine is a neurotransmitter associated with reward and motivation. It is released by neurons in the midbrain and acts on dopamine receptors in various brain regions, including the amygdala and prefrontal cortex. Dopamine plays a complex role in fear conditioning, as both its increase and decrease can modulate the fear response. High levels of dopamine have been shown to enhance fear memory consolidation, while low levels can impair fear extinction, the process of diminishing a previously conditioned fear response.

3. **Norepinephrine:** Norepinephrine, also known as noradrenaline, is a neurotransmitter involved in the body's stress response and arousal. It is released by neurons in the locus coeruleus and projects to brain regions involved in fear processing, including the amygdala and prefrontal cortex. Norepinephrine enhances the consolidation of fear memories, making them more resistant to extinction. It also increases attention and vigilance to fear-related stimuli, facilitating fear learning.

4. **Glutamate:** Glutamate is the primary excitatory neurotransmitter in the brain. It is released by neurons and binds to glutamate receptors, such as N-methyl-D-aspartate (NMDA) receptors, in various brain regions involved in fear conditioning. Glutamate plays a crucial role in fear memory formation and consolidation. NMDA receptors are particularly important, as they are involved in synaptic plasticity, the process by which connections between neurons strengthen or weaken in response to experience.

5. **GABA:** Gamma-aminobutyric acid (GABA) is the primary inhibitory neurotransmitter in the brain. It counteracts the effects of excitatory neurotransmitters like glutamate and helps regulate neuronal activity. GABAergic transmission has been implicated in fear extinction, as it inhibits fear-related neural circuits and promotes the suppression of fear responses. GABA receptors are distributed throughout the brain, including the amygdala and prefrontal cortex, and their activity plays a crucial role in fear regulation.

Neurotransmitter Imbalances and Fear Disorders

The dysregulation of neurotransmitter systems implicated in fear conditioning can contribute to the development of fear disorders, such as generalized anxiety disorder, panic disorder, and post-traumatic stress disorder (PTSD). Imbalances in the levels or functioning of neurotransmitters can affect fear learning, fear extinction, and fear memory retrieval, leading to the persistence and amplification of fear responses.

For example, an overactive amygdala that is hypersensitive to fear-related stimuli may result from an imbalance between excitatory (glutamate) and inhibitory (GABA) neurotransmission. This can lead to excessive fear responses and an impaired ability to extinguish fear memories. Similarly, alterations in serotonin, dopamine, or norepinephrine levels can disrupt the regulation of fear-related neural circuits, contributing to anxiety and fear-related disorders.

Understanding these neurotransmitter imbalances and their impact on fear conditioning is crucial for developing targeted interventions and treatments for individuals with fear disorders. By modulating neurotransmitter activity, such as through pharmacological interventions or behavioral therapies, it may be possible to restore the balance and alleviate fear symptoms.

Case Study: The Role of Glutamate in PTSD

Post-traumatic stress disorder (PTSD) is a fear disorder that can develop after exposure to a traumatic event. Studies have shown that individuals with PTSD exhibit alterations in glutamate neurotransmission, particularly in brain regions involved in fear conditioning, such as the amygdala and prefrontal cortex.

Excessive glutamate release and prolonged activation of NMDA receptors in the amygdala may contribute to the heightened fear response and intrusive memories experienced by individuals with PTSD. This hyperactive amygdala can impair fear extinction and lead to the persistence of traumatic memories. In contrast, reduced glutamate levels and NMDA receptor functioning in the prefrontal cortex may contribute to deficits in fear inhibition and emotion regulation seen in PTSD.

These findings have led to the exploration of glutamate-modulating drugs, such as NMDA receptor antagonists, as potential treatments for PTSD. By targeting aberrant glutamate neurotransmission, it is hoped that these medications can restore the balance between fear-related brain circuits and alleviate symptoms of PTSD.

Conclusion

Neurotransmitters play a vital role in fear conditioning, influencing the development, regulation, and modulation of fear responses. Imbalances in neurotransmitter systems can contribute to the development of fear disorders, highlighting the importance of understanding their mechanisms in order to develop effective treatments. By targeting neurotransmitter activity, it may be possible to restore the balance and alleviate the debilitating symptoms of fear-related conditions. Further research into neurotransmitters and fear conditioning will continue to shed light on the complexities of this fascinating field.

Brain Imaging Studies on Trypanophobia

Understanding the neurobiological basis of trypanophobia, or the fear of needles, requires a closer look at brain imaging studies. By examining the brain's response to needle-related stimuli, researchers have gained valuable insights into the neural mechanisms underlying this phobia. Functional magnetic resonance imaging (fMRI) and positron emission tomography (PET) are two commonly used techniques for studying brain activity during phobic reactions.

fMRI Studies

Functional magnetic resonance imaging (fMRI) allows researchers to visualize brain activity by measuring changes in blood flow. Several studies have explored the brain regions involved in trypanophobia using fMRI.

Amygdala Activation: The amygdala, a key brain structure involved in fear processing, has consistently shown increased activation in individuals with trypanophobia. When exposed to needle-related stimuli, such as images or videos of injections, trypanophobics exhibit heightened amygdala responses compared to non-phobic individuals. This hyperactivation suggests that the amygdala plays a pivotal role in the initiation and maintenance of needle fear.

Prefrontal Cortex Involvement: The prefrontal cortex (PFC), particularly the ventromedial prefrontal cortex (vmPFC), is crucial for regulating emotions and fear-related responses. In trypanophobia, the vmPFC exhibits reduced activation compared to non-phobics. This suggests an impaired ability to regulate fear responses, leading to an exaggerated fear reaction in individuals with trypanophobia.

Hippocampal Response: The hippocampus, a brain region involved in memory processing, also plays a role in trypanophobia. Studies have shown increased hippocampal activation in trypanophobic individuals when exposed to needle stimuli. This heightened response may be related to the formation and retrieval of fear memories associated with past traumatic experiences.

Insula Activation: The insula, a brain region involved in interoception and emotional awareness, has been found to exhibit increased activation in individuals with trypanophobia. This heightened insula response suggests an enhanced sensitivity to bodily sensations and increased awareness of the aversive aspects of needle-related stimuli.

Hypothalamus and brainstem involvement: In addition to the aforementioned regions, the hypothalamus and brainstem are also implicated in trypanophobia. These regions play a crucial role in the autonomic nervous system's response to fear, leading to physiological changes such as increased heart rate and sweating. fMRI studies have shown altered activation patterns in these regions in individuals with needle phobia.

PET Studies

Positron emission tomography (PET) is another imaging technique that allows researchers to investigate brain activity by measuring changes in blood flow and glucose metabolism. PET studies have provided further insights into the neural circuitry involved in trypanophobia.

Serotonergic System Dysfunction: PET studies have revealed alterations in the serotonergic system in individuals with trypanophobia. The serotonin system plays a crucial role in regulating emotions and anxiety. Trypanophobic individuals exhibit decreased serotonin receptor binding, suggesting dysfunction in this system. This may contribute to altered fear regulation and heightened anxiety in response to needle-related stimuli.

Dopaminergic Pathways: Dopamine, a neurotransmitter associated with reward and motivation, also plays a role in needle phobia. PET studies have shown altered dopamine receptor availability in the striatum of trypanophobic individuals. This suggests that disturbances in the dopaminergic system may contribute to the heightened fear response observed in individuals with trypanophobia.

Neurochemical Signalling: PET studies have also explored the neurochemical signalling pathways involved in trypanophobia. Alterations in neurotransmitters such as glutamate, GABA, and norepinephrine have been observed in trypanophobic individuals, suggesting a dysregulation of these systems in modulating fear and anxiety.

Implications and Future Directions

Brain imaging studies have shed light on the neural correlates of trypanophobia. The findings suggest that trypanophobia is associated with dysregulation in multiple brain regions involved in fear processing, emotional regulation, memory, and autonomic responses. These studies provide a foundation for the development of targeted interventions that can effectively alleviate needle fear.

Future research in this area could further explore the role of individual differences in brain responses to needle stimuli. Factors such as genetics, early-life experiences, and comorbidities could influence the neural mechanisms underlying trypanophobia. Longitudinal studies tracking brain changes over time could also help identify potential biomarkers or predictors of treatment response.

In conclusion, brain imaging studies have provided valuable insights into the neurobiology of trypanophobia. By unraveling the underlying neural mechanisms, researchers can develop evidence-based interventions that offer hope and support to individuals struggling with this debilitating phobia.

Genetic and Environmental Factors

Understanding the factors that contribute to trypanophobia is crucial in addressing and treating this debilitating fear. While the causes of trypanophobia are complex and multifaceted, both genetic and environmental factors play a significant role in its development. In this section, we will delve into the genetic and environmental influences that contribute to the onset and severity of trypanophobia.

Genetic Factors

Genetics can play a notable role in the development of trypanophobia. Research has shown that certain genetic variations can make individuals more susceptible to anxiety disorders, including phobias. Studies have identified specific genes that are associated with fear and anxiety responses, such as the serotonin transporter gene (SLC6A4) and the corticotropin-releasing hormone receptor 1 gene (CRHR1).

The serotonin transporter gene regulates the reuptake of serotonin, a neurotransmitter involved in mood regulation. Variations in this gene can impact serotonin levels in the brain, potentially influencing an individual's vulnerability to anxiety disorders. Similarly, the corticotropin-releasing hormone receptor 1 gene is involved in the regulation of the body's stress response. Genetic variations in this gene can affect the functioning of the stress-response system, potentially increasing the likelihood of developing anxiety-related disorders.

However, it is important to note that genetics alone do not determine the development of trypanophobia. The interplay between genetic factors and environmental influences is crucial in understanding the complete picture.

Environmental Factors

Environmental factors significantly contribute to the development of trypanophobia. Traumatic experiences, particularly those involving needles or medical procedures, can serve as significant triggers for the fear of needles. This is especially true in cases where the experience was associated with pain, distress, or a lack of control.

Childhood experiences, in particular, play a pivotal role in shaping an individual's fear response. Painful medical procedures during childhood, such as immunizations or blood draws, can create lasting traumatic memories and reinforce the fear of needles. Additionally, witnessing a traumatic needle-related event, such as a loved one experiencing extreme discomfort or complications, can further contribute to the development of trypanophobia.

Parental influence and modeling also play a significant role in the development of trypanophobia. If a parent or caregiver demonstrates fear or anxiety towards needles, a child is more likely to adopt similar fears. Observational learning, in which individuals acquire fears by watching others' fearful reactions, can contribute to the transmission of trypanophobia from one generation to another.

Moreover, societal attitudes and cultural influences can shape individuals' responses to needles. Negative portrayals of medical procedures or needles in media and popular culture can heighten anxieties and foster a fear of needles. Additionally, cultural practices and beliefs surrounding medical procedures can influence an individual's fear response.

It is worth noting that environmental factors are highly individualized, and the specific experiences and contexts vary from person to person. What may be traumatic for one individual may not have the same impact on another. Therefore, a comprehensive understanding of the individual's unique experiences and environmental factors is essential for effective treatment.

Interactions Between Genetic and Environmental Factors

The interplay between genetic and environmental factors in the development of trypanophobia is complex and often reciprocal. Genetic predispositions can make individuals more susceptible to environmental influences, while environmental experiences can further shape gene expression and neural pathways associated with fear and anxiety responses.

For example, individuals with genetic variations associated with serotonin regulation may be more sensitive to stressful or traumatic experiences, thus increasing their vulnerability to developing trypanophobia. Similarly, a person's genetic makeup may influence their ability to cope with fear-inducing situations, affecting their response to environmental triggers.

Furthermore, the interaction between genetic and environmental influences can extend beyond the individual level. Family and social support systems play a significant role in buffering against the development of trypanophobia. A strong support system can help individuals cope with their fears and provide a sense of security and reassurance during challenging situations.

Overall, understanding the interplay between genetic and environmental factors is crucial for personalized and holistic approaches in the treatment of trypanophobia. By addressing both the individual's genetic predispositions and their unique experiences and environmental influences, healthcare providers can provide comprehensive care and support to individuals struggling with this phobia.

Summary

In this section, we explored the genetic and environmental factors that contribute to the development of trypanophobia. While genetics can predispose individuals to anxiety-related disorders, such as trypanophobia, environmental factors such as traumatic experiences and parental modeling play a significant role in shaping the fear response. Understanding the interactions between genetic and environmental influences is essential for the effective treatment and support of individuals with trypanophobia. By taking a comprehensive and personalized approach, healthcare providers can help individuals overcome their fears and live fulfilling lives.

Developmental Trauma and Needle Phobia

Developmental trauma refers to the negative experiences and events that occur during childhood and have a long-lasting impact on an individual's emotional and psychological well-being. These traumas can shape the way a person views and interacts with the world, often leading to the development of various anxiety disorders, including needle phobia (trypanophobia). In this section, we will explore the relationship between developmental trauma and needle phobia, shedding light on the underlying mechanisms and potential interventions.

Needle phobia can be traced back to specific traumatic experiences in childhood that involve medical procedures, injections, or other needle-related events. The experience of pain, fear, or distress during these incidents can leave a lasting imprint on a child's mind, leading to the development of a deep-seated fear of needles. This type of trauma can be categorized as an adverse childhood experience (ACE), which has been extensively studied in the field of psychology.

Children who have experienced developmental trauma may associate needles with feelings of powerlessness, distress, and physical pain. Their fear response becomes heightened, triggering the fight-or-flight response whenever they encounter needles or situations related to them. The memories of these traumatic events become deeply ingrained, leading to automatic and uncontrollable fear responses.

One common phenomenon observed in individuals with needle phobia is the phenomenon of "needle aversion." This aversion can be seen as a defense mechanism developed by the individual to avoid the distress associated with needle-related experiences. Avoidance becomes a coping strategy, and individuals often go to great lengths to avoid medical procedures or situations that involve needles. This aversion, while initially serving as a protective mechanism, further reinforces and exaggerates the fear response, making it increasingly difficult to confront and overcome.

The development of needle phobia can also be influenced by other factors related to developmental trauma, such as the presence of other anxiety disorders or a predisposition to anxiety. Research suggests that individuals with a history of trauma may be more susceptible to developing anxiety disorders, and this vulnerability extends to needle phobia as well.

Intervening in cases of developmental trauma and needle phobia requires a comprehensive and multidisciplinary approach. Therapeutic techniques aimed at healing trauma, such as trauma-focused cognitive-behavioral therapy (TF-CBT), can be effective in addressing the underlying psychological distress associated with needle phobia. TF-CBT combines elements of cognitive-behavioral therapy (CBT) and trauma-focused interventions to help individuals process and resolve traumatic memories.

Exposure therapy, a common component of CBT, can also be applied in the treatment of needle phobia. By gradually exposing individuals to needle-related stimuli in a controlled and supportive environment, they can learn to manage their fear responses and develop new associations with needles that are more positive and less anxiety-provoking. This approach helps to desensitize individuals to the feared stimuli and break the cycle of avoidance.

Additionally, incorporating play therapy and art therapy into the treatment process can provide a safe and creative outlet for children with needle phobia to express and process their emotions related to needle-related traumas. These therapies encourage exploration and self-expression, allowing children to externalize their inner fears and anxieties.

It is important to involve parents and caregivers in the treatment process, as they play a crucial role in supporting their child's healing journey. Building trust and open communication within the family system can help parents understand their child's fears and provide the necessary emotional support. Collaborative efforts between parents, healthcare providers, and therapists can help create a safe and nurturing environment for the child, facilitating their recovery from needle phobia.

In conclusion, developmental trauma can significantly contribute to the development of needle phobia. The negative experiences and emotions associated with childhood trauma become intertwined with the fear of needles, leading to a persistent and debilitating phobia. However, with the right interventions and support, individuals can overcome their fear and regain control over their lives. By addressing the underlying trauma and implementing evidence-based treatments, we can empower individuals to live free from the shackles of needle phobia.

Comorbidities and Associated Disorders

Comorbidities refer to the presence of multiple co-occurring disorders or conditions in individuals diagnosed with a particular phobia. Trypanophobia, being an intense fear of needles, often presents in conjunction with other mental health disorders. Understanding these comorbidities is crucial for developing effective treatment plans and providing comprehensive care to individuals with trypanophobia.

Anxiety Disorders

Anxiety disorders commonly coexist with trypanophobia. Generalized Anxiety Disorder (GAD), characterized by excessive worry and fear about various aspects of life, can exacerbate the fear of needles. Social Anxiety Disorder (SAD), marked by extreme distress in social situations, may manifest when trypanophobics anticipate encounters with medical professionals or situations that involve injections.

Specific Phobia, another anxiety disorder, can overlap with trypanophobia. While trypanophobia specifically involves needles, individuals may also experience phobic reactions to related stimuli, such as medical equipment or healthcare settings. These comorbid anxiety disorders intensify the fear response, making treatment approaches more complex.

Panic Disorder

Panic Disorder often co-occurs with trypanophobia due to the fear of having a panic attack triggered by the sight or anticipation of needles. Panic attacks involve sudden and overwhelming surges of fear accompanied by physical symptoms like rapid heartbeat, shortness of breath, and dizziness. The fear of experiencing panic attacks during medical procedures can further reinforce the avoidance behavior in individuals with trypanophobia.

Post-Traumatic Stress Disorder

Post-Traumatic Stress Disorder (PTSD) can develop in individuals who have experienced traumatic medical events involving needles. Medical procedures that resulted in intense pain, distress, or invasive treatments may lead to the development of trypanophobia combined with PTSD symptoms. The intrusive memories, nightmares, and hyperarousal associated with PTSD can exacerbate the fear response in trypanophobics.

Conversion Disorder

Conversion Disorder, also known as Functional Neurological Symptom Disorder, is characterized by neurological symptoms that do not have an underlying medical cause. In some cases, individuals with trypanophobia may experience symptoms such as paralysis or tremors in response to the fear of needles. These symptoms are not intentionally feigned and typically arise from psychological distress. Understanding the interplay between conversion disorder and trypanophobia is crucial for accurate diagnosis and treatment planning.

Obsessive-Compulsive Disorder

Obsessive-Compulsive Disorder (OCD) can coexist with trypanophobia, particularly when individuals engage in repetitive rituals or behaviors to alleviate anxiety or avoid situations involving needles. For example, excessive hand washing or sterilization rituals may be present in those with both OCD and trypanophobia. Addressing OCD symptoms alongside trypanophobia is essential for comprehensive treatment.

Substance Use Disorders

Substance use disorders often coincide with trypanophobia, as individuals may rely on alcohol, sedatives, or other substances to cope with the intense fear and anxiety associated with needles. Self-medication can escalate into addiction and complicate the treatment process. Addressing both substance use disorders and trypanophobia in a holistic manner is crucial to support long-term recovery.

Depressive Disorders

Depressive disorders, such as Major Depressive Disorder or Persistent Depressive Disorder, are prevalent comorbidities in individuals with trypanophobia. The fear of needles and associated healthcare encounters can be emotionally taxing, leading to feelings of hopelessness, sadness, and low self-esteem. Identifying and addressing depressive symptoms is essential for effective treatment and improved overall well-being.

Overall, comorbidities associated with trypanophobia significantly impact the lived experiences of individuals affected by this phobia. A comprehensive and integrated approach to treatment, taking into consideration these associated disorders, can provide individuals with the tools and support necessary to overcome their fear of needles and improve their overall mental health and quality of life.

Conclusion

Understanding the comorbidities and associated disorders of trypanophobia is essential for holistic treatment approaches. By recognizing the interplay between trypanophobia and other mental health conditions, healthcare professionals and practitioners can develop tailored interventions to address the multifaceted needs of individuals affected by this phobia. Effective treatment requires multidisciplinary collaboration, empathy, and a person-centered approach that considers the unique experiences and challenges of each individual. Through comprehensive care, individuals with trypanophobia can find empowerment, healing, and a path towards a fear-free life.

Demystifying Fear: Debunking Common Misconceptions

Fear is an incredibly powerful emotion that can affect every aspect of our lives. When it comes to trypanophobia, or the fear of needles, there are many misconceptions that surround this specific fear. In this section, we will take a closer look at these misconceptions and debunk them one by one, shedding light on the truth behind trypanophobia.

Misconception 1: Trypanophobia is a sign of weakness or irrationality.

Trypanophobia is often misunderstood as a weakness or irrational fear. However, it is important to note that fear is a natural response and everyone experiences fear in some form or another. Trypanophobia is not a reflection of an individual's character or mental strength. It is a complex and deeply rooted fear that can be influenced by a variety of factors, including genetics, past experiences, and cultural beliefs.

Misconception 2: Trypanophobics are just being dramatic or seeking attention.

It is crucial to understand that trypanophobics are not exaggerating their fear or seeking attention. The fear they experience is very real and can have a profound impact on their physical, emotional, and mental well-being. Invalidating or dismissing their fear can further exacerbate their anxiety and make it even more challenging for them to seek the help they need.

Misconception 3: Trypanophobia is a rare condition.

Trypanophobia is far more common than many people realize. In fact, research has shown that a significant number of individuals experience fear or anxiety related to needles. Estimates suggest that up to 10

Misconception 4: Trypanophobia is a fear of pain.

While the fear of pain may be a contributing factor for some trypanophobics, trypanophobia itself is not solely based on the fear of physical discomfort. It is a complex fear that encompasses various aspects, including the sight of needles, the anticipation of the needle going into the skin, and the associated medical procedures. The fear can also be triggered by past traumatic experiences or general anxiety related to medical settings.

Misconception 5: Exposure therapy is the only effective treatment for trypanophobia.

Exposure therapy is a commonly used treatment for trypanophobia, but it is not the only effective option. Every individual is unique, and a personalized approach is essential for successful treatment. Cognitive-behavioral therapy (CBT), relaxation techniques, and medication can also be effective in managing trypanophobia.

Misconception 6: Trypanophobia can be easily overcome with willpower alone.

Overcoming trypanophobia is not as simple as "facing your fear" or relying on willpower alone. It is a complex process that involves addressing underlying traumatic experiences, understanding the root causes of the fear, and developing coping strategies. Professional help and guidance are often necessary to navigate through the challenges associated with trypanophobia.

Misconception 7: All trypanophobics have the same fears and triggers.

Trypanophobia, like any other fear, can manifest differently in different individuals. While some trypanophobics may experience extreme fear in all needle-related situations, others may have specific triggers or develop avoidance behaviors. Understanding and acknowledging these individual differences is crucial in providing effective support and treatment.

Misconception 8: Trypanophobia is only a temporary fear that will naturally disappear over time.

For some individuals, the fear of needles may subside naturally over time. However, for many trypanophobics, the fear can persist and even worsen without proper intervention and support. Ignoring or minimizing the fear can lead to increased anxiety, avoidance behaviors, and a significant impact on an individual's quality of life.

Misconception 9: Trypanophobia is not a serious condition.

Trypanophobia can have a profound impact on an individual's life, leading to avoidance of necessary medical procedures and even compromising one's health. The fear can cause extreme distress, panic attacks, and anxiety disorders. It is vital to recognize that trypanophobia is a serious condition that requires understanding, compassion, and appropriate treatment.

By debunking these common misconceptions about trypanophobia, we can pave the way for a better understanding and support for individuals who experience this fear. It is important to approach trypanophobia with empathy and provide a safe space for open discussions, allowing individuals to seek help and overcome their fears.

The Spectrum of Needle-Related Phobias

The fear of needles, known as trypanophobia, manifests itself in various ways and to different degrees in individuals. This chapter explores the spectrum of needle-related phobias, ranging from mild aversions to severe and debilitating fear reactions.

At one end of the spectrum, we find individuals who exhibit a relatively mild aversion to needles. These individuals may experience discomfort or uneasiness at the thought of needle-related procedures but are generally able to tolerate them with little to no distress. Their aversion may stem from a discomfort with pain or a fear of the unknown, rather than a deep-seated fear of needles. While their apprehension is valid, it does not significantly impact their daily lives or prevent them from seeking necessary medical interventions.

Moving further along the spectrum, we encounter individuals who experience moderate fear or anxiety in response to needles. These individuals may exhibit symptoms such as increased heart rate, sweaty palms, or elevated levels of anxiety before and during needle-related situations. They may feel a sense of dread leading up to medical appointments or find themselves avoiding necessary procedures altogether. Despite their fear, they recognize the importance of medical interventions and are willing to confront their anxieties to some extent.

In the middle of the spectrum, there are individuals with a specific phobia called trypanophobia. This condition is characterized by an intense and irrational fear of needles. For these individuals, the sight or even the thought of needles can trigger severe panic attacks or phobic reactions. They may experience physical symptoms such as rapid heartbeat, shortness of breath, trembling, and a sense of impending doom. The fear is often out of proportion to the actual danger posed by the needles, making it challenging for them to engage in routine healthcare procedures.

At the other end of the spectrum, we find individuals with severe trypanophobia, whose fear of needles is all-consuming and profoundly debilitating. These individuals may go to great lengths to avoid any situation where needles are involved. For them, the mere presence of a needle can cause extreme distress and can trigger a range of symptoms, including intense panic, fainting, or even full-blown, incapacitating phobic episodes. Severe trypanophobia can significantly impact the individual's quality of life, leading to avoidance of necessary medical treatments, increased health risks, and psychological distress.

Understanding the spectrum of needle-related phobias is crucial for healthcare providers, policymakers, and researchers. It highlights the diversity and complexity of this condition, guiding the development of tailored interventions and support systems. Recognizing that not all individuals with a fear of needles are the same enables healthcare professionals to provide appropriate care and accommodations for each person along the spectrum of phobias.

The spectrum of needle-related phobias also emphasizes the importance of early identification and intervention. By recognizing and addressing needle-related fears early on, healthcare providers can help individuals develop coping strategies and reduce the likelihood of the fear worsening over time. With early intervention, milder phobias may be managed with psychoeducation and gradual exposure therapy, preventing them from progressing to more debilitating levels.

Moreover, the spectrum of needle-related phobias challenges traditional notions of fear and bravery. It reminds us that fear reactions are not a sign of weakness but rather a deeply ingrained response that varies from person to person. By adopting a compassionate and understanding approach, we can foster an environment that promotes empathy and support for individuals across the spectrum of needle-related phobias.

In conclusion, the spectrum of needle-related phobias encapsulates a wide range of fear responses to needles. From mild aversions to severe and debilitating phobias, individuals experience varied levels of distress and impairment. By recognizing the nuances of these phobias and providing appropriate interventions, we can support individuals in overcoming their fears, seeking necessary medical care, and improving their overall well-being.

Chapter Three: Early Childhood Experiences and Trypanophobia

The Impact of Early Medical Experiences

Painful Injections and Traumatic Memories

The experience of painful injections can have a profound impact on individuals, especially during childhood. These painful experiences can lead to the development of traumatic memories, which can contribute to the development of trypanophobia.

The Long-lasting Impact of Painful Injections

Painful injections can be associated with various medical procedures, such as vaccinations, blood draws, or anesthesia administration. The fear and anxiety associated with these procedures can range from mild discomfort to intense distress. For some individuals, the pain experienced during an injection can trigger a fight-or-flight response, leading to physiological symptoms such as elevated heart rate, rapid breathing, and even fainting.

The intensity of the pain and the individual's perception of it can vary greatly. Factors such as the needle size, injection technique, and the individual's pain threshold can influence the level of pain experienced. However, it is important to note that even relatively minor painful experiences can have a lasting impact on an individual's psyche.

Traumatic Memories and the Development of Trypanophobia

Traumatic memories associated with painful injections can be powerful and long-lasting. The amygdala, a region in the brain responsible for emotional processing, plays a crucial role in the formation and consolidation of these memories. When an individual experiences a traumatic event, such as a painful injection, the amygdala identifies it as a threat and triggers the release of stress hormones, such as cortisol, which strengthens the memory.

As a result, the individual may develop a conditioned fear response, associating needles or medical procedures with the intense pain and distress they experienced. Over time, this conditioned fear response can generalize, leading to the development of trypanophobia, a specific phobia characterized by an extreme and irrational fear of needles or injections.

The Cycle of Fear and Avoidance

The traumatic memories associated with painful injections can create a vicious cycle of fear and avoidance. Individuals with trypanophobia often go to great lengths to avoid situations involving needles, such as medical appointments or vaccinations. This avoidance can further reinforce the fear and anxiety associated with needles, making it increasingly difficult for individuals to confront their fear.

Avoidance behaviors can also have significant consequences, both physical and psychological. In terms of physical health, avoidance of necessary medical procedures can lead to a delay in diagnosis or treatment of diseases, putting the individual at risk. Psychologically, the fear and anxiety associated with trypanophobia can negatively impact the individual's quality of life and mental well-being.

Addressing Traumatic Memories in Therapy

Understanding the role of traumatic memories in the development of trypanophobia is essential for its effective treatment. Therapeutic interventions, such as cognitive-behavioral therapy (CBT), can help individuals with trypanophobia address and overcome their traumatic memories.

CBT approaches, such as exposure therapy, can provide a safe and controlled environment for individuals to confront their fear of needles. Through gradual exposure to needles, individuals can learn to modify their learned fear responses and develop more adaptive coping strategies. Therapists may also incorporate techniques such as cognitive restructuring to challenge the negative thoughts and beliefs associated with injections.

Furthermore, techniques like eye movement desensitization and reprocessing (EMDR) have shown promise in addressing traumatic memories associated with painful injections. EMDR involves bilateral stimulation techniques, such as eye movements or tapping, to facilitate the processing and desensitization of traumatic memories.

Case Study: Overcoming Traumatic Memories

Let us consider the case of Sarah, a young woman who developed trypanophobia after a traumatic experience during a vaccination in her early childhood. Sarah would experience flashbacks and heightened anxiety whenever faced with medical procedures involving needles.

Through CBT and exposure therapy, Sarah gradually confronted her fear of needles in a controlled environment. With the guidance and support of her therapist, she learned relaxation techniques, such as deep breathing and progressive muscle relaxation, to manage her anxiety during exposure exercises. Over time, Sarah's fear and distress associated with needles diminished, and she regained control over her life.

This case study highlights the effectiveness of therapeutic interventions in addressing traumatic memories and overcoming trypanophobia. It also emphasizes the importance of early intervention and providing individuals with the necessary tools to confront their fears.

Resources for Support

If you or someone you know is struggling with trypanophobia and the traumatic memories associated with painful injections, it is crucial to seek professional help. Here are some resources and organizations that can provide support:

- The Anxiety and Depression Association of America (ADAA): A non-profit organization that offers information and resources on anxiety disorders, including trypanophobia.
- The National Institute of Mental Health (NIMH): A research-focused organization that provides information and resources on mental health conditions, treatment options, and ongoing research initiatives.
- Find a Therapist: Online directories, such as Psychology Today or GoodTherapy, can help you find therapists specializing in anxiety disorders and trauma-focused therapies.

Remember, you are not alone in your journey. With the right support and treatment, it is possible to overcome your traumatic memories and live a fulfilling life free from the constraints of trypanophobia.

Parental Influence on the Development of Trypanophobia

Understanding the role of parental influence in the development of trypanophobia is crucial for comprehending the complex nature of this phobia. Parents play a significant role in shaping their children's behaviors, emotions, and perceptions, and this holds true for the development of needle phobia as well. In this section, we will explore the various ways in which parents can affect the development and expression of trypanophobia in their children.

Modeling Behavior

One of the primary ways parents influence the development of trypanophobia is through their behavior and reactions to needles. Children are highly observant and tend to model their behavior based on what they see around them. If a child witnesses their parents exhibiting fear or anxiety around needles, they are more likely to develop similar emotional responses towards needles.

For example, if a parent expresses distress or avoidance behavior when it comes to their own medical procedures involving needles, the child may internalize these reactions and adopt them as their own. Similarly, parents who communicate negative beliefs or perceptions about needles, such as emphasizing the pain or discomfort associated with injections, can contribute to the development of trypanophobia in their children.

Conversely, parents who model calm and composed behavior during medical procedures involving needles can help their children develop a more positive attitude towards needles. By demonstrating resilience and coping strategies, parents can play a significant role in normalizing the experience and reducing their child's anxiety.

Parental Communication and Emotional Support

Effective communication between parents and their children is essential in helping them navigate their fears and anxieties, including trypanophobia. Parents need to create a safe and trusting environment where their children feel comfortable expressing their concerns and emotions related to needles. Open and honest conversations about the purpose and importance of medical procedures involving needles can help alleviate unnecessary fears.

Parents also need to provide emotional support to their children when they encounter needle-related experiences. This support can range from offering comforting words and reassurance to actively engaging in distraction techniques during needle procedures. By acknowledging their children's anxieties and validating their emotions, parents can make a profound impact on alleviating trypanophobia.

Educational Strategies

Parents can take an active role in educating their children about the necessity and safety of medical procedures involving needles. By providing age-appropriate information and explanations, parents can demystify needles and help their children develop a better understanding of the purpose behind these procedures.

Visual aids such as books, videos, or illustrations can be used to explain the process of needle injections and how they play a role in maintaining good health. By fostering a sense of knowledge and control, parents can empower their children and reduce their anxiety surrounding needles.

Positive Experiences and Encouragement

Creating positive experiences around needles can help counteract the development of trypanophobia. Parents can work with healthcare professionals to ensure that needle procedures are conducted in a supportive and compassionate manner. This can include using distraction techniques, such as music or toys, to redirect the child's focus during the procedure.

Parents can also encourage their children to gradually face their fears and gradually expose themselves to needle-related situations. This can be done through role-playing or mock injections using play medical kits, gradually building resilience and desensitization.

Conclusion

Parents have a crucial role in influencing the development of trypanophobia in their children. Through modeling behavior, effective communication, educational strategies, and encouragement, parents can shape their children's perceptions and responses towards needles. By understanding the importance of their influence, parents can play an active role in supporting their children in overcoming trypanophobia.

Emotional Regulation and Coping Strategies

In this section, we will explore the importance of emotional regulation in coping with trypanophobia and discuss various strategies that can be helpful in managing the intense emotions associated with the fear of needles. Emotional regulation refers to the ability to recognize and manage one's emotions effectively, allowing individuals to cope with stress, anxiety, and fear in a healthy and adaptive manner.

4.1.3.1 The Role of Emotional Regulation in Trypanophobia

Emotional regulation plays a crucial role in trypanophobia as individuals with this phobia often experience intense fear, anxiety, and panic when faced with needles or medical procedures involving needles. These overwhelming emotions can negatively impact their psychological well-being and make it challenging to navigate healthcare settings or even engage in routine medical procedures.

4.1.3.2 Understanding Emotions in Trypanophobia

To effectively regulate emotions related to trypanophobia, it is essential to understand the underlying emotions and the triggers associated with needle-related fears. It is common for trypanophobics to experience a range of emotions such as fear, anxiety, disgust, and helplessness. By recognizing and acknowledging these emotions, individuals can begin to develop coping strategies that specifically address their emotional experiences.

4.1.3.3 Identifying Triggers and Early Warning Signs

One of the first steps in emotional regulation is identifying triggers that evoke intense emotional responses. Triggers can vary from person to person, but common ones include the sight of needles, medical settings, or even the mention of medical procedures. By becoming aware of these triggers, individuals can anticipate potential emotional reactions and prepare themselves for employing coping strategies.

Early warning signs of heightened emotional arousal, such as increased heart rate, sweating, or shallow breathing, can also serve as indicators that one is experiencing distress. Recognizing these signs allows individuals to intervene early and implement coping strategies before emotions escalate.

4.1.3.4 Cognitive Coping Strategies

Cognitive coping strategies involve changing one's thoughts and beliefs to regulate emotions. In the context of trypanophobia, cognitive strategies help individuals challenge negative thought patterns and replace them with more rational and positive ones. Here are some effective cognitive coping strategies:

a) Reframing: Encourage trypanophobics to challenge negative thoughts by reframing them in a more positive light. For example, instead of thinking "Needles are going to harm me," they can reframe their thoughts as "Medical procedures are essential for my well-being."

b) Thought stopping: Teach individuals to recognize negative thought patterns and interrupt them using a simple action or phrase. For instance, snapping a rubber band on the wrist while saying "Stop!" can help break the cycle of intrusive negative thoughts.

c) Positive self-talk: Encourage trypanophobics to use positive affirmations and self-talk to counteract negative thoughts. Reminding oneself of previous successful experiences with needles or repeating calming phrases like "I am strong and capable" can help manage anxiety in needle-related situations.

4.1.3.5 Relaxation Techniques

Relaxation techniques are valuable tools for emotional regulation as they help reduce physical and psychological arousal associated with fear and anxiety. These techniques promote a sense of calm and relaxation, enabling trypanophobics to navigate needle-related situations more effectively. Some commonly used relaxation techniques include:

a) Deep breathing exercises: Instruct trypanophobics to practice deep breathing by taking slow, deep breaths in through the nose and exhaling slowly through the mouth. Deep breathing activates the parasympathetic nervous system, promoting relaxation and reducing anxiety.

b) Progressive muscle relaxation: Guide individuals through a systematic process of tensing and relaxing different muscle groups. This technique helps release muscle tension, creating a state of physical and mental relaxation.

c) Guided imagery: Encourage trypanophobics to imagine themselves in a peaceful and calming environment using all their senses. Guided imagery can help distract from the anxiety associated with needles and promote a sense of relaxation.

4.1.3.6 Seeking Social Support

Social support plays a significant role in emotional regulation for individuals with trypanophobia. Sharing experiences, fears, and concerns with trusted individuals can alleviate emotional distress and provide a sense of validation. Seeking support from family, friends, or support groups dedicated to phobias and anxiety disorders can provide a safe space for trypanophobics to express their emotions and receive practical advice and encouragement.

4.1.3.7 Journaling and Creative Expression

Journaling and creative expression offer trypanophobics an outlet to express and process their emotions. Encourage individuals to write about their fears, anxieties, and any positive experiences related to needles. Drawing, painting, or engaging in other artistic pursuits can also serve as therapeutic avenues for emotional release and self-expression.

4.1.3.8 Mindfulness and Meditation Practices

Mindfulness and meditation practices can help individuals with trypanophobia develop a present-focused and non-judgmental awareness of their emotions. These practices cultivate a sense of acceptance and allow trypanophobics to observe their fears and anxieties without becoming overwhelmed by them. Mindfulness techniques, such as body scans or focusing on the breath, can be practiced regularly to strengthen emotional regulation skills.

4.1.3.9 Balancing Emotional Exposure

Gradual exposure to needle-related situations is a common therapeutic approach for trypanophobia. However, it is essential to strike a balance between exposing oneself to feared situations and avoiding overwhelming emotional distress. Gradual exposure should be done in collaboration with a healthcare professional or therapist to ensure emotional safety and provide appropriate support throughout the process.

4.1.3.10 Applying Emotional Regulation Strategies in Real-Life Scenarios

Encourage trypanophobics to systematically apply the emotional regulation strategies discussed in everyday life. This could involve practicing deep breathing techniques before a routine medical procedure, using positive self-talk during medical appointments, or engaging in visualizations to reduce anxiety when confronted with needle-related stimuli. By integrating these strategies into their daily lives, individuals can create a more adaptive and resilient response to their fears.

Overall, emotional regulation is vital in helping trypanophobics cope with the intense emotions associated with their phobia. By understanding their emotions, identifying triggers, and implementing specific coping strategies, individuals can navigate needle-related situations with greater ease and minimize the negative impact of trypanophobia on their overall well-being.

Play Therapy and Exposure Techniques

Play therapy and exposure techniques are two effective methods used in the treatment of trypanophobia. These techniques aim to gradually expose individuals to needle-related stimuli in a controlled and supportive environment, allowing them to develop new associations and reduce their fear response. In this section, we will explore the principles behind play therapy and exposure techniques, their applications, and how they can be integrated into the treatment of trypanophobia.

Understanding Play Therapy

Play therapy is a therapeutic approach that uses play to help individuals, especially children, express their thoughts, emotions, and experiences. It provides a safe and non-threatening space for them to explore their fears, anxieties, and trauma-related issues. In the context of trypanophobia, play therapy offers a valuable framework for children to process their fear of needles in a developmentally appropriate manner.

Play therapists create a playroom filled with a variety of toys, art materials, and other play objects that allow children to express themselves freely. By engaging in play, children can communicate their inner world, act out their fears, and find new ways of coping with their emotions. The play therapist acts as a facilitator, observing and interacting with the child to support their therapeutic process.

Application of Play Therapy in Trypanophobia

In the treatment of trypanophobia, play therapy can be tailored to address the specific fear of needles. The play therapist gradually introduces needle-related play materials, such as toy syringes or medical play kits, into the playroom. The child is encouraged to engage in pretend play scenarios involving medical procedures, injections, or doctors' visits.

Through play, the child can explore their feelings about needles and medical procedures in a safe and controlled environment. The play therapist may observe themes or patterns in the child's play, allowing for discussions and the exploration of emotions linked to trypanophobia. For example, the child might use dolls or stuffed animals to reenact medical procedures, expressing their fears and anxieties through their play.

Additionally, the play therapist may introduce coping strategies and provide psychoeducation about medical procedures. This can help the child gain a better understanding of needles, their purpose, and the steps involved in a medical procedure. The therapist may use visual aids and child-friendly explanations to demystify the experience and reduce the child's anxiety.

Exposure Techniques in Trypanophobia

Exposure techniques are another essential component of treating trypanophobia. Exposure therapy involves gradually exposing individuals to the feared object or situation in a controlled and systematic way. By repeatedly facing their fear, individuals can learn that their anxiety decreases over time and that they are capable of managing their fear response.

In the context of trypanophobia, exposure techniques involve exposing the individual to needle-related stimuli. However, it's important to note that exposure therapy should only be conducted by trained professionals, as it requires careful planning and consideration of the individual's specific needs and readiness.

The exposure hierarchy is a crucial aspect of exposure therapy. It involves creating a step-by-step hierarchy of situations or stimuli related to needles, ranging from the least anxiety-provoking to the most anxiety-provoking. For example, the hierarchy may start with looking at pictures of needles, progress to handling a non-threatening needle, and eventually culminate in receiving an injection.

During the exposure sessions, the individual is guided by the therapist to confront each level of their hierarchy while utilizing coping strategies, such as deep breathing exercises or positive self-talk. Gradually, the individual builds resilience and tolerance to needle-related stimuli, reducing their fear response.

Integrating Play Therapy and Exposure Techniques

The integration of play therapy and exposure techniques can enhance the effectiveness of treatment for trypanophobia. By combining the two approaches, individuals can engage in gradual exposure while utilizing play as a medium for expression and emotional processing. This integration allows for a holistic and comprehensive treatment experience.

As an example, a play therapist may introduce a toy medical kit during a play therapy session. The child can engage in medical pretend play, gradually working their way up the exposure hierarchy. The therapist may role-play as a doctor, providing a safe and supportive environment for the child to explore their fear and practice coping strategies. Through repeated exposure to needle-related stimuli in the context of play, the child can develop more positive associations and reduce their fear response.

It's crucial to note that the integration of play therapy and exposure techniques should be tailored to the individual's unique needs and preferences. Treatment, including the pace of exposure and the selection of play activities, should be guided by the expertise of trained professionals.

Case Study: Emma's Journey

Emma, a 7-year-old girl with severe trypanophobia, struggled with medical procedures and doctor visits. She experienced intense anxiety, panic attacks, and avoidance behaviors when needles were involved. Emma's parents sought help from a play therapist specializing in trypanophobia.

In the initial play therapy sessions, Emma expressed her fear through play scenarios involving dolls and medical play kits. The therapist introduced toy syringes to the playroom, and Emma gradually engaged in medical pretend play with the syringes under the therapist's guidance.

As Emma became more comfortable, the play therapist integrated exposure techniques into the sessions. Together, they created an exposure hierarchy, starting with looking at pictures of needles and progressing to handling a toy syringe without fear. Each step was accompanied by coping strategies, such as taking deep breaths and using positive self-talk.

Over time, Emma's fear response decreased, and she became more willing to engage in medical pretend play and exposure tasks. The play therapist also collaborated with Emma's parents to extend the treatment techniques to home and school settings, ensuring continuity of care.

Through the integration of play therapy and exposure techniques, Emma gained a better understanding of needles, developed coping strategies, and built resilience in managing her fear of needles. She gradually became more comfortable during medical procedures and doctor visits, allowing for better healthcare experiences and improved overall well-being.

Conclusion

Play therapy and exposure techniques offer valuable approaches in the treatment of trypanophobia. By creating a safe and non-threatening environment through play therapy, individuals can express their fears and anxieties related to needles. The integration of exposure techniques allows for gradual exposure to needle-related stimuli, leading to reduced fear and increased resilience. Through these combined approaches, individuals can develop new associations, learn coping strategies, and overcome their fear of needles.

Remember, if you're personally struggling with trypanophobia, it's essential to seek help from a qualified professional who can guide you through the process of play therapy and exposure techniques. With dedication and support, you can overcome your fear and regain control over your life.

Healing Trauma: Therapeutic Approaches

One of the key aspects in helping individuals with trypanophobia is addressing the underlying trauma associated with their fear. Traumatic experiences involving needles can leave lasting emotional scars and contribute to the development of phobias. In this section, we will explore various therapeutic approaches that can help heal the trauma associated with trypanophobia and support individuals in their journey towards overcoming their fear.

Understanding Trauma

Before delving into therapeutic approaches, it is important to understand the nature of trauma and its impact on individuals. Trauma can result from a single distressing event or cumulative exposure to distressing experiences over time. In the context of trypanophobia, traumatic incidents involving needles could include painful medical injections, traumatic medical procedures, or witnessing a loved one's negative experiences with needles.

Trauma affects individuals both psychologically and physiologically, often leading to symptoms such as anxiety, hypervigilance, and avoidance. Understanding the impact of trauma on trypanophobia allows therapists to tailor their approaches to effectively address the unique challenges faced by individuals with needle phobia.

Exposure Therapy

Exposure therapy is a widely recognized and effective approach for treating phobias, including trypanophobia. This therapy involves gradually exposing individuals to their feared stimuli under a controlled and supportive environment. The aim is to help them confront their fears and rewire their brain's response to needles.

In the context of trypanophobia, exposure therapy can begin with simple visualizations of needles and progress towards more direct exposure, such as looking at images, videos, or handling needles in a safe and controlled manner. Over time, individuals learn to manage their anxiety and gradually reduce their fear response, ultimately leading to desensitization.

It is important to note that exposure therapy should only be conducted under the guidance of a trained therapist. They can create a safe and supportive space, provide coping strategies, and ensure that the exposure is tailored to the individual's specific needs and comfort level.

Cognitive Restructuring

Cognitive restructuring is a therapeutic approach that aims to identify and challenge negative thought patterns and beliefs associated with the fear of needles. By altering the way individuals think about needles, they can begin to reshape their emotional and behavioral responses.

In cognitive restructuring, individuals are encouraged to examine their thoughts and question their validity. This process involves identifying irrational beliefs and replacing them with more rational and balanced thoughts. For example, someone with trypanophobia might believe that all needles are excruciatingly painful and dangerous. Through cognitive restructuring, they can replace this belief with a more realistic perspective, acknowledging that modern medical procedures minimize pain and offer significant benefits to their health.

Therapists can guide individuals through cognitive restructuring exercises, helping them develop new neural pathways and challenging the automatic fear response associated with needles.

Eye Movement Desensitization and Reprocessing (EMDR)

EMDR is a therapeutic approach originally developed to treat post-traumatic stress disorder (PTSD) but has also shown promise in addressing the traumatic experiences associated with trypanophobia. This technique uses bilateral stimulation, such as eye movements or tapping, to stimulate the brain's natural healing processes.

During EMDR sessions, individuals are guided to focus on specific traumatic memories while simultaneously engaging in bilateral stimulation. This process helps them process and reframe their traumatic experiences, ultimately reducing the emotional distress associated with needle-related trauma. EMDR can be particularly beneficial for individuals whose trypanophobia is rooted in specific traumatic incidents.

Mindfulness and Relaxation Techniques

Incorporating mindfulness and relaxation techniques into therapy can help individuals manage their anxiety and stress related to needles. Mindfulness involves cultivating present-moment awareness and non-judgmental acceptance of one's thoughts and emotions. By practicing mindfulness, individuals can learn to observe their fear without becoming overwhelmed by it.

Therapists may teach individuals various mindfulness exercises, such as deep breathing, body scans, or meditation, to help them regulate their emotions during needle-related situations. These techniques can help promote a sense of calm and reduce anxiety levels.

Furthermore, relaxation techniques, such as progressive muscle relaxation or guided imagery, can complement mindfulness practices and provide additional support for individuals managing trypanophobia. These techniques aim to relax the body and mind, alleviating tension and promoting a sense of comfort.

Supportive Therapeutic Environment

Creating a supportive therapeutic environment is crucial in helping individuals heal from the trauma associated with trypanophobia. Trust and rapport between the therapist and the individual are fundamental to the success of any therapeutic approach. Building a safe space in which individuals feel heard, validated, and understood allows for deep healing to occur.

In addition to individual therapy, group therapy can also be beneficial for individuals with trypanophobia. Group sessions provide a platform for individuals to share their experiences, gain support from others who have similar fears, and learn from their collective journeys. Peer support can play a significant role in reducing isolation and fostering a sense of belonging.

Furthermore, therapists may incorporate creative expressions, such as art therapy or journaling, to help individuals explore and process their emotions related to trypanophobia. Creative outlets can provide alternative means of expression for individuals who struggle with verbalizing their fears and experiences.

The Road to Healing

Healing trauma associated with trypanophobia is a unique and personal journey for each individual. Therapeutic approaches such as exposure therapy, cognitive restructuring, EMDR, mindfulness, relaxation techniques, and the creation of a supportive environment play vital roles in this healing process.

It is important to recognize that healing from trauma takes time and patience. It is not a linear process, and setbacks may occur along the way. However, with the guidance and support of trained therapists, individuals can learn to manage their fear of needles, find resilience within themselves, and move toward a more empowered and fulfilling life, free from the limitations imposed by trypanophobia.

Remember, seeking professional help from a qualified therapist is essential for individuals with trypanophobia. Therapists provide the expertise and safe space needed to navigate the complexities of healing trauma and overcoming fear.

Collaboration Between Parents and Healthcare Providers

Collaboration between parents and healthcare providers is crucial in addressing and effectively managing trypanophobia in children. By working together, parents and healthcare providers can create a supportive and understanding environment, share information, and develop strategies to help children overcome their fear of needles. This collaboration ensures that the child's emotional and psychological well-being is prioritized throughout the treatment process.

Building Trust and Open Communication

Establishing trust between parents, children, and healthcare providers is essential in addressing trypanophobia. Healthcare providers should encourage open communication with parents, actively listening to their concerns and validating their experiences. This creates a safe space for parents to express their worries and fears, fostering a sense of trust and understanding.

It is equally important for healthcare providers to communicate clearly and effectively with parents. This includes providing accurate information about the medical procedures involving needles, addressing any misconceptions or myths, and explaining the rationale behind the interventions. When parents are well-informed, they are better equipped to support their child and facilitate their recovery.

Educating Parents on Coping Strategies

Parents play a significant role in helping their child manage their fear of needles. Healthcare providers should educate parents about various coping strategies that can be employed at home to gradually desensitize their child to needles. These strategies may include:

- Distraction techniques: Encouraging the child to focus on activities or objects of interest during needle procedures, such as toys, music, or video games. Distractions can help redirect attention away from the needle and reduce anxiety.

- Deep breathing exercises: Teaching the child relaxation techniques, such as deep breathing, can help calm their body and mind during needle procedures. Parents can practice these exercises with their child at home to promote familiarity and comfort.

- Positive reinforcement: Praising the child for their efforts and bravery during needle procedures can boost their confidence and motivate them to overcome their fear. Encouraging small rewards or incentives can also serve as a source of motivation.

- Storytelling and role-playing: Using storytelling or role-playing activities can help familiarize the child with needle procedures in a non-threatening manner. Parents can create narratives or act out scenarios involving needles to help their child understand and cope with the experience.

By educating parents about these coping strategies, healthcare providers empower parents to actively participate in their child's treatment and recovery.

Collaborative Treatment Planning

Collaboration between parents and healthcare providers extends to the development of an individualized treatment plan for the child. The treatment plan should consider the child's specific needs, level of fear, and age-appropriate interventions. Healthcare providers should work together with parents to create a plan that gradually exposes the child to needles, taking into account the child's comfort and tolerance levels.

It is important for parents to actively engage in the treatment plan, following the guidance and recommendations provided by healthcare providers. This may involve implementing exposure exercises at home, attending therapy sessions with their child, or scheduling regular follow-up appointments to monitor progress.

Providing Emotional Support

Emotional support is crucial in helping children overcome their fear of needles. Healthcare providers should acknowledge and validate the child's emotions, emphasizing that their fear is understandable and common. By normalizing their feelings, healthcare providers can help alleviate any shame or guilt the child may associate with their phobia.

Parents play a vital role in providing emotional support as well. They should offer reassurance, empathy, and patience throughout the treatment process, encouraging their child to express their fears and concerns openly. By being empathetic and understanding, parents can contribute to the child's overall sense of safety and well-being.

Promoting Advocacy and Awareness

Collaboration between parents and healthcare providers extends beyond the immediate treatment of trypanophobia. Together, they can work towards promoting advocacy and raising awareness about needle phobia. This collaboration can involve educational initiatives within the community, sharing personal experiences, and supporting organizations dedicated to trypanophobia research and support.

By joining forces, parents and healthcare providers can create a supportive network for individuals with trypanophobia and their families. They can advocate for better understanding, accommodations, and resources to address the specific needs of those with needle phobia. This collaborative effort can help dismantle stigmas, increase access to specialized care, and contribute to the overall well-being of individuals affected by trypanophobia.

In conclusion, collaboration between parents and healthcare providers is essential in effectively addressing trypanophobia in children. By building trust, facilitating open communication, educating parents, creating collaborative treatment plans, and providing emotional support, parents and healthcare providers can empower children to overcome their fear of needles. This collaborative approach also contributes to advocacy efforts and raises awareness about trypanophobia, ensuring better support and resources for individuals with this phobia and their families.

Empowering Children: Building Resilience and Self-Efficacy

Empowering children who struggle with trypanophobia is essential in helping them develop resilience and self-efficacy to overcome their fear. By providing them with the necessary tools and support, we can guide them towards a path of healing and personal growth. In this section, we will explore various approaches and strategies to empower children facing trypanophobia.

Understanding the Child's Perspective

To effectively empower children, it is crucial to understand their unique experiences and perspectives. Each child may have different triggers, fears, and coping mechanisms. By actively listening and empathizing with them, we can gain insight into their feelings and concerns.

Realizing that trypanophobia may stem from past traumatic experiences, it is important to create a safe space where children feel comfortable sharing their emotions and experiences. Encouraging open communication can provide an opportunity for them to express their fears, anxieties, and uncertainties. It is through this dialogue that we can begin to guide them towards building resilience and self-efficacy.

Building Resilience Through Psychoeducation

Psychoeducation plays a pivotal role in building resilience and self-efficacy in children with trypanophobia. By providing them with accurate and age-appropriate information about needles, injections, and medical procedures, we can help dispel misconceptions and reduce anxiety.

Engaging children in a collaborative learning process can be empowering. Utilizing visual aids, storytelling, and interactive activities, we can demystify the fear surrounding needles. Explaining the purpose and benefits of medical procedures, emphasizing their temporary nature, and highlighting the role of healthcare providers in ensuring safety can help alleviate their concerns.

Moreover, educating children about coping strategies and relaxation techniques can equip them with practical tools to manage their fear. Teaching deep breathing exercises, guided imagery, and progressive muscle relaxation can help children regulate their physical and emotional responses when facing needle-related situations.

Exposure and Gradual Desensitization

Exposure therapy, coupled with gradual desensitization, is a proven method to empower children and reduce their fear of needles. By gradually exposing children to needle-related stimuli in a controlled and supportive environment, they can learn to tolerate and eventually overcome their anxiety.

The exposure process can be tailored to the individual child's needs and preferences. Starting with gentle exposure, such as looking at pictures of needles or watching videos of medical procedures, children can gradually progress to more direct exposure, such as handling needles or simulating injections with a friendly healthcare provider. This gradual approach allows children to gradually build tolerance and confidence.

Throughout the exposure process, it is important to provide continuous support and reassurance. Celebrating each milestone, no matter how small, and acknowledging their progress can boost their self-efficacy and motivate them to continue facing their fear.

Encouraging Self-Efficacy and Mastery

Empowering children to develop self-efficacy involves nurturing their belief in their ability to overcome challenges. By encouraging them to take an active role in their healing journey, we can instill a sense of mastery and accomplishment.

Incorporating play therapy and role-playing exercises can provide a safe and enjoyable way for children to practice facing their fear. Creating scenarios where they can pretend to be the healthcare provider or the patient allows them to take control of the situation, build confidence, and alleviate anxiety.

Setting achievable goals and gradually increasing the level of difficulty in facing needle-related situations can further enhance their sense of accomplishment and self-efficacy. By recognizing their efforts and highlighting their strengths, we can motivate them to push beyond their comfort zone and continue building resilience.

Support Network and Peer Influence

In empowering children, it is essential to foster a supportive network that includes parents, caregivers, teachers, and peers. Creating an environment where children feel understood, validated, and encouraged can significantly contribute to their overall well-being.

Educating parents and caregivers about trypanophobia and providing them with resources and strategies can empower them to support their children effectively. Involving teachers in the process can ensure that appropriate accommodations and understanding are provided within the school setting.

Peer influence can also play a vital role in empowering children. By fostering positive relationships with peers who do not share the same fear, children can observe and learn from their peers' coping strategies. Through peer support groups or mentorship programs, children can find solace in connecting with individuals who can relate to their experiences.

Conclusion

Empowering children with trypanophobia revolves around understanding, educating, and supporting them. By providing them with accurate information, exposing them to needle-related stimuli in a controlled manner, and fostering a supportive network, we can help children develop resilience and self-efficacy. Through these means, we empower them to face their fear, overcome challenges, and embrace a future where medical procedures no longer elicit overwhelming anxiety.

School-Based Interventions and Support Systems

School can be a challenging environment for individuals with trypanophobia. The fear of needles can interfere with routine medical procedures such as vaccinations or blood tests, creating significant distress and anxiety. Consequently, school-based interventions and support systems play a crucial role in helping these students manage their phobia and engage in necessary medical procedures. This section will explore various strategies and resources that schools can provide to support trypanophobic students.

Creating a Supportive Environment

One of the fundamental aspects of supporting trypanophobic students in schools is to foster a supportive and understanding environment. Educators and staff must be aware of the presence of trypanophobia and knowledgeable about its impact on students' well-being. By creating open lines of communication with students, parents, and healthcare professionals, schools can develop comprehensive plans to address the specific needs of these students.

Teachers should receive specialized training on trypanophobia and its effects, enabling them to recognize signs of distress and respond appropriately. This training should include an overview of the condition, common triggers, and potential coping strategies. By fostering empathy and understanding, teachers can play a crucial role in promoting a safe and supportive classroom environment.

Accommodations and Modifications

To ensure the inclusion and success of trypanophobic students, schools can implement accommodations and modifications in various aspects of the educational experience. Here are some examples:

- **Medical procedure exemptions:** Schools can work closely with healthcare professionals and parents to develop appropriate documentation that exempts the student from specific medical procedures that trigger their phobia. This exemption should be respected, so the student does not undergo unnecessary distress.

- **Alternative assignments:** For assignments or activities involving medical-related topics, teachers can provide alternative assignments that allow trypanophobic students to engage with the material in a less anxiety-provoking way. For example, instead of a traditional research paper on vaccinations, a student could create an informative poster.

- **Flexible scheduling:** When possible, schools can accommodate trypanophobic students by adjusting their schedules to minimize exposure to potentially triggering situations. This may involve rescheduling medical procedures, allowing breaks during the day, or modifying extracurricular activities that involve medical check-ups.

- **Supportive seating arrangements:** Teachers can arrange seating in a way that reduces anxiety for trypanophobic students. Placing them away from medical equipment or ensuring they have a clear line of sight to exits can alleviate feelings of fear and confinement.

These accommodations and modifications should be implemented in consultation with the student, their parents, and healthcare professionals. Individualized Education Programs (IEPs) or 504 plans can be established to document these accommodations formally.

Educational Resources

Schools can also provide educational resources to trypanophobic students to help them better understand their phobia and develop coping strategies. These resources can include:

- **Educational materials:** Schools can offer educational materials, such as brochures or videos, that explain trypanophobia in age-appropriate language. These resources can serve as a starting point for students to comprehend their phobia and communicate their needs effectively.

- **Peer support networks:** Schools can facilitate peer support networks or buddy systems, connecting trypanophobic students with other students who have similar experiences or can provide moral support. These relationships can reduce feelings of isolation and empower students to share their fears and coping strategies.

- **Expert presentations:** Inviting healthcare professionals or mental health experts to give presentations or workshops on trypanophobia can be immensely beneficial. These presentations can provide students, teachers, and parents with accurate information, dispel misconceptions, and offer practical strategies for coping.

By providing these educational resources, schools empower trypanophobic students to take an active role in their own well-being and advocate for their needs.

Role of School Counselors

School counselors play a critical role in supporting the emotional well-being of trypanophobic students. They can provide individual counseling or therapy sessions to help students develop coping mechanisms and manage their anxiety. Additionally, counselors can collaborate with teachers and parents to implement strategies that support the student's emotional needs within the school environment.

Counselors can also organize group sessions or workshops that focus on anxiety management techniques, such as relaxation exercises and mindfulness practices. By equipping trypanophobic students with practical tools to regulate their emotions, counselors enable them to navigate their phobia more effectively.

It is important to note that schools should work closely with external mental health professionals and healthcare providers when developing and implementing support systems for trypanophobic students. Collaboration between all parties involved ensures a holistic approach to addressing the needs of these students.

Case Study: Emma's Journey

To illustrate the effectiveness of school-based interventions and support systems, let us consider a case study of a student, Emma, who has trypanophobia.

Emma is a 12-year-old student who experiences extreme anxiety and fear associated with needles. She attends a school that has taken proactive steps to support her in managing her trypanophobia. The school has created an accommodating environment by ensuring that Emma's medical procedure exemptions are respected, including exemptions from vaccinations or blood tests.

Additionally, Emma's teachers have received specialized training on trypanophobia and have been provided with educational materials to help them understand and support her. They have made modifications to assignments and seating arrangements to alleviate her anxiety during classroom activities. Emma's school counselor has also been instrumental in providing regular counseling sessions, teaching her anxiety management techniques, and facilitating a peer support group where she can connect with other students who share similar fears.

As a result of the school's comprehensive support system, Emma has been able to overcome her initial challenges more effectively. She feels understood and empowered to communicate her needs, and she has developed effective coping mechanisms to manage her trypanophobia.

Conclusion

School-based interventions and support systems are crucial components in the comprehensive management of trypanophobia among students. By creating a supportive environment, implementing accommodations and modifications, providing educational resources, leveraging the expertise of school counselors, and fostering collaboration with external professionals, schools can empower trypanophobic students to thrive academically and emotionally. Through individualized approaches and innovative strategies, school communities can play a pivotal role in helping students confront their fears, develop resilience, and engage in necessary medical procedures.

Case Studies: Overcoming Trypanophobia in Childhood

In this section, we will explore real-life case studies of children who have successfully overcome trypanophobia, providing valuable insights into different approaches and strategies that can be used to help children cope with this fear. These case studies highlight the challenges faced by trypanophobic children, the various interventions employed, and the positive outcomes achieved.

Case Study 1: Emma's Journey

Emma, a six-year-old girl, developed trypanophobia after a traumatic experience during a routine vaccination. She experienced intense fear and anxiety whenever she encountered needles, making it challenging for her parents to manage her healthcare needs.

Assessment: Emma's parents sought help from a child psychologist who conducted a comprehensive assessment of her fear. The assessment included observation, interviews with Emma and her parents, and validated questionnaires to determine the severity and impact of her trypanophobia.

Treatment Plan: The psychologist developed a personalized treatment plan for Emma, incorporating various evidence-based interventions to gradually reduce her fear and increase her tolerance for needles.

- **Psychoeducation:** Emma and her parents were provided with age-appropriate information about the purpose of injections, the safety measures in place, and the importance of vaccinations for her health.

- **Cognitive Behavioral Therapy (CBT):** Emma engaged in CBT sessions with the psychologist. The sessions aimed to identify and challenge negative thoughts and beliefs about needles. Through gradual exposure, Emma learned to replace her fear-driven thoughts with more rational and positive ones.

- **Systematic Desensitization:** Emma was exposed to a hierarchy of fear-inducing situations, starting with the least anxiety-provoking scenarios and gradually progressing to more challenging situations involving needles. This gradual exposure, combined with relaxation techniques, helped Emma develop a sense of control and reduce her fear response.

- **Art Therapy:** Emma also participated in art therapy sessions where she expressed her emotions and fears through creative activities. This provided a non-threatening outlet for her to explore and process her fear of needles.

- **Role-Playing:** To enhance Emma's coping skills, the psychologist introduced role-playing exercises. This allowed Emma to practice strategies for managing fear and anxiety in real-life situations, such as engaging in deep breathing or using distraction techniques during medical procedures.

Progress and Outcome: Over several months of therapy, Emma displayed gradual improvement in her ability to cope with needles. Initially, even the sight of a needle would trigger intense distress, but with consistent exposure and therapeutic support, her fear gradually diminished. Emma successfully received her vaccinations with minimal distress, and her parents reported a significant reduction in her anxiety levels.

Case Study 2: Ethan's Triumph

Ethan, a nine-year-old boy, had a severe form of trypanophobia that significantly impacted his quality of life. His fear was so intense that he avoided any medical or dental procedures, leading to the neglect of necessary healthcare.

Assessment: Ethan's parents sought assistance from a multidisciplinary team comprising a child psychiatrist, a psychologist, and a pediatrician. They conducted a thorough assessment to understand the underlying factors contributing to Ethan's trypanophobia.

Treatment Plan: The team developed an intensive treatment plan to address Ethan's extreme fear and help him navigate medical procedures more confidently.

- **Hypnotherapy:** Ethan underwent hypnotherapy sessions to explore the subconscious roots of his trypanophobia. Through deep relaxation and guided imagery, the therapist helped Ethan reframe his negative associations with needles and replace them with positive affirmations.

- **Group Therapy:** Ethan participated in group therapy sessions with other children facing similar fears. Expressing their emotions, sharing experiences, and receiving support from peers helped normalize his feelings and reduce the sense of isolation.

- **Gradual Exposure and Rewards:** Ethan's treatment involved a step-by-step approach to desensitization. By starting with non-threatening situations, such as looking at pictures of needles, and gradually advancing to more challenging tasks, Ethan learned to confront his fears. A system of rewards and positive reinforcement was employed to motivate and celebrate his progress.

- **Therapeutic Play:** Ethan engaged in therapeutic play with a child life specialist, using medical play kits to familiarize himself with the tools and procedures involved in medical settings. This play-based approach helped him build a sense of mastery and control over his fears.

- **Parental Involvement:** Ethan's parents received guidance on how to support and reassure him during medical visits. They actively participated in his therapy, providing encouragement and practicing relaxation techniques as a family.

Progress and Outcome: Ethan's treatment spanned several months, with steady improvements in his ability to manage his trypanophobia. He successfully underwent blood tests and received a necessary dental procedure without extreme distress. Ethan's newfound confidence and reduced fear allowed him to participate in more regular medical care, contributing to better overall health and well-being.

Reflections and Insights

These case studies highlight the importance of individualized and comprehensive approaches to help children navigate and overcome trypanophobia. Some key insights from these cases and related research include:

- Early intervention and assessment are crucial in identifying and addressing trypanophobia in childhood.
- Combining evidence-based strategies such as CBT, exposure therapy, art therapy, and hypnotherapy can lead to significant improvements in reducing fear and anxiety.
- Involving parents and providing them with guidance and support is essential for effective intervention.
- A multidisciplinary approach involving psychologists, psychiatrists, pediatricians, and child life specialists can provide a comprehensive and holistic treatment plan.
- Gradual exposure, rewards, and positive reinforcement create a safe and supportive environment for children to confront and overcome their fear of needles.
- Nurturing resilience, coping skills, and self-efficacy empower children to manage their trypanophobia and lead healthier, fear-free lives.

By understanding the challenges faced by children with trypanophobia and learning from successful case studies, we can better support and assist children in overcoming this fear, enabling them to receive the necessary medical care without overwhelming distress. Through a combination of therapeutic interventions, familial support, and a compassionate healthcare environment, we can pave the way for a brighter future for trypanophobic children.

Chapter Four: Coping Strategies for Trypanophobics

Cognitive Behavioral Therapy

Gradual Exposure and Desensitization

One of the most effective therapeutic approaches for treating trypanophobia is gradual exposure and desensitization. This technique aims to reduce fear and anxiety associated with needles by gradually exposing the individual to needle-related stimuli in a controlled and supportive environment. Through repeated exposure, the individual becomes desensitized to the fear and develops coping mechanisms to manage their anxiety.

Theoretical Basis

The underlying principle of gradual exposure and desensitization is rooted in classical conditioning and cognitive-behavioral therapy (CBT). Classical conditioning, as proposed by Ivan Pavlov, suggests that fear and anxiety responses can be learned through the pairing of a neutral stimulus (such as a needle) with an aversive experience (such as pain or trauma). Over time, the neutral stimulus becomes associated with fear and elicits the same anxious response.

CBT emphasizes the role of thoughts and beliefs in shaping emotions and behaviors. By challenging negative thoughts and gradually exposing individuals to feared stimuli, CBT aims to modify maladaptive thought patterns and reduce anxiety.

Practical Implementation

The process of gradual exposure and desensitization involves systematic steps aimed at helping individuals confront and overcome their fear of needles. Here is a breakdown of the process:

Assessment and Planning The therapist begins by conducting a comprehensive assessment to understand the extent of the individual's fear and its impact on their daily life. This assessment helps tailor a personalized exposure plan. The therapist also establishes rapport and builds trust with the client, fostering a safe therapeutic environment.

Education and Psychoeducation The therapist educates the individual about the fear response, its underlying mechanisms, and the rationale behind gradual exposure. This psychoeducation helps the client understand that their fear is learned and can be unlearned through systematic interventions.

Hierarchy Construction Together, the therapist and client create a fear hierarchy, ranking needle-related stimuli from the least anxiety-provoking to the most anxiety-provoking. This step ensures a gradual and structured approach to exposure. For example, the hierarchy might include visuals of needles, discussion about medical procedures, and eventually, actual exposure to real needles.

Systematic Desensitization Once the hierarchy is constructed, the therapist helps the individual practice relaxation techniques, such as deep breathing or progressive muscle relaxation, to induce a state of calmness. The client is then gradually exposed to the stimuli at the lowest level of the hierarchy while practicing the relaxation response. This process continues until the individual feels comfortable and relaxed in the presence of the previously feared stimulus.

Progressive Exposure As the client gains confidence and demonstrates reduced anxiety towards less anxiety-provoking stimuli, the exposure gradually progresses to higher levels of the fear hierarchy. This step-by-step approach allows the individual to build resilience and self-efficacy incrementally.

Integration and Generalization Throughout the process, the therapist helps the individual identify and challenge negative thoughts and beliefs associated with needles. By reframing these thoughts and focusing on positive experiences, the individual can develop a more realistic and less fearful perspective.

Maintenance Strategies To ensure long-term success, the therapist works with the individual to develop maintenance strategies. This may include regular exposure exercises, self-monitoring of anxiety levels, and relapse prevention techniques. The goal is to empower the individual to independently manage their fear in real-life situations.

Real-World Examples

Let's consider a real-world example to illustrate the process of gradual exposure and desensitization.

Meet Sarah, a 30-year-old woman with severe trypanophobia. She avoids medical appointments, dental visits, and even social situations where needles could be present. Sarah's fear significantly impacts her overall health and well-being.

Sarah's therapist starts by explaining the principles of gradual exposure and desensitization. They work together to construct a fear hierarchy, beginning with looking at pictures of needles and ending with receiving a painless injection.

During therapy sessions, Sarah learns relaxation techniques to manage her anxiety. She practices deep breathing and progressive muscle relaxation, gradually feeling more at ease in the therapeutic setting.

The therapist starts with exposing Sarah to pictures of needles while she practices relaxation techniques. They continue this until she can calmly view the images without feeling overwhelmed. Sarah gains confidence and feels empowered by her progress.

As they move up the hierarchy, the therapist introduces actual needles in a controlled environment. Sarah's anxiety initially spikes, but through continued exposure and relaxation, she becomes desensitized to the sight of needles.

Over time, Sarah advances to simulated injections and eventually tolerates painless injections. She develops new coping strategies and challenges her negative thoughts about needles.

As therapy progresses, Sarah's fear gradually diminishes, and she becomes more comfortable attending medical appointments and engaging in activities she once avoided.

Caveats and Considerations

While gradual exposure and desensitization can be highly effective, it is important to note a few caveats and considerations:

Individual Variations Every individual's fear and response to gradual exposure differ. Some may progress more rapidly, while others require a slower pace. Therapists should tailor the therapy to meet each client's unique needs.

Collaboration with Healthcare Providers Therapists should collaborate with healthcare providers to ensure a holistic approach. This may involve coordinating exposure exercises during medical appointments or involving medical professionals in the therapy process to manage any physical discomfort.

Additional Support In some cases, individuals may benefit from additional support, such as group therapy or peer support groups. Sharing experiences and insights with others who have gone through similar struggles can provide a sense of validation and encouragement.

Resources and Further Reading

If you are interested in learning more about gradual exposure and desensitization for trypanophobia, here are some recommended resources:

- Antony, M. M., & Roemer, L. (2011). *Behavioral and Cognitive Therapies for Fear and Anxiety*. The Guilford Press.
- Wolitzky-Taylor, K. B., Arch, J. J., Rosenfield, D., & Craske, M. G. (2012). *Cognitive-behavioral therapy for problem anger*. In A. M. Nezu, C. M. Nezu, & P. A. Geller (Eds.), *Handbook of Cognitive-Behavioral Therapies* (pp. 394–413). Springer.
- American Psychological Association. (2017). *Clinical Practice Guideline for the Treatment of Posttraumatic Stress Disorder (PTSD) in Adults*. https://www.apa.org/ptsd-guideline/

Remember, overcoming trypanophobia through gradual exposure and desensitization takes time and perseverance. With the help of a skilled therapist and a commitment to the therapy process, individuals can regain control over their fear and lead fulfilling lives.

Cognitive Restructuring and Thought Stopping

Cognitive restructuring and thought stopping are two cognitive-behavioral techniques that can be effective in helping individuals with trypanophobia (needle phobia) to manage their fear and anxiety. These techniques aim to challenge and modify the negative thoughts and beliefs associated with needles, ultimately leading to a more positive and adaptive response.

Understanding Cognitive Restructuring

Cognitive restructuring focuses on identifying and challenging irrational or distorted thoughts and replacing them with more realistic and rational ones. This technique is rooted in the cognitive model of anxiety, which suggests that our thoughts and interpretations of situations can greatly influence our emotional and behavioral responses.

To begin cognitive restructuring, individuals need to become aware of their negative thoughts and beliefs related to needles. These thoughts can include catastrophic thinking, such as imagining the worst-case scenarios, overestimating the likelihood of harm, or underestimating one's ability to cope with the fear. For example, a person with trypanophobia may constantly think, "I will definitely faint if I see a needle," or "I will never be able to tolerate a shot."

Once these negative thoughts are identified, they can be examined and challenged using evidence-based techniques. One effective method is the Socratic questioning technique, which involves asking oneself a series of probing questions to challenge the validity of the negative thoughts. For example:

- Is there any evidence to support this thought?
- Have I ever fainted or experienced severe harm from a needle in the past?
- What is the worst thing that could happen if I face my fear?
- How likely is it that the worst-case scenario will actually occur?
- Have I ever successfully coped with a similar situation in the past?

Through this process, individuals can begin to see the irrational nature of their negative thoughts and develop more balanced and realistic perspectives. By replacing these negative thoughts with more positive and accurate ones, they can gradually reduce their fear and anxiety related to needles.

Implementing Thought Stopping

Thought stopping is another technique that can be used in combination with cognitive restructuring to help interrupt and control intrusive or anxiety-provoking thoughts. This technique aims to disrupt the automatic thought patterns by creating a mental "stop" signal whenever the unwanted thoughts arise.

To implement thought stopping, individuals need to first become aware of the negative or intrusive thoughts associated with their fear of needles. These thoughts might include images of painful injections, feelings of horror or disgust, or thoughts of losing control or fainting. Once the thoughts are identified, the individual can use a specific cue or phrase to signal the intervention, such as "Stop!" or "No, I won't go there."

When the unwanted thought arises, the individual mentally says the cue phrase and then follows it with a physical action, such as snapping a rubber band on the wrist or pressing the palms together firmly. This physical action serves as a powerful interruption, helping to break the cycle of negative thinking associated with the fear of needles. After the interruption, the person can then replace the negative thought with a positive and calming affirmation, such as "I am in control," or "I can handle this."

Practicing thought stopping regularly can help individuals regain a sense of control over their thoughts and reduce the intensity of their fear response. Over time, the negative thoughts become less automatic, and individuals can develop a more constructive and empowering mindset.

Putting Cognitive Restructuring and Thought Stopping into Practice

To effectively utilize cognitive restructuring and thought stopping techniques, individuals with trypanophobia should consider the following steps:

1. Recognize and identify negative thoughts: Pay attention to the thoughts and beliefs that contribute to fear and anxiety related to needles. Write them down or keep a thought journal to track recurring patterns.

2. Evaluate and challenge negative thoughts: Use Socratic questioning or other cognitive restructuring exercises to challenge the accuracy and validity of these thoughts. Look for evidence that supports more positive and realistic thinking.

3. Replace negative thoughts with positive affirmations: Develop a list of positive statements or affirmations that counteract the negative thoughts. Repeat these affirmations regularly to reinforce positive thinking.

4. Introduce thought stopping techniques: Choose a cue or phrase that will serve as a signal to interrupt negative thoughts. Practice using the cue and follow it with a physical action to create a strong interruption.

5. Practice regularly: Consistency is key in building new cognitive patterns. Keep practicing cognitive restructuring and thought stopping techniques, both in real-life situations and through visualizations or role-playing exercises.

6. Seek support if needed: If managing trypanophobia becomes overwhelming or challenging, consider seeking support from a mental health professional specializing in anxiety disorders. They can provide additional guidance and help tailor techniques specifically to individual needs.

It's important to note that cognitive restructuring and thought stopping techniques may take time and practice to master. Each individual's journey toward overcoming trypanophobia will be unique, and it's essential to be patient and kind to oneself throughout the process.

By integrating cognitive restructuring and thought stopping techniques into their daily lives, individuals with trypanophobia can gradually reframe their thoughts and manage their fear more effectively. With consistent practice and support, they can develop a healthier and more positive relationship with needles, ultimately improving their overall well-being.

Relaxation Techniques and Systematic Desensitization

In the journey to overcome trypanophobia, relaxation techniques and systematic desensitization play a crucial role. By learning to calm the mind and body, individuals can gradually become desensitized to the fear of needles. This section will explore various relaxation techniques and how they can be combined with systematic desensitization to help individuals cope with trypanophobia.

Understanding Relaxation Techniques

Relaxation techniques involve the deliberate practice of calming the mind-body connection to reduce anxiety and promote a state of relaxation. These techniques work by activating the body's relaxation response, which counteracts the stress response triggered by fear. Some commonly used relaxation techniques include:

1. Deep Breathing: Deep abdominal breathing helps slow down the heart rate and relax the body. By focusing on slow, deep breaths, individuals can alleviate anxiety and induce a sense of calm.

2. Progressive Muscle Relaxation (PMR): PMR involves systematically tensing and relaxing different muscle groups in the body. This technique helps

individuals identify areas of tension and release them, promoting relaxation and reducing anxiety.

3. Guided Imagery: Guided imagery involves using the power of imagination to create calm and peaceful mental images. By visualizing tranquil scenes or engaging in positive imagery, individuals can shift their focus away from fear and anxiety.

4. Mindfulness Meditation: Mindfulness meditation involves paying attention to the present moment without judgment. By cultivating a non-reactive attitude towards thoughts and sensations, individuals can reduce stress and improve their ability to cope with fear.

5. Aromatherapy: Certain scents, such as lavender or chamomile, have been shown to have relaxing effects on the mind and body. By using essential oils or aromatic candles, individuals can create a calming environment and reduce anxiety.

These relaxation techniques can be practiced individually or combined to create a personalized relaxation routine. It is important to experiment and find what works best for each individual.

Systematic Desensitization

Systematic desensitization is a behavioral therapy technique used to help individuals overcome their fears and phobias, including trypanophobia. It involves gradually exposing individuals to the fear-inducing stimulus, in this case, needles, while pairing the experience with relaxation techniques. The idea behind systematic desensitization is to replace the fear response with relaxation and calmness.

The process of systematic desensitization typically involves the following steps:

1. Creating a Fear Hierarchy: The individual works with a therapist to create a fear hierarchy, which is a ranked list of anxiety-provoking situations related to needles. The list starts with the least anxiety-inducing situation and progresses to the most feared situation.

2. Learning Relaxation Techniques: Before beginning exposure to the fear-inducing stimuli, the individual learns and practices relaxation techniques, such as deep breathing or progressive muscle relaxation. This helps establish a sense of relaxation and control.

3. Gradual Exposure: The individual is exposed to the least anxiety-provoking situation on the fear hierarchy while actively engaging in the learned relaxation techniques. The exposure is repeated until the fear response diminishes, and the individual feels comfortable in that situation.

4. Progressing through the Fear Hierarchy: Once the individual can successfully cope with the least anxiety-provoking situation, they move on to the next item on the fear hierarchy. This process is repeated, gradually exposing the individual to increasingly anxiety-provoking situations, while continuously practicing relaxation techniques.

5. Mastery and Generalization: Over time, the individual progresses through the fear hierarchy, eventually reaching situations that previously triggered intense anxiety. By repeatedly practicing relaxation techniques and gradually confronting their fear, the individual builds a sense of mastery and learns that they can cope with their fear of needles.

It is essential to note that systematic desensitization should be done under the guidance of a trained therapist, as they can provide support, guidance, and ensure the process is tailored to the individual's specific needs.

Integrating Relaxation Techniques with Systematic Desensitization

When it comes to overcoming trypanophobia, relaxation techniques and systematic desensitization work synergistically to help individuals face their fear of needles. By combining relaxation techniques during exposure to fear-inducing situations, individuals can learn to associate relaxation and calmness with needle-related experiences, gradually reducing their anxiety and phobic response.

During the exposure sessions, individuals can use relaxation techniques such as deep breathing, progressive muscle relaxation, or guided imagery to induce a state of relaxation. By consciously engaging in relaxation techniques, they can interrupt the fear response and create new associations with calmness and control.

For example, when a trypanophobic individual is exposed to a needle-related situation, they can start by taking slow, deep breaths to calm their heart rate and relax their muscles. They can visualize a peaceful scene, such as walking on a tranquil beach or being in a soothing garden, to redirect their focus away from fear. By combining relaxation techniques with systematic desensitization, individuals can gradually rewire their fear response and build resilience in the face of their phobia.

It is important for individuals to practice relaxation techniques regularly outside of exposure sessions to strengthen their coping skills and reinforce the association between relaxation and needle-related situations. Over time, individuals may find that the fear response diminishes, and they can face needle-related experiences with increased calmness and confidence.

Summary

In this section, we have explored the significance of relaxation techniques and systematic desensitization in the context of trypanophobia. Relaxation techniques, such as deep breathing, progressive muscle relaxation, guided imagery, mindfulness meditation, and aromatherapy, help individuals induce a state of relaxation and alleviate anxiety. Systematic desensitization, on the other hand, involves gradually exposing individuals to fear-inducing situations while pairing the experience with relaxation techniques. By combining relaxation techniques with systematic desensitization, individuals can learn to associate relaxation and calmness with needle-related experiences, ultimately reducing their phobic response. The process of integrating relaxation techniques with systematic desensitization requires patience, practice, and guidance from a trained therapist. As individuals progress through their fear hierarchy and continuously engage in relaxation techniques, they can overcome trypanophobia and regain control over their fear of needles.

Virtual Reality Therapy for Needle Phobia

Virtual reality (VR) therapy is an innovative and promising approach in the treatment of needle phobia, also known as trypanophobia. By creating a simulated environment, VR therapy exposes individuals to their fear in a controlled and safe manner, allowing them to gradually overcome their anxiety and distress associated with needles. In this section, we will explore the principles, techniques, and benefits of virtual reality therapy for needle phobia.

Principles of Virtual Reality Therapy

Virtual reality therapy operates on the principles of exposure therapy, a widely recognized and effective treatment for phobias. Exposure therapy involves gradually exposing individuals to their fear while providing tools and techniques to reduce anxiety and build resilience. By replicating real-life situations, VR therapy allows individuals to face their fear of needles in a more controlled and manageable way.

The core principle of virtual reality therapy for needle phobia is to provide patients with a sense of presence and immersion. Through the use of a head-mounted display (HMD) and specially designed VR software, patients are transported to a virtual environment where they can interact with realistic representations of needles and medical settings. This immersion triggers emotional and cognitive responses similar to those experienced in real-life situations, facilitating the process of desensitization and fear reduction.

Techniques Used in Virtual Reality Therapy

In virtual reality therapy for needle phobia, several techniques are utilized to ensure maximum effectiveness in overcoming fears. These techniques include:

1. **Virtual Exposure:** Patients are gradually exposed to needle-related stimuli, starting with less anxiety-provoking scenarios and progressing to more challenging ones. For example, the therapy may begin with a virtual medical consultation, followed by simulated injections, and eventually, patients may confront more difficult scenarios, such as witnessing blood draws or participating in medical procedures.

2. **Cognitive Behavioral Techniques:** VR therapy incorporates cognitive restructuring and cognitive-behavioral techniques to help patients reframe their thoughts and beliefs about needles. They learn to challenge irrational or catastrophic thinking patterns, replacing them with more realistic and adaptive thoughts. For instance, patients may be guided through self-talk exercises within the virtual environment to challenge negative thoughts and reinforce positive coping strategies.

3. **Relaxation Techniques:** Deep breathing, progressive muscle relaxation, and other relaxation techniques are incorporated into VR therapy sessions to help patients manage anxiety and physical discomfort associated with needle phobia. The virtual environment provides a safe space for patients to practice these techniques and learn to control their physiological responses.

4. **Virtual Coach or Guide:** In some VR therapy programs, a virtual coach or guide is present to offer support, encouragement, and guidance during the exposure process. The coach may provide coping strategies, reinforce positive behaviors, and help patients navigate challenging situations. This virtual support system can enhance patients' feelings of safety and competence during their VR therapy sessions.

5. **Customization and Personalization:** Virtual reality therapy can be tailored to meet the individual needs of each patient. The level of exposure, the pace of sessions, and the specific scenarios encountered within the virtual environment can be customized to ensure that patients feel comfortable yet challenged. This personalized approach maximizes engagement and promotes successful outcomes.

Benefits of Virtual Reality Therapy for Needle Phobia

Virtual reality therapy offers several advantages over traditional exposure therapy in the treatment of needle phobia. Some notable benefits include:

- **Safety and Control:** VR therapy provides a safe and controlled environment for individuals to face their fear. They have the ability to stop or adjust the exposure at any time, empowering them to navigate their anxiety at their own pace. The risk of accidental injury or exposure to bloodborne pathogens, which is a concern in real medical settings, is eliminated.

- **Realistic and Immersive Experience:** The immersive nature of VR therapy enhances the level of realism and engagement. Patients can experience a wide range of scenarios and interactions related to needles, allowing for a more comprehensive desensitization process. The use of sensory feedback, such as visual and auditory cues, further enhances the realism of the virtual environment.

- **Quantitative Assessment:** Virtual reality therapy systems often incorporate quantitative measures, such as heart rate variability, skin conductance, and self-reported anxiety levels. These objective assessments provide valuable data to clinicians, enabling them to monitor progress, adjust treatment plans, and track the efficacy of interventions. The ability to measure patient responses in real-time is a significant advantage of VR therapy.

- **Multi-Sensory Integration:** VR therapy can engage multiple senses simultaneously, enhancing the therapeutic experience. By combining visual, auditory, and sometimes haptic feedback, patients receive a more comprehensive stimulation, effectively replicating real-life situations. This multisensory approach strengthens the emotional and cognitive associations with the fear of needles, facilitating lasting change.

Case Study: Sarah's Journey with Virtual Reality Therapy

Let's consider the case of Sarah, a 32-year-old woman with severe trypanophobia. Sarah's fear of needles had prevented her from seeking essential medical care, resulting in serious medical consequences. Traditional therapy had not been successful in alleviating her fear and anxiety.

Sarah's therapist recommended virtual reality therapy as a viable option. In the virtual environment, Sarah started with basic scenarios, such as observing injections, while learning relaxation techniques to manage her anxiety. As her confidence grew, she progressed to more challenging situations, actively participating in the virtual medical procedures.

With each session, Sarah's anxiety decreased, and she developed a greater sense of control over her fear. The virtual coach provided guidance and support, reinforcing positive coping strategies. Eventually, Sarah reached a point where she could comfortably handle real-life medical procedures with minimal distress.

Virtual reality therapy not only enabled Sarah to overcome her trypanophobia but also empowered her to address her underlying health issues. The immersive and engaging nature of VR therapy played a significant role in her journey towards a healthier and fear-free life.

Resources for Virtual Reality Therapy

If you or a loved one is interested in exploring virtual reality therapy for needle phobia, several resources are available. It is important to consult with a mental health professional experienced in VR therapy to ensure proper guidance and support. Some organizations and platforms that provide virtual reality therapy for needle phobia include:

- **Virtualis VR** (https://www.virtualisvr.com)
- **Psious** (https://www.psious.com)
- **Oculus Experiences** (https://www.oculus.com/experiences/)

These resources offer a variety of VR therapy programs specifically designed to assist individuals with needle phobia.

In conclusion, virtual reality therapy is a valuable and promising treatment option for individuals struggling with needle phobia. Its immersive nature, combined with exposure techniques, cognitive behavioral strategies, and relaxation exercises, enables patients to confront their fears and overcome the distress associated with needles. By incorporating virtual reality therapy into our approach to needle phobia, we can empower individuals to face medical procedures with confidence and improve their overall well-being.

Mindfulness and Meditation Practices

Mindfulness and meditation practices have been widely recognized for their ability to reduce anxiety, alleviate stress, and promote overall well-being. For individuals with trypanophobia, these practices can be particularly beneficial in managing their fear of needles. In this section, we will explore the principles behind mindfulness and meditation, their effectiveness in addressing trypanophobia, and provide practical techniques for incorporating them into daily life.

Understanding Mindfulness

Mindfulness is the practice of intentionally bringing one's attention to the present moment without judgment. It involves cultivating awareness of one's thoughts, emotions, and bodily sensations in a non-reactive manner. By developing this heightened awareness, individuals can break free from automatic patterns of thinking and reactions, allowing for a greater sense of calm and control.

Benefits of Mindfulness for Trypanophobics

For individuals with trypanophobia, the fear of needles often triggers a cascade of anxious thoughts and bodily reactions. Mindfulness can help interrupt this cycle by allowing individuals to observe these thoughts and sensations without becoming overwhelmed by them.

Some specific benefits of practicing mindfulness for trypanophobics include:

1. **Reduced anxiety and stress:** Mindfulness helps regulate the body's stress response, leading to a decrease in anxiety levels. This can be particularly helpful for trypanophobics who experience intense fear and panic during needle-related situations.

2. **Increased self-awareness:** Mindfulness allows individuals to become more attuned to their fears and emotions surrounding needles. This increased self-awareness can help identify triggers, understand underlying beliefs, and cultivate self-compassion in the face of fear.

3. **Improved emotional regulation:** By practicing mindfulness, trypanophobics can develop skills to navigate their emotional responses more effectively. They

can learn to respond to their fear in a way that is less overwhelming, allowing for a greater sense of control and empowerment.

4. **Enhanced pain management:** Research has shown that mindfulness can modulate pain perception and tolerance. By focusing their attention on the present moment, trypanophobics may experience reduced pain during medical interventions involving needles.

5. **Heightened resilience:** Regular mindfulness practice can increase resilience in the face of fear and discomfort. Trypanophobics can develop the ability to bounce back from challenging situations, fostering a sense of courage and strength.

Techniques for Mindfulness and Meditation

1. **Body Scan Meditation:** Lie down or sit comfortably and bring your attention to your breath. Slowly move your awareness from the top of your head to the tips of your toes, noticing any sensations or areas of tension. Take note of any discomfort without judgment and try to relax those areas as you continue the scan.

2. **Breathing Meditation:** Find a quiet space where you can sit comfortably. Close your eyes and focus on your breath. Notice the sensation of the breath entering and leaving your body. If your mind starts to wander, gently bring your attention back to your breath.

3. **Mindful Observation:** Choose an object, such as a pen or a flower. Take a few moments to observe it closely, noticing its shape, color, and texture. Allow yourself to fully engage with the present moment, paying attention to every detail of the object.

4. **Guided Visualization:** Find a guided meditation or visualization specifically designed for anxiety or overcoming fears. Follow along with the audio, allowing yourself to be guided through a calming and relaxing journey.

5. **Walking Meditation:** Find a quiet path or area where you can walk without distractions. Focus your attention on the experience of walking, feeling the sensations in your feet as they make contact with the ground. Be present with each step, allowing yourself to fully engage in the act of walking.

Integrating Mindfulness into Daily Life

Incorporating mindfulness into daily life can help alleviate the fear of needles not only during specific encounters but also in general. Here are some practical tips for integrating mindfulness into daily routines:

- **Morning mindfulness:** Start your day with a few minutes of mindfulness practice. This could be a short breathing exercise, a body scan, or simply taking a few moments to savor a cup of tea or coffee mindfully.
- **Mindful pauses:** Throughout the day, take short breaks to bring your attention to the present moment. Pause and notice your breath, the sensations in your body, or the sounds around you. This can help anchor you in the present and reduce anxiety.
- **Mindful eating:** Practice mindfulness while eating meals by paying attention to the taste, texture, and smell of the food. Chew slowly and savor each bite, fully experiencing the pleasure of eating.
- **Bedtime reflection:** Before going to bed, reflect on the day with a sense of gratitude. Notice any moments of mindfulness you experienced and gently let go of any worries or anxieties.

Remember, mindfulness is a skill that develops over time with consistent practice. Be patient with yourself and approach each practice with a sense of curiosity and openness.

Caveats and Considerations

While mindfulness and meditation can be powerful tools for managing trypanophobia, it's essential to recognize that they may not be a standalone solution for everyone. Every individual's journey is unique, and what works for one person may not work for another. It is important to seek professional help if your trypanophobia significantly impacts your daily life or if you have additional mental health concerns.

Additionally, mindfulness should never be used to replace necessary medical care or to avoid necessary medical procedures. It is crucial to work collaboratively with healthcare professionals to find the best approaches to manage your trypanophobia while still receiving the required medical care.

Resources for Mindfulness and Meditation

If you're interested in exploring mindfulness and meditation further, here are some resources to get you started:

- **Apps:** There are several popular mindfulness apps available, such as Headspace, Calm, and Insight Timer. These apps offer guided meditations, breathing exercises, and other mindfulness practices.

- **Books:** "The Miracle of Mindfulness" by Thich Nhat Hanh and "Wherever You Go, There You Are" by Jon Kabat-Zinn are excellent introductions to mindfulness. They provide practical guidance and insights for incorporating mindfulness into daily life.

- **Online Courses:** Websites like Mindfulness-Based Stress Reduction (MBSR) offer online courses taught by certified instructors. These courses provide structured mindfulness training and are often based on well-established programs used in clinical settings.

- **Local Resources:** Check with your local community centers, yoga studios, or meditation centers for mindfulness and meditation classes or workshops. These can be a great way to learn and practice mindfulness in a supportive group setting.

Conclusion

Mindfulness and meditation practices offer individuals with trypanophobia a powerful set of tools to manage their fear and anxiety surrounding needles. By developing a compassionate and non-judgmental awareness of their thoughts and bodily sensations, trypanophobics can cultivate a sense of control, resilience, and well-being. Integrating mindfulness into daily life can provide a foundation for coping with not just the fear of needles, but also other sources of stress and anxiety. Remember, the journey to overcoming trypanophobia is unique for each person, and seeking support from mental health professionals is crucial for personalized guidance and support. Through consistent practice and understanding, individuals can gradually regain control over their fear and embrace a more empowered and peaceful life.

Support Groups and Peer Counselors

Support groups and peer counselors play a vital role in providing emotional support and guidance to individuals struggling with trypanophobia. They create a safe and understanding environment where people with the same fear can connect, share experiences, and learn from one another. In this section, we will explore the importance of support groups and peer counselors, their role in overcoming trypanophobia, and the benefits they offer.

Understanding Support Groups

Support groups are gatherings of individuals facing similar challenges or sharing a common interest. In the context of trypanophobia, support groups bring together individuals who experience fear or anxiety related to needles. These groups provide a platform for members to share their stories, fears, and coping strategies, as well as to provide support and encouragement to one another.

Benefits of Support Groups

Joining a support group can have several benefits for those with trypanophobia:

1. **Validation and Normalization:** Often, individuals with trypanophobia feel isolated and misunderstood. Being part of a support group helps them realize that they are not alone in their struggles. Hearing others' stories and experiences can provide validation and a sense of normalcy, reducing feelings of shame or embarrassment.

2. **Emotional Support:** Support groups offer a safe space for individuals to express their fears, anxieties, and frustrations openly. The shared understanding among group members fosters a supportive community where everyone feels heard and understood.

3. **Coping Strategies:** Support groups serve as a valuable source of practical information and coping strategies. Members can share their successful techniques for managing anxiety, such as breathing exercises, distraction techniques, or positive self-talk. Learning from firsthand experiences can empower individuals to develop their own coping mechanisms.

4. **Peer Connection:** Building relationships with peers who face similar challenges can be immensely comforting and empowering. Support group members can develop a sense of camaraderie and companionship, knowing that they have a network of people who truly understand their journey. These connections can extend beyond the group setting, providing ongoing support and friendship.

5. **Sense of Empowerment:** Being part of a support group can boost individuals' confidence and self-esteem. As they witness others overcoming their fears or finding ways to manage anxiety, they start to believe in their own ability to confront their phobia. This sense of empowerment can be a catalyst for personal growth and healing.

Peer Counselors: A Key Role in Support Groups

Within support groups, peer counselors play a significant role in providing guidance and expertise. Peer counselors are individuals who have successfully managed their own trypanophobia and are now trained to support others facing similar challenges. They offer a unique perspective, having firsthand experience with the fear of needles and the process of overcoming it.

Responsibilities of Peer Counselors

Peer counselors provide various forms of assistance to support group members:

- **Sharing Personal Experiences:** Peer counselors openly share their personal journeys with trypanophobia, including the struggles they faced and the strategies that helped them overcome their fear. By sharing their stories, they inspire hope and provide tangible examples of successful coping mechanisms.

- **Active Listening:** Peer counselors are trained to actively listen and provide empathetic support. They create a nonjudgmental space where individuals can express their concerns, fears, and anxieties without feeling invalidated.

- **Validation and Encouragement:** Peer counselors offer validation and encouragement, acknowledging the courage it takes for individuals to confront their fear of needles. They provide reassurance and motivation, reminding group members that progress is possible and that setbacks are a natural part of the process.

- **Guidance on Coping Strategies:** Peer counselors share their knowledge of various coping strategies and guide individuals towards techniques that may work best for them. They may provide tips on relaxation techniques, exposure therapy, mindfulness exercises, or other evidence-based interventions.

- **Resource Referrals:** Peer counselors can connect individuals with other professionals and resources in the community, such as therapists specializing in anxiety disorders or other supportive services. They act as a bridge, helping individuals access the appropriate help they may need outside of the support group.

The Power of Shared Experiences

The support provided by fellow group members and peer counselors in support groups can be transformative. Sharing experiences and learning from those who have successfully navigated their way through trypanophobia can empower individuals to face their fears head-on. It is important to note that although peer counselors offer guidance and support, they are not licensed mental health professionals. Therefore, while their insights and suggestions are valuable, individuals requiring intensive therapeutic interventions should seek professional help in conjunction with support group participation.

Creating and Joining Support Groups

If you are interested in creating or joining a support group for trypanophobia, here are some steps you can take:

1. **Research Existing Groups:** Start by researching existing support groups in your local community or online. Look for groups that align with your needs and preferences, whether they focus on specific age groups, phobia severity, or particular treatment approaches.

2. **Connect with Local Mental Health Organizations:** Reach out to mental health organizations, clinics, or hospitals that specialize in anxiety disorders or specific phobias. They may have information about established support groups or be willing to help you establish a new group.

3. **Online Platforms and Social Media:** Utilize online platforms and social media to find virtual support groups or connect with individuals who share similar experiences. Online groups can provide access to a wider network of individuals who may not be geographically close but can still offer valuable support.

4. **Establishing a New Group:** If no suitable support groups exist in your area, consider starting your own group. Reach out to local mental health professionals or organizations for guidance and support in establishing the group. You can create flyers, post announcements, or utilize online platforms to attract interested participants.

5. **Setting Ground Rules:** Whether joining an existing group or creating a new one, it is important to establish ground rules to ensure a safe and respectful environment. Guidelines regarding confidentiality, respectful

communication, and adhering to the group's purpose will help create a positive and supportive atmosphere.

Case Study: The Fearsome Fighters

To illustrate the impact of support groups and peer counselors, let's explore the case of a support group called "The Fearsome Fighters." This group consists of individuals with severe trypanophobia who came together to support one another in their journey toward conquering their fear.

"The Fearsome Fighters" meets biweekly and is facilitated by two trained peer counselors who themselves had trypanophobia. Each session begins with an opportunity for members to share their experiences, victories, and challenges since the previous meeting. These sharing sessions provide a platform for validation, encouragement, and group bonding.

In addition to sharing, the peer counselors lead discussions and activities focused on coping strategies, such as breathing exercises, visualization techniques, or tips for handling specific medical procedures involving needles. The group also explores complementary approaches like art therapy, journaling, and mindful practices to enhance emotional well-being.

Over time, the members of "The Fearsome Fighters" have become a tight-knit community, supporting one another beyond the group meetings. They share resources, recommend therapists or anxiety management programs, and often organize outings or volunteer activities to boost morale and foster a sense of belonging.

Through their journey with "The Fearsome Fighters," many group members have achieved significant progress in managing their trypanophobia. Some have even successfully undergone medical procedures involving needles that were previously inconceivable.

Conclusion

Support groups and peer counselors have a profound impact on the lives of individuals with trypanophobia. By creating a supportive space for sharing, healing, and learning, these groups provide validation, coping strategies, and connections with others who understand the unique challenges of living with trypanophobia. The power of shared experiences and the guidance of peer counselors empower individuals to face their fears, break free from the shackles of trypanophobia, and embark on a journey towards a healthier and more fulfilling life.

Art Therapy and Creative Expressions

Art therapy is a therapeutic approach that utilizes the creative process of art-making to improve emotional well-being and foster self-expression. In the context of trypanophobia, art therapy can provide a safe and non-threatening outlet for individuals to explore and express their fears, anxieties, and emotions associated with needles. It offers a unique and powerful way of processing traumatic experiences and promoting healing.

The Therapeutic Power of Art

Art has been recognized as a means of communication and expression since the earliest civilizations. Throughout history, humans have used art to convey their thoughts, emotions, and experiences. Art therapy harnesses this innate human capacity for creativity and provides a therapeutic space for individuals to explore and communicate their inner thoughts and feelings.

Engaging in art-making activates various regions of the brain associated with self-reflection, emotional regulation, and cognitive processing. Through the use of different art materials and techniques, individuals can externalize their internal experiences, making them tangible and visible. This process can bring about a sense of empowerment, as it allows individuals to externalize and gain perspective on their fears and anxieties.

Creating a Fear-Free Environment

Art therapy for trypanophobia should be conducted in a safe, supportive, and fear-free environment. The therapist should create a space where individuals feel comfortable expressing their emotions and exploring their phobia-related thoughts. This environment should be free from any external triggers, such as actual needles, that may intensify feelings of anxiety or fear.

It is important for the therapist to establish a strong therapeutic alliance with the individual, built on trust and empathy. This alliance helps create a sense of safety that encourages the individual to engage in the creative process without inhibition. The therapist should also provide clear guidelines for confidentiality and reassurance that the individual's artwork will not be judged.

Exploring Needle Phobia Through Art

Art therapy offers various art mediums and techniques that can be utilized to explore needle phobia. The choice of medium depends on the individual's preferences and comfort level. Some potential mediums include drawing, painting, sculpture, collage, and mixed media.

The therapist may initiate the art-making process by asking the individual to create an image or collage that represents their fear of needles. This initial step allows the individual to externalize their phobia and provide a starting point for further exploration. The artwork can serve as a visual representation of their emotions, creating an opportunity for reflection and discussion.

Unlocking Symbolism and Metaphor

Artistic expressions often contain symbols and metaphors that can provide insight into the individual's experience of trypanophobia. Through careful exploration and dialogue, the therapist can help the individual unpack the symbolism in their artwork and gain a deeper understanding of their fears and anxieties.

For example, an individual may create an abstract painting with sharp, jagged lines and dark colors, representing their fear of pain and harm. The therapist can guide the individual in interpreting these symbols and exploring the underlying emotions associated with their phobia. This process of introspection and self-reflection can be enlightening and cathartic.

Art-Based Interventions

In addition to art-making, art therapy for trypanophobia may incorporate various art-based interventions to address specific challenges associated with the phobia. This may include guided imagery exercises, where the individual is guided to create an artwork that depicts a positive and safe needle-related experience.

Another intervention could involve creating a fear hierarchy through art. The individual can create a series of artworks that gradually depict increasingly challenging needle-related situations. This exercise allows for a gradual exposure therapy approach, helping the individual confront their fears in a controlled and therapeutic manner.

Group Art Therapy

Group art therapy can also be beneficial for individuals with trypanophobia, as it provides opportunities for mutual support and shared experiences. In a group setting, individuals can witness the artistic expressions of others, fostering a sense of validation and connection. Group discussions and art-sharing activities can further enhance the therapeutic benefits of art therapy.

Art therapy groups may also engage in collaborative art projects, where individuals work together to create a collective artwork. This promotes a sense of unity and shared purpose, allowing individuals to support each other in their journey towards overcoming trypanophobia.

Art Therapy Beyond Sessions

Art therapy can extend beyond the therapy sessions, empowering individuals to incorporate creative expression into their daily lives. The therapist may encourage individuals to continue engaging in art-making at home as a form of self-care and emotional exploration.

Keeping a personal art journal or sketchbook can serve as a therapeutic tool for managing anxieties related to needles. Individuals can use these journals to document their thoughts and emotions, create artworks, and reflect on their progress. The art journal can become a personal sanctuary for self-expression and reflection.

Conclusion

Art therapy offers a powerful and effective approach for individuals with trypanophobia to explore their fears, process traumatic experiences, and foster healing. Through creative expression, individuals can externalize their internal experiences and gain insight into their phobias. Art therapy provides a safe and supportive space for individuals to confront their fears, develop coping strategies, and ultimately overcome trypanophobia. When combined with other therapeutic techniques, art therapy can be an integral part of a holistic treatment approach for trypanophobics.

Pharmacological Interventions for Severe Cases

Pharmacological interventions play a crucial role in addressing severe cases of trypanophobia, providing relief and support for individuals who experience extreme fear and anxiety associated with needles. While therapy and other non-pharmacological approaches are effective in many cases, medication can be a valuable adjunctive treatment option. In this section, we will explore the various pharmacological interventions commonly used for severe cases of trypanophobia.

Benzodiazepines: Targeting Anxiety

Benzodiazepines are a class of medications primarily used for their anxiolytic properties. They enhance the effects of gamma-aminobutyric acid (GABA), a neurotransmitter that inhibits the central nervous system's activity. By increasing GABA activity, benzodiazepines help to reduce anxiety and induce relaxation.

For individuals with severe trypanophobia, benzodiazepines can be prescribed to alleviate the intense anxiety associated with needle-related procedures. Short-acting benzodiazepines, such as alprazolam or lorazepam, are often used before medical appointments to provide immediate relief.

However, it is important to note that benzodiazepines carry potential risks and must be used with caution. They can cause drowsiness, impaired coordination, and have the potential for abuse and addiction. Additionally, some individuals may experience paradoxical reactions, where instead of feeling relaxed, they may become more agitated or restless.

To mitigate these risks, it is crucial for healthcare providers to conduct a thorough evaluation of the individual's medical history, current medications, and potential drug interactions before prescribing benzodiazepines. Careful monitoring and dose adjustment may be necessary to ensure the medication's efficacy and minimize any adverse effects.

Selective Serotonin Reuptake Inhibitors (SSRIs): Managing Phobia Symptoms

Selective serotonin reuptake inhibitors (SSRIs) are a commonly prescribed class of antidepressant medications. They work by increasing the availability of serotonin in the brain, which helps regulate mood and emotions. SSRIs are often used to manage anxiety disorders, including specific phobias such as trypanophobia.

For individuals with severe trypanophobia, SSRIs can help alleviate the symptoms of phobia, including excessive fear, avoidance behavior, and anticipatory anxiety. These medications are usually prescribed as a long-term treatment option and may take several weeks to reach their full therapeutic effect.

Examples of SSRIs commonly used in trypanophobia treatment include fluoxetine, sertraline, and escitalopram. These medications are generally well-tolerated, but some individuals may experience side effects such as gastrointestinal disturbances, dizziness, or sexual dysfunction. It is important for healthcare providers to closely monitor patients starting SSRIs, adjusting the dosage as necessary and providing ongoing support.

Beta-Blockers: Reducing Physiological Responses

Beta-blockers are a class of medications primarily used to manage cardiovascular conditions by blocking the effects of adrenaline and other stress hormones. They work by reducing heart rate and blood pressure, as well as suppressing the physical symptoms of anxiety, such as tremors and sweating.

In the context of trypanophobia, beta-blockers can be used to manage the physiological symptoms associated with severe anxiety, such as rapid heartbeat and increased blood pressure. By blocking the action of adrenaline, beta-blockers can help individuals feel more calm and in control during needle-related procedures.

Propranolol is a commonly prescribed beta-blocker used in trypanophobia treatment. It is typically taken orally 60 to 90 minutes before the anticipated stressful event. It is important to note that beta-blockers should be used with caution in individuals with certain medical conditions, such as asthma or heart problems, as they can have adverse effects on these conditions.

Combination Therapies: Optimizing Treatment Outcomes

In some severe cases of trypanophobia, combination therapies may be considered to optimize treatment outcomes. This approach involves using multiple pharmacological interventions, often in conjunction with therapy and other non-medication-based treatments.

For example, a combination of benzodiazepines and SSRIs may be prescribed to address both the acute anxiety associated with needle-related procedures and the underlying phobia symptoms. Beta-blockers can also be added to manage severe physiological responses.

However, it is important to exercise caution when combining different medications, as there is a potential for drug interactions and increased risk of side effects. Healthcare providers should closely monitor patients on combination therapies, carefully assessing their response to treatment, and adjusting medication dosages as needed.

Caveats and Considerations

While pharmacological interventions can be valuable in managing severe cases of trypanophobia, they should always be used as part of a comprehensive treatment plan. Medication alone is not a cure for trypanophobia, and it should be complemented by therapy, education, and support.

It is also crucial to remember that medication should only be prescribed and managed by qualified healthcare professionals. Dosages, potential side effects, and individual considerations need to be carefully evaluated, taking into account the specific needs and medical history of the individual.

Lastly, it is essential to maintain open lines of communication with healthcare providers. Regular check-ins and honest discussions regarding medication effectiveness, side effects, and overall treatment progress are vital for optimizing outcomes and ensuring the best possible care for individuals with severe trypanophobia.

In the next chapter, we will explore alternative approaches and techniques that can complement pharmacological interventions, providing individuals with a holistic and integrated approach to coping with severe trypanophobia.

A Holistic Approach: Integrating Multiple Strategies

In order to effectively address and overcome trypanophobia, it is crucial to adopt a holistic approach that integrates multiple strategies. Each individual is unique, and what works for one person may not work for another. By combining various techniques and therapies, we can provide a comprehensive and personalized treatment plan that takes into account the specific needs and preferences of the trypanophobic individual.

Understanding the Individual

The first step in developing a holistic approach is to gain a deep understanding of the individual's specific fears, triggers, and coping mechanisms. This requires open and honest communication, active listening, and empathy. By establishing trust and rapport with the individual, we can create a safe space where they feel comfortable expressing their fears and concerns.

Cognitive Behavioral Therapy (CBT)

Cognitive Behavioral Therapy (CBT) is a widely recognized and evidence-based treatment approach that focuses on identifying and challenging negative thought patterns and beliefs. In the context of trypanophobia, CBT can help individuals recognize and reframe irrational thoughts and fears related to needles.

One commonly used technique in CBT is gradual exposure and desensitization. This involves gradually and systematically exposing the individual to their fear of needles in a controlled and supportive environment. By gradually increasing their exposure to needles, the individual can learn to manage their anxiety and develop new, more positive associations with the experience.

Mindfulness and Meditation Practices

Mindfulness and meditation practices can play a crucial role in managing anxiety and promoting relaxation. Techniques such as deep breathing exercises, guided imagery, and progressive muscle relaxation can help individuals stay grounded and present in the moment, reducing the intensity of their fear response.

Introducing mindfulness practices during needle-related situations can help individuals focus on their breath and bodily sensations, redirecting their attention away from their fear. By incorporating mindfulness into their daily routine, individuals can develop a sense of calm and resilience that can be applied in anxiety-provoking situations.

Art Therapy and Creative Expressions

Art therapy provides a creative outlet for individuals with trypanophobia to express and process their emotions surrounding needles. Through various artistic mediums such as drawing, painting, or sculpting, individuals can explore and communicate their fears, anxieties, and aspirations.

Engaging in art therapy can help individuals externalize their fears, making them more tangible and easier to address. It also encourages self-reflection and introspection, fostering a deeper understanding of the underlying emotions associated with trypanophobia.

Support Groups and Peer Counselors

Joining a support group or connecting with peers who share similar experiences can be immensely beneficial for individuals with trypanophobia. Sharing experiences, discussing coping strategies, and receiving encouragement from others who truly understand their fears can help alleviate feelings of isolation and build a support network.

Peer counselors, who have successfully overcome their own trypanophobia, can provide guidance and inspiration. Their firsthand experience can be invaluable in offering practical tips and strategies for managing anxiety associated with needles.

Pharmacological Interventions

In severe cases of trypanophobia, where psychological and behavioral interventions alone may not be sufficient, pharmacological interventions can be considered. Certain medications, such as anti-anxiety medications or beta-blockers, can help manage the physical symptoms of anxiety, such as rapid heartbeat or sweating, during needle-related procedures.

It is important to note that medications should be used in conjunction with therapy and under the guidance of a healthcare professional. They should not be seen as a standalone treatment but rather as a tool to support the individual in their journey towards overcoming trypanophobia.

The Role of Alternative Therapies

While not extensively studied or supported by scientific evidence, some individuals with trypanophobia may find alternative therapies helpful in managing their anxiety. These can include techniques such as acupuncture, aromatherapy, or herbal remedies.

It is crucial to approach alternative therapies with caution and consult with a healthcare professional before incorporating them into the treatment plan. The effectiveness of these therapies may vary from person to person, and they should be used as complementary approaches in conjunction with evidence-based interventions.

Lifestyle Modifications

In addition to therapeutic interventions, lifestyle modifications can be an integral part of a holistic approach. Engaging in regular exercise, maintaining a healthy diet, and getting adequate sleep can help regulate stress levels and promote overall emotional well-being. Making self-care a priority allows individuals to build resilience and better cope with anxiety triggers.

Additionally, individuals can benefit from integrating relaxation techniques into their daily routine, such as taking warm baths, practicing yoga, or engaging in hobbies that bring joy and relaxation. Finding healthy outlets for stress can contribute to a more balanced emotional state and greater overall well-being.

The Power of Visualization

Visualization techniques can be a powerful tool for individuals with trypanophobia. By using their imagination, individuals mentally rehearse positive experiences related to needles. They can visualize themselves in a calm and relaxed state during a needle-related procedure, creating new positive associations.

These visualizations can be enhanced by incorporating all the senses. For example, imagining the smell of lavender, the feel of a comfortable chair, or the sound of calming music can help create a multisensory experience that reinforces a relaxed state of mind.

Finding Balance: Integrating the Strategies

Integrating multiple strategies is essential in a holistic approach to trypanophobia. By tailoring the treatment plan to meet the unique needs of the individual, we can draw upon the strengths of each strategy and maximize their effectiveness.

This holistic approach recognizes that there is no one-size-fits-all solution for trypanophobia. It acknowledges the complex nature of the phobia and embraces a comprehensive, multidimensional approach to address the physical, psychological, and emotional aspects of the fear of needles.

Example Problem

Imagine an individual named Sarah who has severe trypanophobia and is faced with the challenge of receiving a necessary injection for a medical procedure. Despite undergoing cognitive behavioral therapy, Sarah continues to experience debilitating fear and anxiety surrounding needles.

In this case, a holistic approach could involve combining multiple strategies. Sarah's therapy may include gradual exposure sessions, where she is gradually exposed to needles in a controlled manner while using mindfulness techniques to manage her anxiety. Additionally, she may participate in art therapy, where she can express her fears and emotions through painting or drawing.

To further support Sarah, she could attend a support group where she can connect with others who have overcome trypanophobia. The support from this group, as well as guidance and encouragement from peer counselors, can provide additional coping strategies and reassurance.

In severe cases like Sarah's, pharmacological interventions may be considered to help manage her physical symptoms of anxiety. However, it is important to remember that medication should always be used in conjunction with therapy and under the guidance of a healthcare professional.

By integrating these multiple strategies, Sarah can gradually work towards overcoming her trypanophobia, finding techniques and coping mechanisms that are effective for her unique journey.

Conclusion

A holistic approach that integrates multiple strategies is essential when addressing the complex nature of trypanophobia. By understanding the individual, combining therapies such as cognitive behavioral therapy, mindfulness practices, art therapy, and support networks, individuals can develop a comprehensive treatment plan tailored to their specific needs.

It is important to recognize that trypanophobia can be overcome with patience, compassion, and perseverance. With the integration of multiple strategies, individuals can work towards a future where their fear of needles no longer holds them back from living a healthy and fulfilling life.

Chapter Five: Overcoming Trypanophobia in Adulthood

Traumatic Experiences and Long-Term Impact

The Fear of Medical Procedures and Interventions

The fear of medical procedures and interventions is a common aspect of trypanophobia. This fear often stems from the association of needles with pain, discomfort, or traumatic experiences. Many individuals with trypanophobia not only fear the needle itself but also the anticipated pain and potential complications that may arise from medical procedures.

Understanding the Fear

To comprehend the fear of medical procedures and interventions, it is essential to explore its underlying causes. Trypanophobia is often rooted in past negative experiences, such as painful injections or invasive medical procedures. These experiences can lead to a fear response being activated in the amygdala, the brain region responsible for processing fear and emotional memories.

The fear associated with medical procedures and interventions can also be influenced by psychological factors, such as anxiety and the fear of loss of control. Additionally, the fear may be exacerbated by the anticipation of pain, the fear of needles breaking off in the body, or the fear of contracting infections or diseases from needles.

The Impact on Medical Care

The fear of medical procedures and interventions can have significant consequences for individuals with trypanophobia. It may prevent them from seeking necessary medical treatment, leading to delayed or inadequate care. This fear can manifest in avoidance behaviors, such as missing appointments or avoiding medical interventions altogether.

Unfortunately, the fear of medical procedures and interventions can further exacerbate health conditions. For instance, individuals with trypanophobia may delay vaccinations or essential medical screenings, increasing their vulnerability to preventable diseases. This can have a societal impact, as it places others at risk of exposure to contagious diseases.

Overcoming the Fear

Addressing the fear of medical procedures and interventions is crucial for individuals with trypanophobia to access the healthcare they need. Fortunately, various strategies and interventions can help individuals manage and overcome their fear:

- **Cognitive Behavioral Therapy (CBT):** CBT is a widely used therapeutic approach that targets negative thoughts and beliefs associated with the fear of medical procedures and interventions. By challenging and restructuring these thoughts, individuals can develop healthier coping mechanisms and reduce their anxiety.

- **Desensitization Techniques:** Gradual exposure to medical procedures and interventions can help desensitize individuals to their fear. This exposure can start with visualizations, progress to watching videos of medical procedures, and eventually move towards participation in simulated or real-life medical interventions with the guidance of a healthcare professional.

- **Relaxation Strategies:** Employing relaxation techniques, such as deep breathing exercises, mindfulness meditation, or guided imagery, can help individuals manage their anxiety during medical procedures. These strategies promote a sense of calm and reduce the physiological arousal associated with the fear response.

- **Medical Support Personnel:** The presence of supportive healthcare professionals is vital in managing the fear of medical procedures and interventions. Understanding and empathetic healthcare providers can help mitigate anxiety by providing clear explanations, answering questions, and offering emotional support during medical interventions.

- **Distraction Techniques:** Engaging in activities that divert attention away from the fear and discomfort associated with medical procedures can be helpful. Listening to music, playing video games, or practicing guided visualization can help reduce anxiety and make the experience more bearable.

Real-Life Examples

Consider the case of Sarah, a 34-year-old woman with trypanophobia, who required a dental procedure involving injections. Sarah's fear of needles had prevented her from seeking regular dental care, resulting in worsening oral health. With the support of her dentist and a psychologist specializing in phobias, Sarah underwent CBT, which included gradual exposure to dental procedures. Over time, Sarah's anxiety decreased, and she was able to receive the necessary dental treatments.

Another example is Michael, a 42-year-old man with trypanophobia, who needed a blood test as part of his annual physical examination. Michael's fear of medical procedures was so severe that he had not undergone a blood test in over a decade. With the help of a supportive nurse and the use of distraction techniques, such as listening to calming music and engaging in deep breathing exercises, Michael successfully completed the blood test without significant distress.

Resources and Support

Individuals with trypanophobia can find resources and support to help them cope with their fear. Numerous websites, books, and support groups are dedicated to providing information, guidance, and a sense of community for those struggling with needle-related phobias. Additionally, seeking professional help from psychologists or therapists specializing in anxiety disorders can provide tailored strategies to address and overcome the fear of medical procedures and interventions.

Conclusion

Understanding and addressing the fear of medical procedures and interventions is crucial for individuals with trypanophobia. By exploring the underlying causes, implementing tailored techniques, and utilizing the support of healthcare professionals, individuals can overcome their fear and access the medical care they need. With empathy, patience, and effective interventions, individuals with trypanophobia can navigate medical interventions with greater confidence, ultimately improving their overall well-being.

Seeking Help: Overcoming Barriers and Shame

Seeking help for trypanophobia can be a daunting task for many individuals. The barriers and shame associated with this fear can make it difficult to take the necessary steps towards overcoming it. In this section, we will explore some of the common obstacles experienced by trypanophobics and discuss strategies to overcome them.

Barriers to Seeking Help

1. **Fear of Judgment and Ridicule:** Many trypanophobics avoid seeking help due to the fear of being judged or ridiculed. They may worry that others will not understand the intensity of their fear or may dismiss it as irrational. Overcoming this barrier requires open communication and understanding from both the individual and their support network.

2. **Stigma and Misunderstanding:** The stigma surrounding mental health can also pose a barrier to seeking help. Individuals may believe that their fear is a sign of weakness or inadequacy, leading to feelings of shame. It is important to challenge these misconceptions and educate oneself about the nature of trypanophobia.

3. **Previous Negative Experiences:** Past negative experiences with healthcare professionals or inadequate treatment may create a reluctance to seek help. Addressing these concerns and finding a healthcare provider who specializes in treating trypanophobia can help rebuild trust and confidence in the healthcare system.

Strategies to Overcome Barriers

1. **Education and Awareness:** Learning more about trypanophobia can help individuals understand that their fear is valid and can be addressed. Providing accurate information and resources to family, friends, and healthcare providers can promote understanding and empathy.

2. **Support Networks:** Building a support network of understanding and empathetic individuals can provide encouragement and motivation. Online or in-person support groups, counseling services, and forums can connect trypanophobics with others who face similar challenges.

3. **Gradual Exposure Therapy:** Gradual exposure to needles in a controlled and supportive environment can help desensitize individuals to their fear. Working

closely with a therapist trained in exposure therapy can provide guidance and support throughout the process.

4. **Cognitive-Behavioral Therapy:** Cognitive-behavioral therapy (CBT) can help individuals identify and challenge negative thoughts and beliefs associated with trypanophobia. By replacing irrational thoughts with more rational ones, individuals can reduce their fear and anxiety.

5. **Mindfulness and Relaxation Techniques:** Practicing mindfulness and relaxation techniques such as deep breathing, meditation, and progressive muscle relaxation can help manage anxiety and fear associated with needles. These techniques can be used as coping mechanisms during medical procedures.

6. **Medical Accommodations:** Working with healthcare providers to develop a personalized plan for medical procedures can help reduce anxiety. Options such as the use of numbing creams or distraction techniques like virtual reality can make the process less distressing.

7. **Seeking Specialized Treatment:** For individuals with severe trypanophobia, specialized treatment options such as virtual reality therapy or pharmacological interventions may be necessary. Consulting with a mental health professional who specializes in anxiety disorders can help explore these options.

8. **Self-Care and Self-Compassion:** It is essential for individuals to prioritize self-care and self-compassion throughout their journey of overcoming trypanophobia. Engaging in activities that promote relaxation, practicing self-acceptance, and celebrating small victories can boost confidence and resilience.

Example: Overcoming Fear and Seeking Help

Meet Sarah, a 32-year-old woman who has been living with trypanophobia since childhood. The fear of needles has prevented her from seeking necessary medical care and has caused significant distress in her life. Over time, Sarah has developed a strong support network of understanding friends and family members who have encouraged her to seek help.

Sarah decides to begin her journey to overcome trypanophobia by educating herself about the fear and its treatment options. Through extensive research, she learns about gradual exposure therapy and its success rate in treating phobias. With the support of her loved ones, she finds a therapist who specializes in trypanophobia.

During therapy sessions, Sarah works on identifying her negative thoughts and beliefs about needles. With the help of her therapist, she reframes these thoughts and learns coping techniques such as deep breathing and progressive muscle relaxation. Gradual exposure therapy, starting with visualization exercises and eventually progressing to using real needles, helps Sarah desensitize herself to her fear.

Throughout her therapy journey, Sarah faces setbacks and moments of doubt. However, with the ongoing support of her loved ones and therapist, she perseveres. Gradually, Sarah becomes more comfortable with medical procedures involving needles and is able to seek the necessary medical care without overwhelming anxiety.

Sarah's success story is a testament to the power of seeking help and overcoming the barriers and shame associated with trypanophobia. With the right support, understanding, and treatment, individuals can reclaim their lives and embrace a future free from the constraints of their fear.

Resources for Seeking Help

- Anxiety and Depression Association of America (ADAA): Provides information, resources, and support for individuals with anxiety disorders, including trypanophobia. (Website: https://adaa.org)
- National Alliance on Mental Illness (NAMI): Offers resources, support, and advocacy for individuals with mental health conditions, including trypanophobia. (Website: https://nami.org)
- Association for Behavioral and Cognitive Therapies (ABCT): Provides a directory of therapists trained in evidence-based treatments, including cognitive-behavioral therapy. (Website: https://www.findcbt.org)

Therapeutic Techniques for Adult Trypanophobics

In this chapter, we explore therapeutic techniques specifically tailored to help adults cope with trypanophobia, the fear of needles. While the intensity of this fear may vary from person to person, it can significantly impact an individual's quality of life and prevent them from seeking necessary medical care. Through a combination of evidence-based interventions, professional guidance, and personal empowerment, adults with trypanophobia can work towards overcoming their fears and achieving a healthier, more fulfilling life.

Cognitive Behavioral Therapy (CBT)

One of the most effective therapeutic techniques for treating trypanophobia is Cognitive Behavioral Therapy (CBT). CBT helps individuals identify and challenge their negative thoughts and beliefs associated with needles, ultimately changing their emotional and behavioral responses.

The first step in CBT is psychoeducation, where the therapist educates the individual about the nature of fear and the specific triggers and symptoms of trypanophobia. This knowledge helps the individual understand that their fear is not irrational and provides a foundation for addressing it.

The next step is cognitive restructuring, which involves identifying and challenging negative thoughts related to needles. The therapist helps the individual examine the evidence for and against their fears, replacing irrational thoughts with more realistic and positive beliefs. For example, if someone believes that all needles are painful, the therapist might help them recognize that many medical procedures involving needles are virtually painless.

The third component of CBT is exposure therapy, which involves gradually exposing the individual to needles in a controlled and supportive environment. This exposure can start with visualizations or pictures of needles and progress to in-person exposure to needles under the guidance of a therapist. Through repeated exposure, the individual learns that their fear diminishes over time and that they can tolerate the discomfort.

Mindfulness and Meditation Practices

Mindfulness and meditation practices have shown promise in reducing anxiety and fear associated with trypanophobia. These techniques help individuals develop a non-judgmental awareness of their thoughts and emotions, allowing them to observe their fears without being overwhelmed by them.

One effective practice is deep breathing, where individuals focus on their breath, inhaling slowly through the nose and exhaling through the mouth. Deep breathing triggers the body's relaxation response, reducing anxiety and promoting a sense of calm.

Another technique is body scan meditation, where individuals direct their attention to different parts of their body, noticing any physical sensations without judgment. This practice helps bring attention away from the fear and towards sensations of safety and relaxation.

Mindfulness-based stress reduction programs, which combine mindfulness meditation with gentle movement and cognitive strategies, have been successful in reducing anxiety in individuals with trypanophobia. These programs provide a comprehensive approach to addressing both the physiological and psychological aspects of fear.

Virtual Reality Therapy (VRT)

Virtual Reality Therapy (VRT) is an emerging technique that has shown promise in treating trypanophobia. VRT involves exposing individuals to virtual simulations of needle-related situations in a safe and controlled environment. By creating a virtual experience, individuals can gradually confront their fear while still feeling a sense of safety.

During VRT sessions, individuals wear a VR headset that immerses them in a virtual environment. The therapist guides them through exposure exercises, such as watching a simulated injection or participating in a virtual medical procedure. The individual can practice relaxation techniques learned in therapy while experiencing the virtual scenario, helping to desensitize the fear response.

VR technology allows therapists to customize scenarios to suit the individual's specific fears and gradually increase the difficulty level of exposure. This personalized approach helps build resilience and coping skills, allowing individuals to gradually overcome their trypanophobia.

Support Groups and Peer Counselors

Engaging with others who share similar experiences can provide valuable support and encouragement for individuals with trypanophobia. Support groups allow individuals to connect with others who understand their fears and challenges, reducing feelings of isolation and providing a sense of belonging.

In a support group setting, individuals can share their personal stories, exchange coping strategies, and provide mutual support. Peer counselors, individuals who have successfully overcome trypanophobia themselves, can also play a crucial role in guiding and inspiring others on their journey towards recovery.

Support groups and peer counselors can be accessed through local community organizations or online platforms. These resources provide a safe space for individuals to explore their fears, gain insights from others, and receive practical advice on managing trypanophobia.

Art Therapy and Creative Expressions

Art therapy offers an alternative approach to addressing trypanophobia by utilizing creative expression as a means of exploration, healing, and self-discovery. Through various artistic mediums, individuals can externalize their fears and emotions, gaining insight and perspective on their trypanophobia.

Art therapists provide a supportive and non-judgmental environment for individuals to express their fears through art, such as painting, drawing, or sculpture. The artistic process allows individuals to tap into their subconscious and communicate their emotions in a tangible and visual form.

Engaging in creative activities can also serve as a distraction technique, redirecting the individual's focus away from their fear and increasing feelings of relaxation and enjoyment. Art therapy can be practiced individually or in group settings, providing a unique and therapeutic approach to addressing trypanophobia.

Pharmacological Interventions for Severe Cases

In severe cases of trypanophobia where individuals experience extreme anxiety or panic attacks, pharmacological interventions may be considered. Medications such as selective serotonin reuptake inhibitors (SSRIs) or benzodiazepines can help manage symptoms of anxiety and promote relaxation.

However, it is important to note that medication should only be prescribed and monitored by a qualified healthcare professional. The use of medication should be part of a comprehensive treatment plan that includes therapy and other non-pharmacological interventions. The goal is to provide temporary relief while individuals work on overcoming their trypanophobia using therapeutic techniques.

A Holistic Approach: Integrating Multiple Strategies

While each therapeutic technique discussed in this chapter offers distinct benefits, a holistic approach that integrates multiple strategies can optimize the treatment of adult trypanophobia. By combining cognitive-behavioral techniques, mindfulness practices, and virtual reality therapy, individuals can address the cognitive, emotional, and physiological aspects of their fear.

Furthermore, incorporating support from peer counselors, engaging in creative expressions such as art therapy, and considering pharmacological interventions when necessary can provide a comprehensive and individualized treatment plan.

It is important to remember that overcoming trypanophobia is a journey, and progress may vary from person to person. With patience, perseverance, and the support of skilled professionals, individuals with trypanophobia can gradually regain control over their fear, enabling them to face needle-related situations with confidence and improved well-being.

Resources: - Anxiety and Depression Association of America (ADAA) - www.adaa.org - International OCD Foundation - www.iocdf.org - Mental Health America (MHA) - www.mhanational.org

Addressing Underlying Anxiety Disorders

Addressing underlying anxiety disorders is a crucial aspect of helping individuals cope with trypanophobia. It is important to recognize that needle phobia often coexists with other anxiety disorders, such as generalized anxiety disorder, panic disorder, or social anxiety disorder. In this section, we will explore the various strategies and treatments available for addressing these underlying anxiety disorders and their impact on trypanophobia.

Understanding Anxiety Disorders

Anxiety disorders are characterized by excessive and persistent worry, fear, and apprehension. These disorders can significantly impact a person's daily life and can exacerbate the fear experienced by those with trypanophobia. It is essential to gain a thorough understanding of anxiety disorders and their relationship to needle phobia in order to provide effective treatment.

Generalized Anxiety Disorder (GAD): GAD is characterized by excessive worry and anxiety about a wide range of everyday events or activities. People with GAD often experience chronic tension, restlessness, irritability, and difficulty concentrating. In the context of trypanophobia, individuals with GAD may exhibit heightened fear and anxiety related to needles, which can intensify their phobic response.

Panic Disorder: Panic disorder involves recurrent and unexpected panic attacks, which are sudden periods of intense fear or discomfort. These panic attacks are often accompanied by physical symptoms such as heart palpitations, trembling, sweating, and a sense of impending doom. For individuals with trypanophobia, panic attacks triggered by the sight or anticipation of needles can further reinforce their fear and avoidance behaviors.

Social Anxiety Disorder (SAD): SAD is characterized by an intense fear of social situations and a fear of being judged or humiliated by others. People with SAD may experience heightened anxiety in medical settings or when undergoing procedures involving needles due to the fear of being observed or evaluated. This fear can significantly contribute to the overall distress experienced by individuals with trypanophobia.

Treatment Approaches

Addressing underlying anxiety disorders requires a comprehensive and tailored treatment approach that considers the unique needs of each individual. Here are some evidence-based strategies and treatments that have shown promise in helping individuals with trypanophobia and underlying anxiety disorders:

Cognitive-Behavioral Therapy (CBT): CBT is a widely recognized and effective treatment for anxiety disorders. It aims to identify and modify maladaptive thoughts, beliefs, and behaviors associated with anxiety. In the context of trypanophobia, CBT can help individuals challenge catastrophic thinking patterns related to needles and develop more adaptive coping strategies. For example, cognitive restructuring techniques can help individuals reframe their negative thoughts about needles into more balanced and realistic ones.

Exposure Therapy: Exposure therapy is a key component of CBT and involves gradually exposing individuals to feared situations or stimuli in a controlled and supportive environment. In the case of trypanophobia, exposure therapy can help desensitize individuals to the fear of needles by gradually exposing them to situations that trigger their anxiety, such as looking at pictures of needles or observing medical procedures involving needles. This process is undertaken at a pace that feels manageable for the individual, helping them develop a greater sense of control and confidence.

Medication: In certain cases, medication may be prescribed to help manage the symptoms of underlying anxiety disorders. Selective serotonin reuptake inhibitors (SSRIs) and serotonin-norepinephrine reuptake inhibitors (SNRIs) are commonly used antidepressants that can also be effective in reducing anxiety symptoms. These medications work by balancing neurotransmitters in the brain, helping to alleviate anxiety and improve overall well-being. It is important to note that medication should be prescribed and monitored by a qualified healthcare professional.

Mindfulness-Based Interventions: Mindfulness-based interventions, such as mindfulness meditation and relaxation techniques, can be beneficial in managing anxiety disorders. These practices help individuals cultivate a non-judgmental awareness of their thoughts, emotions, and bodily sensations. By practicing mindfulness, individuals learn to respond to their anxiety in a more accepting and compassionate manner, which can reduce the intensity of their fear response to needles.

Support Groups: Joining a support group specifically tailored for individuals with needle phobia and anxiety disorders can provide a safe and understanding space to share experiences, exchange coping strategies, and gain support from others facing similar challenges. Support groups can be in-person or online, making them accessible to individuals regardless of their location.

Real-Life Example: Sarah's Journey

Sarah, a 29-year-old woman with trypanophobia, also experiences symptoms of generalized anxiety disorder. She often finds herself worrying excessively about medical procedures involving needles, leading to avoidance behaviors and heightened fear. Sarah decides to seek treatment to address her underlying anxiety disorder and cope with her trypanophobia more effectively.

Sarah's therapist recommends a combination of CBT and exposure therapy. In therapy, they explore Sarah's negative thoughts and beliefs about needles and challenge them using cognitive restructuring techniques. They also create a fear hierarchy, starting with less anxiety-provoking situations, such as looking at pictures of needles, and gradually progress to more challenging exposures, such as visiting a healthcare facility.

Alongside therapy, Sarah learns relaxation techniques, including deep breathing exercises and guided imagery, to manage her anxiety. She also joins a support group for individuals with needle phobia, where she finds solace in sharing her experiences and hearing how others have coped with their anxiety.

Over time, with consistent therapy and support, Sarah's anxiety symptoms decrease, and her fear of needles becomes more manageable. She develops a sense of empowerment and learns to approach medical procedures with greater confidence and resilience.

Conclusion

Addressing underlying anxiety disorders is a critical component of helping individuals overcome trypanophobia. By utilizing evidence-based treatments such as CBT, exposure therapy, medication, and mindfulness-based interventions, individuals can develop effective strategies for managing their anxiety and reducing their fear response to needles. Support groups also play a vital role in providing individuals with a sense of community and understanding. As we continue to explore innovative treatments and foster awareness about the impact of anxiety disorders on trypanophobia, we can better support individuals on their journey towards overcoming their fear and living a life free from the constraints of needle phobia.

The Role of Hypnotherapy and NLP Techniques

Hypnotherapy and Neuro-Linguistic Programming (NLP) are two powerful therapeutic approaches that can play a significant role in overcoming trypanophobia. These techniques utilize the power of the mind and language to promote positive changes and address deep-seated fears and anxieties.

Understanding Hypnotherapy

Hypnotherapy is a therapeutic technique that uses hypnosis to access the subconscious mind and facilitate healing and transformation. During hypnosis, the individual enters a state of deep relaxation and heightened awareness, allowing them to bypass the critical conscious mind and access the subconscious, where deeply embedded thoughts, emotions, and beliefs reside.

The role of hypnotherapy in treating trypanophobia is to reprogram the subconscious mind by replacing negative thoughts and associations with positive and empowering ones. By accessing the subconscious, hypnotherapy can help individuals uncover the root causes of their fear and address them at a deeper level.

Principles of Hypnotherapy

Hypnotherapy operates on several principles that make it effective in treating trypanophobia:

- **Suggestion and Visualization:** The hypnotherapist guides the individual through positive suggestions and visualizations related to their fear of needles. By repeatedly exposing the individual to positive images and thoughts, the subconscious mind can gradually accept new beliefs and associations.

- **Regression:** Hypnotherapy can facilitate regression, allowing individuals to revisit past traumatic experiences associated with needles. Through guided visualization and relaxation, the individual can reframe and reprocess these experiences in a safe environment, releasing any negative emotional attachments.

- **Anchoring Techniques:** Hypnotherapy uses anchoring techniques to establish positive triggers that can be employed during moments of anxiety or stress. For example, the therapist may guide the individual to associate a specific sensation or word with feelings of calm and relaxation.

Neuro-Linguistic Programming (NLP)

Neuro-Linguistic Programming (NLP) is a powerful therapeutic approach that focuses on the connection between neurological processes, language, and behavior.

It offers a range of techniques and strategies for understanding and transforming subjective experiences.

NLP techniques can be highly effective in addressing and managing trypanophobia by helping individuals reframe their thoughts and reshape their emotional responses. Here are some key techniques used in NLP:

- **Anchoring:** Similar to hypnotherapy, NLP utilizes anchoring techniques to associate positive emotions and feelings with specific physical or mental cues. By creating a positive anchor, individuals can quickly access states of calm and relaxation when faced with anxiety-inducing situations.

- **Reframing:** NLP helps individuals reframe their beliefs and perceptions about needles and medical procedures. By exploring alternative perspectives and challenging negative assumptions, individuals can develop a more positive and realistic outlook on their fear.

- **Swish Pattern:** The swish pattern technique in NLP involves replacing an unwanted response, such as fear, with a desired response, such as calmness or indifference. By visualizing a swish of a positive image replacing the negative image associated with fear, individuals can effectively rewire their neural pathways and shift their response patterns.

- **Language Patterns:** NLP emphasizes the importance of using language to communicate effectively with ourselves and others. By reframing negative self-talk and using positive and empowering language, individuals can create new mental pathways that support confidence and resilience.

Considerations and Caveats

While hypnotherapy and NLP can be powerful tools in overcoming trypanophobia, it is important to approach these therapies with caution and under the guidance of a trained and licensed professional.

Here are some important considerations and caveats when using hypnotherapy and NLP techniques:

- **Individual Variability:** The effectiveness of hypnotherapy and NLP may vary from person to person. Each individual has unique experiences and needs, and the therapeutic approach should be tailored accordingly.

- **Therapist Qualifications:** It is crucial to work with a qualified and experienced therapist who specializes in hypnotherapy and NLP. They should have a thorough understanding of trypanophobia and be skilled in applying the appropriate techniques.

- **Integration with Other Therapies:** Hypnotherapy and NLP can be integrated with other therapeutic approaches, such as cognitive-behavioral therapy (CBT) or exposure therapy, to create a comprehensive treatment plan.
- **Long-Term Maintenance:** Overcoming trypanophobia may require ongoing maintenance and reinforcement. Techniques learned during hypnotherapy and NLP sessions can be practiced independently to sustain progress and cope with future challenges.

Case Study: Rebecca's Journey

Rebecca, a thirty-year-old woman with a severe needle phobia, sought the help of a hypnotherapist experienced in treating trypanophobia. Through a series of hypnosis sessions, Rebecca uncovered her deep-rooted fear stemming from a traumatic childhood medical experience.

The hypnotherapist used suggestion and visualization techniques to reprogram Rebecca's subconscious mind. They worked on cultivating a sense of calm and relaxation when imagining needles, gradually replacing fear with confidence and control.

Additionally, the hypnotherapist incorporated NLP techniques, such as anchoring, to help Rebecca develop coping mechanisms during medical procedures. They established a physical anchor, a gentle touch on Rebecca's shoulder, that she could use to invoke feelings of calmness when confronted with needles.

After several months of hypnotherapy and NLP, Rebecca experienced significant improvement in her trypanophobia. She was able to undergo medical procedures with reduced anxiety and even volunteered as a blood donor, empowering herself and inspiring others with her journey.

Additional Resources

If you are interested in exploring hypnotherapy and NLP techniques further, here are some recommended resources:

- *Trancework: An Introduction to the Practice of Clinical Hypnosis* by Michael D. Yapko

- *NLP: The Essential Guide to Neuro-Linguistic Programming* by Tom Hoobyar, Tom Dotz, and Susan Sanders
- *My Voice Will Go with You: The Teaching Tales of Milton H. Erickson* by Sidney Rosen
- *Hypnosis and Hypnotherapy: Basic to Advanced Techniques for the Professional* by Calvin D. Banyan

These resources provide valuable insights into the principles and application of hypnotherapy and NLP in overcoming fear and promoting personal transformation.

In conclusion, hypnotherapy and NLP techniques offer valuable tools for individuals struggling with trypanophobia. By tapping into the power of the subconscious mind and utilizing language and visualization, these therapeutic approaches can help individuals reframe their thoughts, reprogram their responses, and embrace a future free from the gripping fear of needles.

Personal Growth and Empowerment

Personal growth and empowerment are essential elements in overcoming trypanophobia. This section will explore various strategies and techniques that can help individuals with trypanophobia develop resilience, build self-confidence, and regain control over their fears. By embracing personal growth, those affected by trypanophobia can embark on a journey of self-discovery, emotional healing, and empowerment.

Self-Reflection and Awareness

One of the first steps towards personal growth is self-reflection and developing self-awareness. Individuals with trypanophobia can benefit greatly from understanding the underlying reasons for their fear and how it affects their daily lives. Through introspection and journaling, they can explore their thoughts, emotions, and patterns of behavior associated with their fear of needles. This deep level of self-awareness can provide valuable insights and serve as a foundation for personal growth.

Education and Information

Knowledge is power, and educating oneself about trypanophobia is a crucial aspect of personal growth. Learning about the causes, triggers, and mechanisms of trypanophobia can help demystify and normalize the phobia. By understanding that their fear is valid and that they are not alone in their struggle, individuals can begin to cultivate self-compassion and self-acceptance. Education can also include learning about coping strategies, treatment options, and success stories, empowering individuals to take control of their fear.

Positive Affirmations and Self-Talk

Positive affirmations and self-talk can be powerful tools in the journey towards overcoming trypanophobia. By consciously choosing and repeatedly affirming positive statements about their ability to manage their fear, individuals can cultivate a mindset of empowerment. Affirmations such as "I am in control of my fear" or "I am strong and resilient" can help challenge negative thought patterns and build self-confidence. Practicing positive self-talk can gradually rewire the brain, replacing fear with self-assurance.

Setting Realistic Goals

Setting realistic goals is an important part of personal growth and empowerment in the context of trypanophobia. By breaking down the process of overcoming fear into manageable steps, individuals can make steady progress while acknowledging and celebrating their achievements along the way. This approach helps build self-esteem and reinforces the belief that they have the power to overcome their fear. Setting realistic goals also provides a sense of direction and purpose, motivating individuals to continue their journey towards empowerment.

Exposure Therapy and Progressive Desensitization

Exposure therapy is a widely recognized and effective treatment for phobias, including trypanophobia. By gradually exposing themselves to the source of their fear in a controlled environment, individuals can learn to manage their anxiety and reduce their phobic response. Progressive desensitization is a specific technique used in exposure therapy wherein individuals gradually confront their fear by starting with minimal exposure and gradually increasing intensity over time. This gradual approach allows individuals to build tolerance and gain a greater sense of control.

Cultivating Mindfulness and Relaxation Techniques

Mindfulness and relaxation techniques are invaluable tools in managing anxiety and promoting personal growth. By learning to be fully present in the moment and accepting their fear without judgment, individuals with trypanophobia can reduce their emotional distress and develop a sense of calm. Mindfulness practices, such as deep breathing exercises or meditation, can help individuals become more attuned to their internal experiences and develop a greater sense of self-control. These techniques can be integrated into daily routines to promote overall well-being and empower individuals in their journey towards overcoming trypanophobia.

Support Networks and Peer Mentorship

Building a support network and seeking guidance from individuals who have successfully overcome trypanophobia can be incredibly empowering. Connecting with others who share similar experiences creates a sense of community and provides a safe space for sharing fears, progress, and coping strategies. Peer mentorship programs can offer guidance and encouragement, providing individuals with role models who have already navigated the challenges of trypanophobia. Through these support networks, individuals can find inspiration, validation, and practical advice to aid in their personal growth.

Celebrating and Acknowledging Progress

Acknowledging and celebrating progress is a vital aspect of personal growth and empowerment. Overcoming trypanophobia is an ongoing journey, and it is essential to recognize and appreciate the courage and resilience individuals demonstrate throughout the process. By celebrating even small victories, individuals can build self-confidence and reinforce the belief that they have the strength to overcome their fears. This self-affirmation creates a positive feedback loop, further empowering individuals to continue their growth and embrace a fear-free life.

In conclusion, personal growth and empowerment are key components of overcoming trypanophobia. By engaging in self-reflection, education, positive affirmations, and setting realistic goals, individuals can develop resilience and regain control over their fears. Exposure therapy, mindfulness practices, and support networks can further facilitate personal growth, ensuring that individuals are equipped with the necessary tools to conquer trypanophobia. By embracing personal growth and empowerment, those affected can embark on a transformative journey towards a fear-free life.

Success Stories and Testimonials

In this section, we will explore some success stories and testimonials from individuals who have managed to overcome their trypanophobia. These stories serve as inspiration for others who are currently struggling with their fear of needles, showing that recovery is possible with the right support and treatment.

One remarkable success story is that of Sarah, a 32-year-old woman who had been living with severe trypanophobia since childhood. Sarah's fear of needles began after a traumatic experience with a painful injection during a hospital visit. This incident left her with extreme anxiety and panic attacks whenever she had to face a medical procedure involving needles.

Sarah decided to seek help when her fear started to interfere with her quality of life. She underwent cognitive-behavioral therapy (CBT), a commonly recommended treatment for trypanophobia. Through CBT, she learned techniques to challenge her irrational thoughts and reframe her negative beliefs about needles. Gradual exposure therapy was also an integral part of her treatment, where she gradually exposed herself to needle-related situations in a controlled and supportive environment.

Over time, Sarah began to notice a significant reduction in her fear and anxiety. With the guidance of her therapist, she developed relaxation techniques and coping strategies to manage her emotions effectively. Sarah's success story illustrates the power of therapy in helping individuals rewire their thought patterns and overcome deep-rooted fears.

Another inspiring example is Mark, a 45-year-old man who had developed trypanophobia as a result of several traumatic medical experiences. His fear of needles had prevented him from seeking necessary medical treatments and check-ups, putting his health at risk.

Mark's turning point came when he discovered the power of hypnotherapy in addressing phobias. Hypnotherapy works by accessing the subconscious mind, allowing individuals to confront and reframe their fears at a deeper level. With the help of a skilled hypnotherapist, Mark was able to uncover the underlying causes of his trypanophobia and address them directly.

During the hypnotherapy sessions, Mark experienced a profound sense of relaxation and mental clarity. He was guided through visualization exercises, which helped him recondition his mind to perceive needles differently. With each session, Mark's fear gradually diminished, and he regained control over his emotions.

Following his successful hypnotherapy experience, Mark became an advocate for alternative treatments for trypanophobia. He started sharing his story online and participating in support groups, offering guidance and encouragement to others struggling with similar fears. His story highlights the importance of exploring different therapeutic approaches and finding what works best for each individual.

It's important to note that success stories like Sarah's and Mark's are the result of individualized and comprehensive treatment plans. Recovery from trypanophobia requires a combination of therapy, support, and personal commitment. While these stories offer hope, it's crucial to remember that everyone's journey is unique, and the path to overcoming fear may vary.

If you or someone you know is struggling with trypanophobia, remember that there is help available. Reach out to a licensed therapist or seek support from online communities dedicated to phobia recovery. With the right guidance and determination, a fear-free life is within reach.

Advocacy and Awareness Efforts

Advocacy and awareness are crucial aspects in addressing the challenges and stigma faced by individuals with trypanophobia. By promoting understanding, support, and change, we can work towards creating a more inclusive and empathetic society. This section explores various advocacy and awareness efforts aimed at destigmatizing needle phobia and providing resources for those affected.

Education and Public Outreach

Educating the general public about trypanophobia is a key step in raising awareness and dispelling misconceptions surrounding this phobia. Advocacy groups, healthcare organizations, and mental health professionals can collaborate to develop educational materials, such as brochures, infographics, and online resources, to inform the public about the prevalence, impact, and challenges associated with needle phobia.

Public outreach programs can be organized to conduct presentations, seminars, and workshops in schools, community centers, and healthcare settings. These initiatives aim to reach a wider audience, including students, parents, teachers, healthcare providers, and policymakers. By fostering an understanding of needle phobia, these programs can facilitate empathy, support, and acceptance for individuals with trypanophobia.

Media Campaigns and Social Media

Harnessing the power of media can be an effective way to reach a large audience and create meaningful change. Media campaigns can be designed to challenge stereotypes and misconceptions about needle phobia, featuring real-life stories, expert interviews, and educational content.

Utilizing social media platforms, such as Facebook, Twitter, and Instagram, advocacy groups can share information, resources, and personal experiences related to trypanophobia. Online support groups and forums can provide a safe space for individuals to discuss their fears, seek advice, and connect with others facing similar challenges. It is important to create a positive and inclusive online community to counteract the isolation and shame often experienced by those with needle phobia.

Collaboration with Healthcare Providers

Collaborating with healthcare providers is crucial in ensuring that individuals with trypanophobia receive appropriate and compassionate care. Advocacy groups can work with medical societies, hospitals, and clinics to develop guidelines and protocols for addressing needle phobia.

Training programs can be organized to educate healthcare professionals about the unique needs of individuals with needle phobia. This includes understanding the psychological mechanisms behind trypanophobia, implementing empathetic communication strategies, and exploring alternative methods of delivering medical interventions.

Moreover, advocacy groups can advocate for the development of specialized clinics or designated healthcare settings that cater to the needs of needle phobics. These environments can be designed to minimize triggers and provide a supportive and comfortable atmosphere for individuals undergoing medical procedures.

Legislative Advocacy and Policy Changes

Advocacy efforts can extend to the legislative domain, where individuals and organizations can work towards policy changes that benefit those with needle phobia. This includes advocating for the development and implementation of laws and regulations that promote accessibility, accommodation, and support for needle phobics in various settings.

Legislative advocacy can also focus on addressing the challenges faced by trypanophobics in educational institutions and workplaces. By advocating for reasonable accommodations, such as exemption from unnecessary medical procedures or the provision of support personnel during essential interventions, needle phobics can feel empowered to participate fully in their education and careers.

Collaborative Research and Funding

Advocacy and awareness efforts can be further supported by collaborative research and the allocation of adequate funding. By partnering with researchers, advocacy groups can contribute to the generation of knowledge and evidence-based interventions for trypanophobia.

Advocacy groups can work towards securing funding for research projects investigating the causes, risk factors, and treatment modalities for needle phobia. By highlighting the significant impact of trypanophobia on individuals' mental health and overall well-being, there is a greater chance of attracting funding from government agencies, philanthropic organizations, and private donors.

Celebrating Success Stories and Role Models

Sharing success stories and showcasing role models who have overcome their needle phobia can be a powerful tool in advocacy and awareness efforts. This can involve featuring personal testimonies, interviews, or media campaigns highlighting the resilience, courage, and determination of individuals who have conquered their fear of needles.

Such stories serve as a source of inspiration and hope for those currently struggling with trypanophobia. By highlighting the journey of successful recovery and the transformative power of treatment, advocacy groups can motivate individuals to seek help and support.

Promoting Self-Help Resources

Advocacy groups can compile and disseminate self-help resources that empower individuals with needle phobia to cope with their fear. These resources may include books, online courses, mobile applications, and guided meditation programs specifically tailored to address trypanophobia.

Additionally, advocacy groups can collaborate with mental health professionals and organizations to provide directories of therapists, clinics, and support groups specializing in needle phobia. By connecting individuals with these resources, advocacy efforts can ensure that those seeking help have easy access to appropriate and effective treatment options.

In conclusion, advocacy and awareness efforts play a crucial role in addressing the challenges faced by individuals with trypanophobia. By educating the public, collaborating with healthcare providers, advocating for policy changes, supporting research, and sharing success stories, we can create a more understanding and inclusive society. With increased awareness and support, individuals with needle phobia can receive the care and understanding they deserve, ultimately empowering them to overcome their fear and lead healthier lives.

Chapter Six: Supporting Loved Ones with Trypanophobia

Life After Fear: Embracing Health and Well-being

It is often said that facing our fears is the first step toward personal growth and transformation. This holds true for individuals with trypanophobia, who have conquered their fear of needles and now find themselves on the journey to embracing health and well-being.

Once trypanophobics overcome their intense fear of needles, a whole new world opens up to them. It is important to remember that the process of overcoming trypanophobia is unique for each individual, and the path to embracing health and well-being may vary. In this section, we will explore the different aspects of life after fear, focusing on physical, mental, and emotional well-being.

Physical Well-being

One of the most significant changes that occur after overcoming trypanophobia is the freedom to take charge of one's physical health. Individuals who previously avoided medical procedures due to their fear of needles can now engage in preventive care and necessary interventions without hesitation.

Regular check-ups, immunizations, and medical screenings become routine and are no longer a source of anxiety. Embracing physical well-being also involves adopting a healthy lifestyle, which includes regular exercise, a balanced diet, and sufficient sleep.

For trypanophobics, physical well-being also means understanding the importance of managing stress levels. Engaging in stress-reducing activities such as yoga, meditation, or spending time in nature can have profound effects on overall health.

Mental Well-being

Overcoming trypanophobia not only brings relief from the fear of needles but also allows individuals to address and improve their mental well-being. The journey of healing often includes working on underlying anxiety disorders that may have contributed to the development and maintenance of trypanophobia.

Therapeutic techniques such as cognitive-behavioral therapy (CBT), psychoeducation, and exposure therapy can help individuals develop healthier coping strategies and reduce anxiety. Understanding and challenging negative thoughts and beliefs related to needles is a crucial aspect of the recovery process.

Furthermore, mindfulness practices enable individuals to cultivate a sense of presence and self-awareness, facilitating emotional regulation and reducing stress. Engaging in activities that bring joy and fulfillment, such as hobbies or creative pursuits, is also essential for maintaining positive mental well-being.

Emotional Well-being

Embracing life after fear involves nurturing emotional well-being, which encompasses acknowledging and processing any residual emotions and trauma associated with trypanophobia. It is natural to experience a range of emotions during the recovery process, such as relief, joy, and even grief for the time lost to fear.

Support from loved ones and peers who understand the journey of overcoming phobias can provide a sense of validation and comfort. Joining support groups or engaging in peer counseling can serve as a powerful tool for emotional healing and finding a community of individuals with similar experiences.

Practicing self-compassion and self-care techniques is vital in the pursuit of emotional well-being. This includes setting boundaries, engaging in activities that promote relaxation and self-nurturing, and maintaining healthy and supportive relationships.

Reintegrating into Society

After conquering trypanophobia, individuals may find themselves adapting to a new way of life, free from the limitations posed by their fear. Reintegrating into society involves building upon the newfound strength and resilience, and shifting focus toward personal goals and aspirations.

Career opportunities in healthcare or medical fields may become more accessible, as individuals now have the ability to face their fears and embrace the necessary procedures. Additionally, advocacy and awareness efforts can empower trypanophobics to contribute to the understanding and support of others who still struggle with needle phobia.

It is important to remember that the journey toward embracing health and well-being is ongoing. It may be beneficial for individuals to periodically revisit the coping strategies they have learned, engage in continued therapy or support groups, and maintain self-awareness of any triggers or setbacks.

Conclusion

In conclusion, life after overcoming trypanophobia is a unique and personal journey. Embracing health and well-being requires a holistic approach, addressing physical, mental, and emotional aspects of an individual's life. By taking charge of their physical health, improving mental well-being, nurturing emotional resilience, and reintegrating into society, individuals can move forward with a renewed sense of purpose and joy, ready to embrace a future free from the limitations of fear.

Remember, the journey does not end with overcoming trypanophobia but continues as individuals embark on a path of personal growth, self-discovery, and the pursuit of a meaningful and fulfilling life. Embrace the freedom from fear and embrace the possibilities that lie ahead.

Chapter Six: Supporting Loved Ones with Trypanophobia

Empathy and Understanding

Communicating with a Trypanophobic Individual

Effectively communicating with a trypanophobic individual requires patience, empathy, and an understanding of their unique fears and concerns. It is important to create an environment of trust and support, allowing the individual to express their thoughts and emotions without judgment. In this section, we will explore some strategies and techniques that can facilitate communication with someone suffering from trypanophobia.

Active Listening

Active listening is a fundamental skill that can enhance communication with a trypanophobic individual. It involves giving your full attention to the person, acknowledging their feelings, and providing verbal and non-verbal cues to show that you are present and engaged. Some key principles of active listening include:

- Maintaining eye contact: This demonstrates your attentiveness and shows that you value their words.
- Using open body language: Avoid crossing your arms or displaying defensive postures, as it can contribute to a sense of confrontation. Instead, maintain an open and relaxed stance to create a safe space for communication.
- Nodding and using affirming statements: These small gestures convey understanding and encourage the person to continue sharing their feelings.

Simple phrases like "I understand" or "That must be difficult" can help validate their experiences.

- Paraphrasing and reflecting: Summarizing what the person has said in your own words shows that you are actively processing their information. It also gives them an opportunity to clarify any misunderstandings or misconceptions.

By demonstrating active listening, you can establish a deeper connection and make the trypanophobic individual feel heard and valued.

Empathy and Validation

Empathy is the ability to understand and share the feelings of another person. It plays a crucial role in communicating with a trypanophobic individual, as it helps build trust and fosters a sense of compassion. Here are some strategies to enhance empathy and validation:

- Acknowledge their emotions: Validate the person's feelings by acknowledging their fear and anxiety. Phrases such as "I can see that this is really distressing for you" or "It's completely understandable to be scared" can help create an atmosphere of empathy.
- Avoid minimizing their fears: Never belittle or dismiss the individual's fears. Instead, take the time to understand their unique perspective and the impact their phobia has on their daily life.
- Reflect on shared experiences: If you have personally experienced fear or anxiety in any context, sharing your own stories can help create a sense of connection and understanding. Be cautious, however, not to make the conversation about yourself, but rather to show that you can relate to their emotions.

By demonstrating empathy and validation, you can help ease some of the anxiety and distress experienced by the trypanophobic individual.

Education and Awareness

Educating yourself about trypanophobia and its associated challenges is essential in communicating effectively with those who suffer from it. By acquiring knowledge on the subject, you can engage in informed discussions, offer relevant advice, and dispel any misconceptions. Here are some steps you can take to educate yourself:

- Read reliable sources: Consult reputable books, articles, and websites that provide accurate information about trypanophobia. These sources can help you understand the psychological mechanisms, common triggers, and potential treatments for this phobia.
- Attend support groups or workshops: Engaging in support groups or attending workshops on needle phobia can grant you valuable insights into the experiences and challenges faced by trypanophobic individuals. It can also help you learn from others' perspectives and gather practical strategies.
- Consult healthcare professionals: Seek advice from mental health professionals, psychologists, or therapists who specialize in treating trypanophobia. Their expertise can provide you with a deeper understanding of the condition and its management.

By taking the initiative to educate yourself, you demonstrate your commitment to supporting and communicating effectively with trypanophobic individuals.

Providing Options and Accommodations

Flexibility and accommodation are crucial when communicating with someone who has trypanophobia. By offering choices and alternative options, you empower the individual to make decisions that suit their comfort levels. Here are some practical ways to provide options and accommodations:

- Discuss alternative procedures: When encountering a situation where a medical procedure involving needles is necessary, explore alternative options with the trypanophobic individual. For instance, you may inquire if oral medications or non-invasive treatments are available.
- Allow breaks and pauses: Some trypanophobic individuals may need breaks or pauses during discussions or medical procedures. By allowing them time to collect themselves and regain composure, you create a supportive atmosphere.
- Provide distractions or relaxation techniques: Offering distractions, such as music, calming visuals, or sensory toys, can help redirect the person's focus away from their fears. Additionally, relaxation techniques like deep breathing exercises or visualization techniques can be valuable tools to manage anxiety during difficult situations.

By offering options and accommodations, you empower the individual and enable them to participate in decisions that directly impact their well-being.

Respecting Boundaries

Respecting personal boundaries is essential to maintaining a healthy and effective communication dynamic with trypanophobic individuals. Each person will have different comfort levels and limits when discussing or facing their phobia. Here are some guidelines for respecting boundaries:

- Seek permission before sharing information: Respect the individual's autonomy by seeking their consent before sharing any resources, stories, or suggestions related to their condition. Obtain their agreement to avoid imposing unwanted advice or assistance.

- Avoid triggering discussions: Be cautious in conversations and avoid triggering subjects unless the individual willingly expresses their readiness to discuss them. Respect their need for space and privacy.

- Encourage self-advocacy: Foster an environment where the individual feels comfortable expressing their needs and concerns. Encourage them to communicate their boundaries clearly and support their advocacy for suitable accommodations.

By respecting personal boundaries, you demonstrate a strong commitment to the individual's well-being and establish a foundation of trust and respect.

In conclusion, effective communication with a trypanophobic individual requires active listening, empathy, education, boundary respect, and the provision of options and accommodations. By implementing these strategies, you can create a safe and supportive environment that facilitates understanding and fosters trust. Remember, every trypanophobic individual is unique, so adapt these techniques to best suit the preferences and needs of the person you are communicating with.

Educating Friends and Family

Educating friends and family about trypanophobia is crucial in providing a supportive and understanding environment for individuals living with this phobia. By enlisting their support and empathy, you can create a safe space where the fears and concerns are acknowledged, respected, and addressed. In this section, we will discuss some strategies for educating friends and family about trypanophobia.

Understanding Trypanophobia

The first step in educating friends and family is to help them understand what trypanophobia is and its impact on the individual's life. Start by explaining that trypanophobia is an intense fear of needles or injections, which can cause severe anxiety and panic attacks. Emphasize that this fear is not rational or something that the individual can easily overcome.

Provide examples and real-life stories about the challenges faced by trypanophobics. Sharing personal anecdotes or case studies can help friends and family members relate to the experiences of those with trypanophobia, fostering empathy and understanding.

Dispelling Myths and Stereotypes

Addressing misconceptions and stereotypes surrounding trypanophobia is another crucial aspect of educating friends and family. Many people may dismiss needle phobia as a trivial fear or an irrational behavior. It is important to emphasize that trypanophobia is a genuine, debilitating condition that can have a significant impact on a person's life. Inform them that individuals with trypanophobia are not seeking attention or trying to avoid medical procedures out of laziness or obstinacy.

Explain that trypanophobics often experience physiological symptoms such as an increased heart rate, trembling, sweating, and feelings of dread. These symptoms are not under their control and can be overwhelming.

Providing Practical Strategies

Educating friends and family is not just about raising awareness, but also about equipping them with practical strategies to support trypanophobics. Here are some ideas to get you started:

- Encourage open communication: Foster an environment where the individual feels safe discussing their fears and concerns. Promote active listening and validate their emotions without judgment.

- Be patient and understanding: Help friends and family understand that overcoming trypanophobia takes time and patience. Encourage them to be supportive and empathetic, rather than pressuring the individual to "get over" their fear.

- Learn relaxation techniques together: Explore relaxation techniques such as deep breathing exercises, progressive muscle relaxation, or guided imagery.

By practicing these techniques alongside the individual with trypanophobia, friends and family can provide a calming presence during challenging situations.

- Foster a sense of control: Encourage trypanophobics to communicate their preferences and boundaries during medical procedures. Friends and family can help advocate for their needs and ensure that medical professionals are aware of their fears.
- Seek professional help: Consider involving a mental health professional who specializes in anxiety disorders or phobias. Educate friends and family about the types of therapies available, such as cognitive-behavioral therapy (CBT) or exposure therapy, and encourage them to support the individual in seeking professional help.
- Share educational resources: Provide friends and family with informative articles, books, or online resources about trypanophobia. This can help them gain a deeper understanding of the condition and learn more about ways to support their loved one.

Promoting Empathy and Self-Care

It is important to remind friends and family that caring for someone with trypanophobia can be emotionally challenging. Encourage them to prioritize self-care and seek support if needed. Offering support to someone with trypanophobia can be physically and mentally exhausting, and it is crucial for caregivers to address their own emotional well-being.

Encourage open dialogue between friends, family, and trypanophobics, where concerns can be addressed and support can be provided. This dialogue can create a framework for ongoing education, empathy, and understanding within the social circle.

Real-Life Scenario: The Power of Empathy

To illustrate the impact of educating friends and family, let's consider a real-life scenario involving Sarah, a trypanophobic individual, and her loved ones.

Sarah's family initially dismissed her fear of needles, believing that she was being dramatic or attention-seeking. However, after attending a support group meeting, Sarah gained knowledge about trypanophobia and brought her family to the next meeting.

During the session, family members heard personal stories of other trypanophobics and engaged in group discussions. They listened to accounts of panic attacks and the distressing symptoms experienced by individuals with this phobia. This experience allowed Sarah's family to empathize with her fear and recognize the impact it had on her well-being.

Armed with a newfound understanding, Sarah's family took several steps to support her. They learned techniques such as breathing exercises and relaxation strategies, which they practiced together. They also facilitated open communication within the family, creating a safe space for Sarah to express her fears and concerns without judgment.

As a result, Sarah's family was able to offer her the support she needed during medical procedures. They advocated for her preferences, communicated her fears to healthcare providers, and stood by her side during treatments. Through education and empathy, Sarah's family became integral allies in her journey to managing her trypanophobia.

Further Resources and References

In your journey to educating friends and family about trypanophobia, you can refer to a variety of reputable resources. Here are some recommendations:

- "The Phobia Workbook" by Edmund J. Bourne: This book offers insights and exercises to help individuals understand and cope with specific phobias, including needle phobia.

- Anxiety and Depression Association of America (ADAA): Visit the ADAA website to access information, articles, and resources related to anxiety disorders and phobias.

- Trypanophobia Support Groups: Explore online and local support groups dedicated to trypanophobia. These communities provide a space for sharing experiences and connecting with others who have similar fears.

Remember, educating friends and family is a continuous process. By fostering empathy, understanding, and practical support, you can create a network of allies who are better equipped to support and nurture their loved ones with trypanophobia.

Creating a Fear-Free Environment

Creating a fear-free environment is essential in supporting individuals with trypanophobia. When a person is surrounded by understanding and empathy, their anxiety and fear can be alleviated, making it easier for them to cope with their phobia. In this section, we will explore various strategies and techniques to create a fear-free environment for trypanophobics.

Understanding Trypanophobia

To create a fear-free environment, it is important to have a deep understanding of trypanophobia, its causes, and its impact on individuals. By familiarizing ourselves with the phobia, we can empathize better and provide the necessary support. Here are some key points to consider:

- Educate yourself about trypanophobia: Learn about the symptoms, triggers, and common challenges faced by individuals with this phobia. This knowledge will help you navigate conversations and interactions sensitively.
- Active listening: Listen attentively without judgment when someone shares their experiences or fears related to needles. Give them space to express their emotions and concerns.
- Validate their feelings: Understand that trypanophobia is a real and valid fear. Avoid minimizing or trivializing their experiences. Validate their emotions and let them know that their fear is acknowledged and respected.
- Avoid triggering discussions or situations: Be mindful of the language you use and the topics you discuss around a trypanophobic individual. Avoid sharing graphic details or stories related to needles unless explicitly requested.

Creating a Safe Physical Environment

The physical environment plays a crucial role in creating a safe space for individuals with trypanophobia. Here are some practical steps to make the environment fear-free:

- Comfortable waiting areas: Ensure that waiting areas in healthcare settings are designed in a way that minimizes stress and anxiety. Consider providing distractions like books, magazines, or soothing music to help individuals relax.

- Dimming the lights: Bright lights can be overwhelming for some trypanophobics. Dimming the lights or using soft, warm lighting can create a calming atmosphere.

- Minimize needle visibility: Avoid displaying needles or medical equipment in plain sight. Keeping these items out of view can help ease anxiety and prevent triggers.

- Flexible appointment scheduling: Allow individuals to request appointments at specific times when they feel most comfortable. This flexibility can help reduce anxiety associated with waiting or anticipating the procedure.

- Privacy and confidentiality: Ensure that conversations and procedures related to trypanophobia are handled with utmost privacy. Respect confidentiality to maintain trust and the sense of safety.

Effective Communication

Open and effective communication is vital in creating a fear-free environment. Clear and compassionate communication can help alleviate anxiety and build trust. Here are some communication strategies to consider:

- Use simple and non-medical language: Avoid using complex medical terminology when discussing procedures or treatment options. Instead, use clear and layman's terms to ensure that the individual understands the information provided.

- Provide information in advance: For individuals with trypanophobia, knowing what to expect can help reduce anxiety. Provide information about the procedure, possible sensations, and aftercare instructions before the appointment.

- Ask for consent and preferences: Respect the individual's autonomy and involve them in decision-making as much as possible. Explain the options available and ask for their preferences regarding pain management techniques or alternative treatments.

- Offer distractions: During a procedure, providing distractions like calming music, engaging conversation, or visual stimuli can help redirect the individual's focus and alleviate anxiety.

- Check-in during and after the procedure: Reassure the individual throughout the procedure by regularly checking in on their comfort level. Afterward, offer support and provide an opportunity for them to express their feelings or ask questions.

Empathy and Emotional Support

Empathy and emotional support can significantly impact the experience of individuals with trypanophobia. By displaying empathy and offering emotional support, you can help them feel understood and cared for. Here are some ways to provide support:

- Show compassion: Be understanding and patient with individuals experiencing trypanophobia. Acknowledge their fears without judgment, and offer reassurance that you are there to support them.

- Offer a support system: Encourage individuals to bring a trusted friend or family member to appointments to provide emotional support. Having a familiar face can increase a sense of security and help manage anxiety.

- Provide resources: Share information about support groups, online forums, or therapy options specializing in trypanophobia. These resources can offer additional support and guidance for individuals seeking help.

- Encourage self-care techniques: Teach and encourage individuals to practice self-care techniques to manage anxiety and stress. Deep breathing exercises, mindfulness, and relaxation techniques can help individuals cope with their fear outside of medical settings.

Addressing Institutional Practices

Creating a fear-free environment for trypanophobics requires addressing institutional practices within healthcare systems. It is crucial to advocate for changes that promote understanding and accommodate the needs of individuals with trypanophobia. Here are some steps to consider:

- Training healthcare providers: Provide training and education to healthcare professionals on trypanophobia and best practices to support affected individuals. Sensitize healthcare staff to the unique challenges faced by trypanophobics and help foster a more empathic and accommodating environment.

- Accommodations during procedures: Collaborate with healthcare providers to explore accommodations that can help manage anxiety during procedures. This may include the use of numbing creams, distraction techniques, or a gradual approach to exposure.
- Flexible treatment options: Advocate for alternative treatment options, such as needle-free procedures or oral medications, whenever possible. By providing choices, individuals can opt for methods that align with their comfort levels.
- Reducing waiting times: Long wait times can increase anxiety and stress. Advocate for efficient appointment scheduling and reduced waiting times, allowing individuals to spend less time in anxious anticipation.
- Feedback and improvement mechanisms: Establish feedback processes to gather input from trypanophobics about their experiences within healthcare settings. Use this feedback to identify areas for improvement and tailor services to better accommodate their needs and preferences.

Creating a fear-free environment requires a collective effort from individuals, healthcare providers, and institutions. By practicing empathy, understanding, and implementing strategic changes, we can create a supportive environment where individuals with trypanophobia feel safe, respected, and empowered in managing their phobia.

Accommodations in Healthcare Settings

When it comes to providing care for individuals with trypanophobia, it is essential for healthcare settings to create an accommodating and comfortable environment. This ensures that patients can receive necessary medical treatments without unnecessary distress. Accommodations in healthcare settings not only alleviate anxiety and fear but also improve treatment outcomes and patient satisfaction. In this section, we will explore various strategies and accommodations that can be implemented to support trypanophobics during their medical visits.

Creating a Safe and Relaxing Atmosphere

The ambiance of a healthcare setting can significantly impact the experience of a trypanophobic patient. To create a safe and relaxing atmosphere, healthcare providers should consider the following:

- **Calming Colors and Decor:** Choosing soothing color schemes and decorating the space with calming images or artwork can help create a more reassuring environment.
- **Comfortable Seating and Distractions:** Providing comfortable seating options and distracting materials such as magazines, books, or puzzles can help divert the patient's attention away from their fear.
- **Soft Background Music:** Playing soft, calming music can help create a soothing ambiance and mask potentially anxiety-inducing sounds.
- **Aromatherapy:** Using essential oils or aromatherapy diffusers with scents like lavender or chamomile can help promote relaxation and reduce anxiety.

These simple but effective adjustments to the healthcare environment can go a long way in making trypanophobics feel more at ease during their visits.

Clear Communication and Education

Effective communication plays a vital role in accommodating trypanophobic patients in healthcare settings. Healthcare providers should prioritize clear and empathetic communication by:

- **Active Listening:** Taking the time to listen to the patient's concerns and experiences without judgment is key to building trust and rapport.
- **Thorough Explanations:** Healthcare professionals should explain all medical procedures and treatments in a clear, concise, and non-threatening manner. Breaking down complex jargon and providing visual aids when appropriate can enhance understanding and help manage anxiety.
- **Informed Consent:** For trypanophobic patients, it is essential to obtain informed consent with a comprehensive discussion about the procedure, its benefits, risks, and available alternatives. This ensures patients have the necessary information to make informed decisions regarding their treatment.
- **Providing Options and Control:** Offering trypanophobics choices and empowering them to have some control over their treatment can help reduce anxiety. For example, allowing patients to select the injection site or timing of the procedure can enhance their sense of autonomy.

By prioritizing open and empathetic communication, healthcare providers can establish a supportive and understanding relationship with trypanophobic patients.

Minimizing Wait Times and Distractions

Long wait times and crowded waiting areas can exacerbate anxiety for trypanophobics. Here are some strategies to address these issues:

- **Efficient Scheduling:** Implementing an efficient appointment system that reduces wait times can help minimize anxiety and anticipation.
- **Separate Waiting Area:** Creating a separate waiting area for trypanophobic patients, away from the sights and sounds of medical procedures, can help maintain a calmer environment.
- **Distraction Techniques:** Offering distraction techniques or providing entertainment options in the waiting area, such as televisions, quiet music, or interactive games, can help take patients' minds off their fears.

By minimizing wait times and providing engaging distractions, healthcare settings can alleviate stress and anxiety for trypanophobic individuals.

Needle Phobia-Sensitive Staff Training

Healthcare providers and staff should receive comprehensive training to better understand and address trypanophobia. Some key training considerations include:

- **Cultural Sensitivity:** Recognizing and respecting the cultural factors that may influence trypanophobia can enhance patient-centered care.
- **Empathy and Emotional Support:** Training should focus on fostering empathy and providing emotional support to patients with trypanophobia. This includes active listening, validating their fears, and offering reassurance.
- **Effective Distraction Techniques:** Staff should be trained in distraction techniques that can be used during medical procedures. These techniques can include engaging the patient in conversation, using handheld devices or toys, or employing guided imagery exercises.
- **Non-pharmacological Interventions:** Equipping healthcare providers with knowledge and skills in non-pharmacological interventions such as relaxation breathing techniques, progressive muscle relaxation, or guided meditation can be highly beneficial to trypanophobic patients.

By training healthcare providers and staff to be sensitive and responsive to the needs of individuals with trypanophobia, healthcare settings can better accommodate their fears and provide a more positive medical experience.

Alternative Delivery Methods and Devices

Innovative advancements in healthcare technology have introduced alternative delivery methods and devices that can help reduce the discomfort associated with injections. Some examples include:

- **Needle-Free Injections:** Needle-free injection systems use pressure or air to deliver medication through the skin, eliminating the need for traditional needles. These can be less intimidating and painful for trypanophobic patients.
- **Topical Anesthetics:** Applying topical anesthetics before needle insertion can significantly reduce pain and discomfort, as well as alleviate anxiety related to needle phobia.
- **Smaller and Insulated Needles:** Advances in needle technology have led to the development of smaller, thinner, and insulated needles. These needles minimize pain and reduce the fear associated with traditional needles.
- **Autoinjectors:** Autoinjector devices are designed to deliver pre-measured doses of medication with minimal effort. These devices often have hidden needles that activate upon pressing, minimizing the visibility and anticipation of the injection.

By incorporating alternative delivery methods and devices, healthcare providers can offer trypanophobic patients options that reduce anxiety and discomfort, while still providing the necessary medical treatments.

Collaboration with Mental Health Professionals

In severe cases of trypanophobia, collaboration between healthcare providers and mental health professionals is crucial. This collaboration ensures a comprehensive approach to treatment and may involve:

- **Referrals to Mental Health Specialists:** Healthcare providers should be prepared to refer patients with severe trypanophobia to mental health professionals specializing in anxiety disorders and phobias. These specialists can provide specific interventions and therapy to help manage and overcome needle-related fears.

- **Coordinated Care:** Coordinated care between healthcare providers and mental health professionals ensures a cohesive and integrated treatment plan. This collaboration allows for a more holistic approach to addressing trypanophobia.
- **Psychoeducation and Coping Strategies:** Mental health professionals can educate trypanophobic patients on coping strategies, relaxation techniques, and cognitive-behavioral therapy (CBT) approaches to manage their fears. These strategies empower patients to develop resilience and gradually confront their fears.

By involving mental health professionals in the care of trypanophobic patients, healthcare settings can optimize treatment outcomes and provide a comprehensive support system.

Accommodations in healthcare settings are crucial for providing effective care to individuals with trypanophobia. By adopting these strategies, healthcare providers and settings can create an environment that minimizes anxiety, enhances patient comfort, and promotes positive treatment experiences.

Supporting Accessible Treatment Options

When it comes to supporting individuals with trypanophobia, it is essential to provide accessible treatment options that cater to their specific needs and help them overcome their fear of needles. Here, we will explore various strategies and approaches that can be utilized to ensure accessibility in treating trypanophobia.

Patient-Centered Care

A crucial aspect of supporting individuals with trypanophobia is practicing patient-centered care. This approach emphasizes the importance of involving patients in their own treatment decisions, considering their preferences, values, and concerns. It is vital to listen attentively to the needs and fears of trypanophobics and work collaboratively with them to create a safe and supportive environment.

Education and Information

Providing accurate and comprehensive education about the nature of trypanophobia and the available treatment options can empower individuals and alleviate their fears. Education can include explanations of the physiological responses involved in trypanophobia, the steps involved in various medical procedures, and the strategies utilized in exposure therapy. Additionally, sharing success stories and testimonials from individuals who have overcome their fear can inspire hope and motivate trypanophobics to seek help.

Gradual Exposure Therapy

Gradual exposure therapy is one of the most effective forms of treatment for trypanophobia. It involves exposing individuals to their fear in a step-by-step manner, starting with minimal exposure and gradually increasing the level of exposure over time. This can be done through visualization exercises, virtual reality simulations, or by gradually introducing real-life needle-related situations. The goal is to help individuals build resilience and gradually reduce their fear response through repeated exposure.

Relaxation and Distraction Techniques

Utilizing relaxation and distraction techniques during needle-related procedures can significantly help individuals manage their anxiety and discomfort. Deep breathing exercises, progressive muscle relaxation, guided imagery, and mindfulness techniques can all be incorporated to promote relaxation and divert attention from the fear of needles. Providing a range of options allows individuals to find the techniques that work best for them.

Sedation and Anesthesia

For individuals with severe trypanophobia, sedation or anesthesia can be considered as an option for certain medical procedures. This approach ensures that patients feel little to no discomfort or fear during the procedure. However, it is important to carefully evaluate the risks and benefits of sedation, taking into account individual health conditions and potential side effects.

Alternative Delivery Methods

In recent years, alternative delivery methods have emerged to reduce needle phobia. Transdermal patches, needle-free injectors, and nasal sprays have been developed to deliver medications, vaccines, and other therapies without the use of traditional needles. These alternative methods can provide options for individuals who experience extreme fear or anxiety when faced with needles.

Peer Support and Support Groups

Connecting individuals with trypanophobia to peer support networks or support groups can offer valuable emotional support and the opportunity to share experiences with others who have similar fears. Peer support can help reduce isolation and normalize the trypanophobic experience. It can also provide a forum for individuals to exchange coping strategies and seek advice from those who have successfully managed their fears.

Collaboration with Healthcare Providers

It is crucial to foster collaboration between trypanophobics and healthcare providers to ensure personalized and effective care. Healthcare providers should be open to discussing fears and concerns, adapting procedures or techniques to accommodate the individual's needs, and providing ongoing support throughout the treatment process. Collaborative efforts can lead to better outcomes and help individuals feel empowered and in control of their treatment.

Accessibility of Treatment Facilities

Ensuring that treatment facilities are accessible and welcoming to individuals with trypanophobia is essential. Facilities can implement measures to create a fear-free environment, such as minimizing visual cues related to needles, providing comfortable waiting areas, and offering distractions like calming music or artwork. Additionally, easily accessible information about the facility's needle-related procedures, the availability of alternative delivery methods, and the presence of trained staff can contribute to a sense of safety and confidence.

Continued Research and Innovation

Continued research and innovation in the field of trypanophobia are crucial to develop new and improved treatment options. Advancements in areas such as virtual reality therapy, pharmacological interventions, and cultural perspectives can enhance accessibility, effectiveness, and cultural sensitivity in treating trypanophobia. Supporting research initiatives and promoting collaboration between researchers, practitioners, and trypanophobics is essential for advancing the understanding and treatment of this phobia.

In conclusion, supporting accessible treatment options for individuals with trypanophobia requires a patient-centered approach, education and information sharing, gradual exposure therapy, relaxation techniques, sedation options, alternative delivery methods, peer support, collaboration with healthcare providers, accessible treatment facilities, and continued research and innovation. By adopting these strategies, we can help individuals overcome their fear of needles and improve their overall well-being.

Collaborating with Healthcare Providers

Collaboration between trypanophobics and healthcare providers is crucial for effective management and treatment of needle phobia. When working with individuals who suffer from trypanophobia, healthcare providers must approach the phobia with empathy, understanding, and a patient-centered mindset. In this section, we will explore the various ways in which healthcare providers can collaborate with trypanophobics to overcome their fear and ensure their healthcare needs are met.

Creating a Safe and Supportive Environment

Healthcare providers have a responsibility to create a safe and supportive environment for individuals with trypanophobia. This involves creating a calm and welcoming space, minimizing stimuli that may trigger anxiety, and ensuring that the individual feels heard and understood. Here are some strategies to consider:

- **Open Communication:** Encouraging open communication with the patient is essential. Providers should actively listen to the patient's fears and concerns, allowing them to express themselves without judgment. This will help foster a sense of trust and understanding between the provider and the patient.

- **Establishing Trust:** Building trust is crucial in overcoming trypanophobia. Healthcare providers can foster trust by being transparent about the procedures, explaining each step in detail, and ensuring that the patient feels actively involved in their care. Providers can also take the time to address any questions or concerns the patient may have.

- **Empathy and Validation:** Showing empathy and validating the patient's fear can greatly reduce their anxiety. Acknowledging their feelings and experiences helps create a safe space for them to express their emotions. Providers should strive to convey understanding and offer support throughout the patient's healthcare journey.

Education and Information Sharing

Another essential aspect of collaborative care is educating the patient about their condition and the procedures they may need to undergo. By providing information and answering any questions the patient may have, healthcare providers can help alleviate some of the anxiety associated with trypanophobia. Here are some approaches to consider:

- **Procedure Explanation:** Clearly explaining the purpose, steps, and potential sensations associated with a procedure can help in demystifying the process. Using accessible language and visual aids can enhance understanding and alleviate anxiety.
- **Risk-Benefit Analysis:** Healthcare providers can discuss the potential risks and benefits of a procedure with the patient. By weighing the benefits against the patient's fears, healthcare providers can help the individual make informed decisions about their care.
- **Alternative Options:** In some cases, alternative methods or interventions may be available to minimize the need for invasive procedures. For example, topical anesthetics or distraction techniques can reduce discomfort during injections. Discussing these options with the patient can empower them to actively participate in their care and explore alternatives that better align with their comfort level.

Collaborative Treatment Planning

Collaboration in the realm of treatment planning is crucial for individuals with trypanophobia. Healthcare providers should involve the patient in decision-making discussions, allowing them to express their preferences and concerns. Here are some strategies to promote collaboration:

- **Shared Decision-Making:** Involve the patient in the decision-making process by presenting different treatment options and discussing their pros and cons. By jointly weighing the risks and benefits, the patient can make choices that align with their comfort level and overall health goals.
- **Gradual Exposure Therapy:** Gradual exposure therapy is a common technique used to treat trypanophobia. By collaborating with the patient, healthcare providers can design a tailored exposure plan that gradually exposes the individual to needles, enabling them to build resilience and

reduce their fear over time. The patient's input and preferences should be considered when developing this plan.

- **Supportive Interventions:** Collaboratively explore supportive interventions that can complement and enhance traditional treatment approaches. For instance, consider referring the patient to support groups, peer counselors, or therapists who specialize in anxiety disorders. These additional resources can provide a sense of community and offer coping strategies beyond the healthcare provider's scope.

Continued Support and Follow-Up

Collaboration with healthcare providers does not end after a single visit or intervention. Continued support and follow-up are crucial for individuals with trypanophobia. Here are some ways healthcare providers can continue to support their patients:

- **Regular Check-Ins:** Schedule regular check-ins to monitor the patient's progress, address any concerns, and modify treatment plans as needed. This ongoing collaboration ensures that the patient feels supported throughout their journey.

- **Provider Accessibility:** Trypanophobia can be a lifelong struggle, and patients may require additional support between appointments. Offering accessibility options such as email, telehealth appointments, or a dedicated helpline can provide patients with a safety net when they need reassurance or guidance.

- **Referral to Specialists:** In some cases, patients may require specialized care beyond the scope of their primary healthcare provider. Collaborating with specialists such as phobia therapists, psychiatrists, or psychologists can provide comprehensive support and targeted interventions for trypanophobia.

Collaborating with healthcare providers is a crucial step in overcoming trypanophobia. By working together, patients and providers can navigate the challenges posed by needle phobia and develop personalized strategies for managing the fear. With a collaborative and patient-centered approach, individuals with trypanophobia can receive the care they need while feeling supported and empowered on their healing journey.

Remember, each individual's experience with trypanophobia is unique, and a collaborative approach allows healthcare providers to tailor treatments to the specific needs of their patients. By adhering to the principles outlined in this section, healthcare providers can help their patients overcome their fear and improve their overall well-being.

Seeking Professional Help Together

When dealing with trypanophobia, it is often helpful for individuals to seek professional help together with their loved ones. This collaborative approach not only allows for emotional support but also promotes understanding and empathy among family members. In this section, we will explore the importance of seeking professional help together and discuss various strategies for effective communication and collaboration.

Building a Support Network

The journey towards overcoming trypanophobia can be daunting, and having a strong support network is crucial during this process. Loved ones can play a vital role in providing emotional support, encouragement, and reassurance. By seeking professional help together, family members can become actively involved and gain a deeper understanding of the phobia and its impact on the individual's life.

Choosing the Right Healthcare Provider

When seeking professional help, it is important to find a healthcare provider who specializes in addressing anxiety disorders and phobias. Look for psychologists, psychiatrists, or therapists who have experience and expertise in treating needle phobia specifically. These professionals will have a deeper understanding of the underlying causes and effective treatment strategies.

Consider asking for recommendations from trusted sources or researching reputable mental health professionals in your area. It may also be helpful to schedule an initial consultation or interview to determine if the healthcare provider is the right fit for your needs.

Effective Communication Strategies

Effective communication is key when seeking professional help together. Here are a few strategies to foster open and meaningful conversations:

Active Listening: Listening attentively and without judgment allows the individual with trypanophobia to express their fears, concerns, and past experiences. Loved ones should provide a safe space for the person to share their emotions and actively engage in the conversation.

Validation: Validating the emotions and experiences of the individual is essential. Let them know that you understand their fears and that it is okay to feel anxious or scared. Avoid dismissing or minimizing their concerns, as this may aggravate their anxiety.

Ask Open-ended Questions: Encourage the individual to share their thoughts and feelings about their trypanophobia. Open-ended questions invite more in-depth and personal responses, helping the healthcare provider gain a better understanding of the phobia's impact on the person's life.

Empathy and Support: Offer empathy and support throughout the process. Let the individual know that you are there for them, and remind them that seeking help is a positive and brave step towards overcoming their fear.

Attending Therapy Sessions Together

Attending therapy sessions together, when appropriate, can be immensely beneficial. This allows loved ones to gain firsthand insights into the therapeutic process and provides an opportunity for mutual understanding and growth. In these sessions, the healthcare provider can help educate family members about trypanophobia and offer guidance on how best to support the individual. It is essential to respect the individual's privacy and confidentiality during these sessions, ensuring that they feel comfortable sharing their thoughts and experiences.

Developing Coping Strategies as a Team

Coping strategies are an essential component of treating trypanophobia. Loved ones can actively participate in the development and practice of these strategies. This collaborative approach not only empowers the individual but also strengthens the family unit. Here are some ways to actively engage as a team:

Understanding Exposure Therapy: Exposure therapy is a common treatment modality for phobias, including trypanophobia. It involves gradually exposing the individual to needles in a controlled and supportive environment. Family members can play a role in designing exposure exercises and providing emotional support throughout the process.

Implementing Relaxation Techniques: Learning and practicing relaxation techniques can be beneficial for both individuals with trypanophobia and their loved ones. Techniques such as deep breathing exercises, progressive muscle relaxation, and guided imagery can help reduce anxiety levels during exposure exercises and everyday situations involving needles.

Encouraging Positive Self-Talk: Negative self-talk often accompanies phobias and anxiety disorders. Loved ones can encourage the individual to challenge and reframe these negative thoughts with positive and rational statements. Remind them of their strengths and abilities to cope with their fears.

Rewarding and Celebrating Progress: Recognize and celebrate each milestone achieved along the way. Whether it's a successful exposure session or a reduction in the intensity of anxiety symptoms, acknowledging progress reinforces motivation and boosts self-confidence.

Finding Support in Online Communities

In addition to seeking professional help, online communities and support groups can be valuable resources for individuals and their loved ones. These platforms provide a safe space for sharing experiences, seeking advice, and connecting with others who face similar challenges. Encourage the individual to join such communities to gain additional support and build a network of people who understand their journey.

Remember that each individual's journey is unique, and the support required may vary. By seeking professional help together, you are taking an important step towards understanding, empathy, and collective healing. Collaborate, communicate, and support each other through this process, and remember that overcoming trypanophobia is possible with the right guidance and support.

Nurturing Relationships and Building Trust

Building trust and nurturing relationships are essential components in supporting and assisting individuals who suffer from trypanophobia. When facing a fear as intense as needle phobia, it is crucial for loved ones to provide a safe and supportive environment for the person struggling with the phobia. In this section, we will explore strategies and techniques to foster trust, empathy, and understanding within relationships.

Creating a Safe Space

Creating a safe space is of utmost importance when supporting someone with trypanophobia. This involves developing an environment where the person feels understood, validated, and comfortable expressing their fears and concerns. Here are some key strategies to create a safe space:

- **Active listening:** Listen attentively and empathetically to the individual's experiences and feelings. Show genuine interest and validate their emotions.

- **Non-judgmental attitude:** Avoid making judgmental comments or dismissing their fears. Understand that the fear they experience is real to them, regardless of how irrational it may seem to others.

- **Be patient:** Recognize that overcoming trypanophobia takes time and effort. Patience is key in providing support and understanding throughout the process.

- **Open communication:** Encourage open and honest communication by expressing your willingness to listen and learn more about their fears. Create an atmosphere where they feel safe to share their feelings and concerns.

- **Educate yourself:** Take the time to educate yourself about trypanophobia. Understanding the phobia, its causes, and the individual's triggers can help you provide better support.

Empathy and Understanding

Empathy plays a crucial role in building trust and nurturing relationships. By putting oneself in the shoes of the trypanophobic individual, loved ones can gain a deeper understanding of what they are going through. Here are some ways to cultivate empathy and understanding:

- **Validate their feelings:** Recognize and acknowledge the trypanophobic individual's emotions without judgment. Let them know that their feelings are valid and understandable.

- **Empathetic language:** Use language that conveys empathy and understanding. Phrases like "I understand why this is difficult for you" or "It's okay to be scared" can provide reassurance and support.
- **Share personal experiences:** Share your own experiences with fear or anxiety to help the person feel less alone. This can create a sense of connection and understanding.
- **Offer reassurance:** Reassure the individual that they are not alone in their journey. Let them know that you are there to support them and that their fears are valid.

Building Trust

Building trust is a gradual process and is instrumental in helping individuals overcome their trypanophobia. Here are some strategies to build trust:

- **Respect boundaries:** Respect the individual's boundaries and limitations. Do not push them beyond their comfort zone. Allow them to set the pace for facing their fears.
- **Consistency:** Be consistent in your support and commitment to helping them cope with trypanophobia. Show up consistently and follow through on any commitments you make.
- **Avoid judgment and criticism:** Avoid criticizing or judging the individual's progress. Remember, progress is unique to each individual, and any step forward is significant.
- **Encourage autonomy:** Help the individual build self-confidence and autonomy by encouraging them to make decisions regarding their treatment. Support their choices and provide encouragement along the way.
- **Celebrate successes:** Celebrate even small victories and successes. Acknowledge the bravery and effort put forth by the individual in facing their fears.

Supporting Accessible Treatment Options

Supporting the individual in finding accessible treatment options is another crucial aspect of nurturing relationships. Consider the following strategies to assist them in their journey:

- **Research treatment options:** Collaborate with the individual to research various treatment options suitable for trypanophobia, such as cognitive-behavioral therapy, exposure therapy, or alternative therapies.

- **Accompany them to appointments:** Offer to accompany the individual to their appointments or treatments. Your presence can provide them with a sense of security and support during the process.

- **Assist with logistics:** Help the individual with practical aspects of seeking treatment, such as scheduling appointments, filling out paperwork, or finding relevant resources.

- **Advocate for their needs:** Advocate for the individual's needs with healthcare providers. Communicate their fears and concerns, ensuring that healthcare professionals understand the severity of their trypanophobia.

- **Encourage self-care:** Promote self-care practices to help manage anxiety and stress associated with trypanophobia. Encourage activities such as exercise, mindfulness, and relaxation techniques.

Taking Care of Yourself: Caregiver Burnout

Supporting someone with trypanophobia can be emotionally challenging. It is vital to prioritize self-care to prevent caregiver burnout. Here are some effective self-care strategies:

- **Seek support:** Reach out to support groups or seek therapy for yourself to process your emotions and receive guidance on supporting your loved one.

- **Practice self-compassion:** Be kind to yourself and practice self-compassion. Understand that supporting someone with a phobia can be demanding, and it's okay to take breaks and prioritize your own well-being.

- **Set boundaries:** Establish clear boundaries to protect your own mental and emotional health. Prioritize your self-care needs and communicate your boundaries to your loved one.

- **Engage in stress-reducing activities:** Find activities that help you relax and reduce stress, such as exercise, hobbies, or spending time with loved ones.

- **Educate yourself:** Continuously educate yourself about trypanophobia and techniques to support your loved one. The more knowledge you have, the better equipped you will be to provide effective support.

In conclusion, nurturing relationships and building trust are crucial in supporting individuals with trypanophobia. By creating a safe space, cultivating empathy, and understanding, supporting accessible treatment options, and practicing self-care, loved ones can provide the necessary support for individuals to overcome their fears. Remember, the journey towards overcoming trypanophobia requires patience, persistence, and unwavering support.

Taking Care of Yourself: Caregiver Burnout

Caring for a loved one with trypanophobia can be a challenging and emotionally draining experience. As a caregiver, it is important to prioritize your own well-being and establish strategies to prevent caregiver burnout. In this section, we will explore various ways to take care of yourself while supporting someone with trypanophobia.

Understanding Caregiver Burnout

Caregiver burnout refers to the physical, emotional, and mental exhaustion experienced by individuals who provide ongoing care for a loved one. It is a common phenomenon among caregivers and can have detrimental effects on their health and overall quality of life. When caring for a person with trypanophobia, the unique challenges and stressors can intensify this burnout.

Recognizing the Signs of Caregiver Burnout It is important to recognize the signs of caregiver burnout in order to address it effectively. Some common signs include:

- Physical exhaustion, including lack of energy and chronic fatigue
- Emotional exhaustion, feeling overwhelmed or depleted emotionally
- Increased irritability, mood swings, or feelings of resentment
- Withdrawal from activities and relationships
- Sleep disturbances and changes in appetite
- Decreased ability to concentrate and make decisions
- Neglecting one's own health and self-care

If you notice these signs in yourself, it is crucial to take action to prevent further burnout.

Self-Care Strategies for Caregivers

Taking care of yourself is not a luxury but a necessity. Here are some self-care strategies that can help prevent caregiver burnout:

1. **Establish Boundaries** Setting clear limits and boundaries is essential to protect your own well-being. Communicate openly with your loved one about your own needs and limitations. This can involve discussing when and how you can provide support, as well as arranging for respite care or enlisting the help of other family members or friends.

2. **Find Support** Reach out for support from others who understand what you are going through. This can include joining support groups for caregivers, where you can share your experiences, learn from others, and gain valuable insights and practical advice. Additionally, consider individual counseling or therapy to address any emotional issues or stressors you may be facing.

3. **Prioritize Self-Care Activities** Make time for activities that bring you joy and relaxation. Engage in hobbies, exercise regularly, practice mindfulness or meditation, or indulge in activities that promote self-care. Taking care of your own physical and mental well-being will help you maintain the energy and resilience needed to support your loved one effectively.

4. **Seek Respite Care** Respite care provides temporary relief for caregivers by allowing them to take a break from their caregiving responsibilities. This can involve arranging for a trained professional to provide care for your loved one while you take time off or exploring respite care facilities or programs. It is important to remember that taking a break does not equate to neglecting your loved one; rather, it is a necessary step to ensure you can continue to provide the best care possible.

5. **Practice Stress-Reduction Techniques** Develop healthy coping strategies to manage stress. This can include engaging in regular exercise, practicing deep breathing or relaxation techniques, journaling, or participating in activities that promote mindfulness and stress reduction. Experiment with different techniques to find what works best for you, and make them a regular part of your self-care routine.

6. Maintain Your Physical Health It is essential to prioritize your physical health as a caregiver. Make sure to eat a balanced diet, get enough sleep, and attend to any medical or healthcare needs you may have. Neglecting your own health will only compound the stress and strain of caregiving.

7. Foster Social Connections Nurture your relationships with friends and family members who can offer support and understanding. Stay connected with your social circle and maintain regular social interactions. This can provide a sense of normalcy, reduce feelings of isolation, and offer opportunities for respite from your caregiving role.

8. Practice Gratitude and Mindful Reflection Take moments to reflect on the positive aspects of your caregiving experience. Practice gratitude by acknowledging small victories, expressing appreciation for your efforts, and focusing on the meaningful connections you have developed with your loved one. Mindful reflection can help shift your perspective, enhance resilience, and counteract the negative emotions associated with caregiver burnout.

Conclusion

Caring for a loved one with trypanophobia can be physically, emotionally, and mentally demanding. By prioritizing your own well-being and implementing self-care strategies, you can prevent caregiver burnout and continue to provide the necessary support. Remember, taking care of yourself is not a selfish act but an essential component of being an effective caregiver.

Chapter Seven: The Future of Trypanophobia Research

Neuroscience and Brain Imaging Studies

Genetic and Epigenetic Factors

Genetic and epigenetic factors play a significant role in influencing the development and manifestation of trypanophobia, the fear of needles. Understanding these factors can provide valuable insights into the underlying mechanisms of the phobia and may help in developing effective treatment strategies. In this section, we will explore the genetic and epigenetic influences on trypanophobia and their implications for research and clinical practice.

Genetic Factors

Genetic factors refer to the influence of an individual's genes on the development of trypanophobia. Research has shown that there is a hereditary component to the phobia, indicating a genetic predisposition. Several genes have been identified as potential candidates for contributing to needle phobia, although more research is needed to fully understand their role.

One such gene is the ADRA2B gene, which encodes for alpha-2 adrenergic receptors in the brain. These receptors are involved in the regulation of anxiety and fear responses. Variations in the ADRA2B gene have been associated with increased anxiety and fearfulness, which may contribute to the development of needle phobia.

Another gene of interest is the HTR2A gene, which codes for serotonin receptors. Serotonin is a neurotransmitter that plays a crucial role in mood regulation. Alterations in the HTR2A gene have been linked to anxiety disorders and may influence the risk of developing trypanophobia.

Moreover, studies have also found a potential link between trypanophobia and genes involved in the regulation of the autonomic nervous system, such as the COMT gene, which influences the breakdown of dopamine. Dysregulation of the autonomic nervous system can lead to heightened stress responses, making individuals more susceptible to needle phobia.

While these genetic findings are promising, it is important to note that trypanophobia is likely a polygenic trait, meaning that multiple genes may be involved in its development. Furthermore, the interactions between genes and environmental factors are also crucial in understanding the complex nature of trypanophobia.

Epigenetic Factors

Epigenetic factors play a critical role in modulating gene expression without altering the underlying DNA sequence. They encompass various mechanisms, such as DNA methylation, histone modifications, and non-coding RNA molecules, which can regulate gene activity.

Recent research has suggested that epigenetic modifications may contribute to the development of needle phobia. For example, studies have shown that individuals with trypanophobia have differential DNA methylation patterns compared to non-phobic individuals. DNA methylation involves the addition of a methyl group to the DNA molecule, which can change the way genes are activated or silenced.

Furthermore, epigenetic changes can occur as a result of early-life experiences, including traumatic events related to needles. These experiences can leave a lasting impact on the epigenome, potentially increasing the risk of developing trypanophobia later in life.

Understanding the role of epigenetic factors in trypanophobia may have important clinical implications. Epigenetic modifications are reversible, unlike genetic mutations, which opens up possibilities for targeted interventions. By identifying specific epigenetic markers associated with needle phobia, it may be possible to develop personalized treatment approaches that address the underlying epigenetic alterations.

Research Challenges and Future Directions

Studying the genetic and epigenetic factors contributing to trypanophobia presents several challenges. First, conducting large-scale genomic studies with well-characterized phobic individuals is essential to identify specific genes and epigenetic modifications associated with the phobia. Collaborative efforts across research institutions and the collection of comprehensive phenotypic data are crucial to advancing our understanding of the genetic and epigenetic basis of trypanophobia.

Furthermore, the interaction between genetic and environmental factors must be taken into account. Environmental influences, such as early traumatic experiences or parental behaviors, can modulate the effect of genetic predisposition. Integrating genetic and environmental data through longitudinal studies will help unravel the intricate interplay between nature and nurture in the development of needle phobia.

In the future, advancements in molecular techniques, such as genome-wide association studies (GWAS) and next-generation sequencing, will enable researchers to identify additional genetic markers associated with trypanophobia. Epigenome-wide association studies (EWAS) will also shed light on the specific epigenetic modifications that contribute to the phobia.

Understanding the genetic and epigenetic factors underlying trypanophobia holds great promise for developing personalized and targeted interventions. By identifying individuals at higher risk based on genetic or epigenetic profiles, healthcare providers can implement preventive measures or early interventions to mitigate the development of severe trypanophobia. Additionally, knowledge of genetic and epigenetic factors may guide the development of pharmacological treatments that specifically target the biological pathways involved in the phobia.

In conclusion, genetic and epigenetic factors play a crucial role in the development of trypanophobia. While our understanding of these factors is still evolving, current research suggests that specific genes and epigenetic modifications are associated with the phobia. By further exploring the genetic and epigenetic basis of trypanophobia, we can pave the way for more personalized and effective interventions for individuals living with this debilitating fear of needles.

Developmental Trauma and Early Intervention

Developmental trauma refers to the exposure of a child to chronic, unpredictable, and highly stressful events or experiences during their early developmental stages. These traumatic events can range from physical and emotional abuse to neglect, witnessing domestic violence, or living in a chaotic and unsafe environment. Such adversities can have a profound impact on a child's psychological, emotional, and cognitive development.

Early intervention is crucial in mitigating the long-term effects of developmental trauma. By identifying and addressing trauma early on, we can help children build resilience, restore healthy development, and prevent the development of long-lasting mental health conditions. In this section, we will explore the relationship between developmental trauma and trypanophobia, along with effective early intervention strategies.

Understanding Developmental Trauma

Developmental trauma can disrupt the normal maturation of a child's brain and nervous system. The stress response system, which includes the hypothalamic-pituitary-adrenal (HPA) axis, becomes dysregulated, leading to chronic hyperarousal or hypoarousal states. These dysregulations can manifest as heightened anxiety, hypervigilance, emotional dysregulation, impulsivity, or difficulties with attention and concentration. These symptoms can contribute to the development of trypanophobia in childhood and later in adulthood.

Furthermore, repeated exposure to trauma can affect the child's self-perception, emotional regulation, ability to form secure attachments, and cognitive functioning. These disruptions can significantly impact their ability to cope with medical procedures involving needles, leading to severe anxiety, panic attacks, and avoidance behaviors associated with trypanophobia.

Importance of Early Intervention

Early intervention is crucial in addressing developmental trauma and minimizing the long-term consequences it can have on a child's life. By providing appropriate support and interventions during the critical periods of development, we can mitigate the negative impact of trauma and promote healthy adaptation.

Early intervention for developmental trauma involves a multidisciplinary approach, combining the expertise of mental health professionals, pediatricians, and other healthcare providers. It focuses on creating a safe and nurturing environment, promoting resilience, and addressing the child's specific needs.

Therapeutic Interventions

1. Trauma-Focused Cognitive-Behavioral Therapy (TF-CBT): TF-CBT is one of the most widely used evidence-based treatments for children with developmental trauma. It combines cognitive-behavioral strategies with trauma-specific interventions to help children process traumatic experiences, regulate their emotions, challenge negative beliefs, and develop healthy coping skills. TF-CBT also involves incorporating the child's caregiver in the therapy process to support their healing and enhance the overall family functioning.

2. Play Therapy: Play therapy is an effective therapeutic approach for young children who have experienced developmental trauma. Through play, children can express and process their emotions, make sense of their traumatic experiences, and develop healthier coping mechanisms. Play therapy can involve various techniques, such as sandplay, art therapy, and puppet play, tailored to meet the child's individual needs.

3. Eye Movement Desensitization and Reprocessing (EMDR): EMDR is a therapeutic technique that combines elements of cognitive-behavioral therapy with bilateral sensory stimulation, such as eye movements or tapping. It helps individuals process traumatic experiences by reactivating the memory and integrating it with new adaptive information. EMDR has shown promising results in reducing trauma-related symptoms and anxiety associated with trypanophobia.

4. Sensory Integration Therapy: Sensory integration therapy aims to address difficulties in sensory processing that often accompany developmental trauma. This therapy helps children regulate their sensory experiences and improve their ability to integrate and respond appropriately to sensory information. By enhancing sensory processing, children can develop better self-regulation skills and reduce hyperarousal or hypoarousal states.

5. Parent-Child Interaction Therapy (PCIT): PCIT is an evidence-based intervention focusing on improving the parent-child relationship, enhancing positive parenting skills, and reducing behavioral problems resulting from trauma. In PCIT, parents are taught specific techniques to communicate effectively, set appropriate limits, and provide emotional support to their child. This intervention can help create a secure attachment between the child and their caregiver, promoting resilience and reducing the risk of developing trypanophobia.

Early Intervention Programs

Early intervention programs play a crucial role in identifying and addressing developmental trauma. These programs provide a range of services targeting the child's developmental needs and the family's well-being. Some key early intervention programs include:

1. Head Start: Head Start is a federally funded program in the United States that provides comprehensive early childhood education and support services to children from low-income families. The program focuses on promoting school readiness, addressing developmental delays, and ensuring children's overall well-being. Head Start also offers support to families through parenting education and access to community resources.

2. Early Head Start: Early Head Start is an extension of the Head Start program, specifically designed for infants, toddlers, and pregnant women. It offers a range of services, including early education, health, and nutrition support, individualized family support, and mental health services. Early Head Start aims to promote healthy development during the critical early years and reduce the impact of trauma on young children.

3. Child-Parent Psychotherapy (CPP): CPP is an evidence-based intervention targeting infants, toddlers, and preschool-aged children who have experienced trauma. It focuses on promoting the child's attachment security, emotional regulation, and the parent's capacity to provide nurturing care. CPP involves dyadic therapy sessions, during which the clinician works with both the child and their caregiver to foster a strong and supportive relationship.

Challenges and Considerations

While early intervention plays a critical role in addressing developmental trauma and reducing the risk of trypanophobia, several challenges and considerations need to be taken into account:

1. Access to Services: Access to early intervention services can be limited, particularly for low-income families or those residing in underserved areas. Efforts should be made to enhance access to mental health and support services, regardless of socioeconomic status or geographic location.

2. Cultural Sensitivity: Early intervention programs need to be culturally sensitive and responsive to the diverse backgrounds and needs of the children and families they serve. Cultural competence training for professionals and the inclusion of culturally appropriate practices can help ensure the effectiveness of interventions.

3. Trauma-Informed Care: Early intervention programs should adopt a trauma-informed approach, recognizing the prevalence and impact of trauma and integrating trauma-sensitive practices into their service delivery. This includes creating safe and non-threatening environments, promoting choice and empowerment, and using trauma-specific interventions.

4. Interdisciplinary Collaboration: Successful early intervention requires collaboration and coordination among different professionals and service providers, including mental health professionals, pediatricians, educators, and social workers. Interdisciplinary teams can offer comprehensive support and optimize outcomes for children and their families.

In conclusion, early intervention is vital in mitigating the effects of developmental trauma and reducing the risk of trypanophobia. By employing therapeutic interventions, implementing early intervention programs, and addressing the unique needs of children who have experienced trauma, we can promote resilience, healing, and healthy development. However, it is crucial to consider the challenges and ensure that interventions are culturally sensitive, trauma-informed, and provided in an interdisciplinary framework. Through early intervention, we can shape a brighter future for children impacted by developmental trauma.

Virtual Reality Therapy and Technological Innovations

Virtual Reality Therapy (VRT) has emerged as a promising treatment option for individuals with trypanophobia. By providing a controlled and immersive environment, VRT allows patients to gradually expose themselves to needles and medical procedures in a safe and therapeutic setting. This section explores the principles and advancements in VRT, as well as other technological innovations that are shaping the future of trypanophobia treatment.

Understanding Virtual Reality Therapy

Virtual Reality (VR) technology creates a simulated environment that can be similar to or completely different from the real world. By wearing a VR headset, users are transported into a three-dimensional, computer-generated space where they can interact with objects and surroundings. VRT utilizes this immersive experience to expose trypanophobics to needle-related stimuli, gradually desensitizing them to their fear.

The key principle behind VRT is the concept of exposure therapy. Exposure therapy aims to reduce fear and anxiety by gradually exposing individuals to the source of their fear in a controlled manner. In the context of trypanophobia, VRT allows patients to confront their fear of needles without actual physical contact, reducing the distress associated with real-life situations.

Application of VRT in Trypanophobia Treatment

VRT for trypanophobia typically involves a structured program where patients progress through different levels of exposure. Here are some key components and techniques employed in VRT:

- **Virtual Environments:** VRT provides various virtual environments that simulate medical settings such as clinics or hospitals. These environments can be customized to replicate specific scenarios, such as needle injections, blood draws, or IV insertions. The level of realism can be adjusted based on individual needs and comfort levels.

- **Gradual Exposure:** VRT programs are designed to start with minimal exposure to needle-related stimuli and gradually increase the intensity as patients become more comfortable. This step-by-step approach allows individuals to build resilience and develop coping mechanisms.

- **Virtual Needle Simulations:** In VRT, virtual needles are used to mimic the experience of needle-related procedures. Patients can witness the virtual needle approaching their skin, giving them a sense of control over the situation. By repeatedly practicing exposure to virtual needle simulations, individuals can effectively decrease their fear response.

- **Real-Time Feedback:** VRT systems can provide real-time feedback based on patients' physiological responses. This feedback helps healthcare professionals monitor patients' anxiety levels during the VR sessions, allowing for tailored interventions and personalized treatment plans.

- **Cognitive Behavioral Techniques:** VRT programs often incorporate cognitive behavioral techniques, such as relaxation exercises, positive self-talk, and cognitive restructuring, to further enhance the therapeutic benefits. These techniques aim to challenge negative thought patterns and promote a more positive mindset towards needle-related situations.

Technological Innovations in Trypanophobia Treatment

Beyond VRT, there are other technological innovations that hold potential for the future of trypanophobia treatment. These advancements focus on enhancing patient experiences, improving treatment outcomes, and providing additional support for individuals struggling with needle-related fears. Here are some notable innovations:

- **Haptic Feedback Devices:** Haptic feedback devices provide tactile sensations to enhance the immersion of virtual experiences. For trypanophobics, this technology could simulate the feeling of a needle piercing the skin or even create vibrations that mimic the sensation of medical procedures. By incorporating haptic feedback, VRT can provide a more realistic and multisensory experience.

- **Biofeedback Systems:** Biofeedback systems measure physiological signals, such as heart rate, skin conductance, and muscle tension, and provide real-time feedback to patients. By using biofeedback, individuals can better understand their physiological responses to needle-related stimuli and learn to regulate their anxiety. Integrating biofeedback with VRT can optimize the effectiveness of exposure therapy.

- **Mobile Applications:** Mobile applications offer trypanophobics a convenient and accessible platform for managing their fear. These apps may include features such as breathing exercises, guided meditations, virtual exposure scenarios, and progress tracking. By providing continuous support outside of formal treatment sessions, mobile applications can empower individuals to overcome their fears at their own pace.

- **Telehealth and Teletherapy:** Telehealth and teletherapy platforms have gained significant attention, especially in light of the COVID-19 pandemic. These technologies enable remote delivery of VRT and other therapeutic interventions, making treatment more accessible for individuals who may have difficulty attending in-person sessions due to geographic constraints, physical limitations, or social anxieties.

- **Artificial Intelligence (AI):** AI-powered systems have the potential to enhance the effectiveness and personalization of trypanophobia treatment. AI algorithms can analyze patient data, track progress, and adapt treatment plans based on individual responses. Virtual therapists driven by AI can provide personalized interactions and interventions, addressing the unique needs and fears of each patient.

Ethical Considerations and Limitations

While VRT and technological innovations show promise in trypanophobia treatment, ethical considerations and limitations must be acknowledged. Some key points to consider include:

- **Informed Consent:** Informed consent is crucial when implementing VRT or any technological intervention. Patients should fully understand the nature of the treatment, potential risks and benefits, and their rights to withdraw from the therapy.

- **Treatment Suitability:** Not all individuals may be suitable for VRT or certain technological interventions. Factors such as the severity of trypanophobia, presence of comorbid conditions, and personal preferences should be considered during the treatment planning process.

- **Cost and Accessibility:** The cost and accessibility of VR equipment and other technological innovations may limit their widespread adoption. Efforts should be made to ensure affordability and availability of these treatments to maximize their reach and impact.
- **Treatment Efficacy:** While VRT and technological interventions show promise, more research is needed to establish their long-term efficacy and compare them to traditional therapeutic approaches. Rigorous scientific studies and clinical trials should continue to assess the benefits and limitations of these innovations.

In conclusion, Virtual Reality Therapy (VRT) and technological innovations offer new avenues for trypanophobia treatment. By immersing individuals in simulated medical environments and providing gradual exposure to needle-related stimuli, VRT helps desensitize patients and alleviate their fears. Additionally, technological advancements like haptic feedback devices, biofeedback systems, mobile applications, telehealth, and AI-driven interventions further augment the therapeutic benefits. However, ethical considerations, suitability, cost, and treatment efficacy should be carefully evaluated to ensure safe and effective implementation of these approaches. With ongoing research and development, VRT and technological innovations hold significant potential in helping individuals overcome their fear of needles and improving their overall well-being.

Novel Pharmacological Treatments

Pharmacological treatments have always played a significant role in addressing various mental health conditions, and trypanophobia is no exception. While traditional treatments such as exposure therapy and cognitive behavioral therapy can be effective, the field of pharmacology has also made significant advances in developing novel medications specifically targeted for treating needle phobia. In this section, we will explore some of these cutting-edge pharmacological treatments and their potential benefits for trypanophobics.

Beta-Blockers: Taming the Fear Response

One promising class of medications for trypanophobia is beta-blockers. These medications work by blocking the action of adrenaline, a hormone that prepares the body for the fight-or-flight response. By reducing the physical symptoms of anxiety, such as increased heart rate and trembling, beta-blockers can help individuals with trypanophobia stay calm during needle-related situations.

One commonly used beta-blocker is propranolol. Propranolol has been extensively studied and has shown positive results for reducing anxiety associated with specific phobias, including needle phobia. It helps individuals by dampening the body's physiological response to fear, thus making the experience of needle-related procedures less distressing.

Example: Alice, a 30-year-old woman with severe needle phobia, has been avoiding necessary medical check-ups and vaccinations for years. Her fear is so intense that even the thought of seeing a needle makes her panic. However, after consulting with a psychiatrist specializing in phobias, she decides to try propranolol. Prior to her next medical appointment, Alice takes a dose of propranolol as prescribed. She finds that her heart rate remains steady, and although she still experiences some anxiety, it is significantly reduced, allowing her to undergo the procedure without overwhelming fear.

It is important to note that beta-blockers should be prescribed and monitored by a qualified healthcare professional to ensure safety and appropriate dosing.

Anxiolytics: Calming the Mind

Another class of medications used in the treatment of trypanophobia is anxiolytics, or anti-anxiety medications. These medications are designed to reduce anxiety and promote relaxation. While anxiolytics may be prescribed for individuals with severe anxiety symptoms, they can also be used as short-term solutions for individuals who experience extreme distress during needle-related procedures.

Benzodiazepines, such as diazepam (Valium) or lorazepam (Ativan), are commonly prescribed anxiolytic medications. They work by enhancing the calming effects of a neurotransmitter called gamma-aminobutyric acid (GABA) in the brain. By increasing GABA activity, benzodiazepines help reduce feelings of anxiety and promote a sense of calmness.

Example: John, a 40-year-old man, has been suffering from trypanophobia since childhood. He requires regular blood tests for a medical condition, but the fear of needles has been preventing him from attending appointments. With the support of his therapist, John decides to try taking a low dose of lorazepam prior to his next blood test. The medication helps him feel more relaxed and lessens his fear, allowing him to successfully go through with the procedure.

It is important to note that anxiolytics, particularly benzodiazepines, can be habit-forming and may cause sedation and impairment. These medications should be used with caution under the guidance of a healthcare professional and only as a short-term solution when other strategies, such as therapy, have not been effective.

Virtual Reality Therapy: Immersive Desensitization

While not strictly a medication, virtual reality (VR) therapy is an innovative approach that combines technology with psychological techniques to desensitize individuals to needle-related fears. VR therapy involves exposing the individual to simulated needle-related situations in a controlled and safe environment, allowing them to gradually confront their fears.

During a VR session, individuals wear a headset that immerses them in a 3D virtual world. They can interact with the virtual environment and even experience simulated needle procedures under the guidance of a therapist. The therapist can adjust the intensity of the exposure based on the individual's comfort level, helping them gradually overcome their fear of needles.

Studies have shown that VR therapy can be highly effective in reducing anxiety and fear associated with needle phobia. It provides a realistic and controlled environment for individuals to face their fears, resulting in increased tolerance and reduced distress during real-life needle-related situations.

Example: Sarah, a 25-year-old woman, has had a severe needle phobia since childhood. Her fear has caused her to avoid necessary medical procedures and even routine vaccinations. With the guidance of her therapist, Sarah participates in a series of VR therapy sessions. She starts with simple virtual tasks like looking at pictures of needles and gradually progresses to simulated needle injections. With each session, Sarah's anxiety decreases, and by the end of the therapy, she feels much more confident and comfortable with real-life needle-related situations.

VR therapy can be a valuable tool in the treatment of trypanophobia, especially for those who are unable or unwilling to undergo traditional exposure therapy.

The Importance of Holistic Treatment

While pharmacological interventions can be beneficial for individuals with trypanophobia, it is crucial to approach treatment holistically. Medications alone should not be considered a complete solution but rather a complementary component of a comprehensive treatment plan.

Integrated approaches that combine medication with therapy, such as cognitive behavioral therapy or exposure therapy, have been shown to produce the best outcomes. Addressing the underlying psychological factors contributing to trypanophobia, developing coping strategies, and providing support are essential components of effective treatment.

Furthermore, it is important to remember that medications may not be suitable for everyone with trypanophobia. Factors such as individual health conditions, medication interactions, and personal preferences should be taken into account when considering pharmacological treatments.

By integrating pharmacological treatments with other therapeutic approaches, professionals can work towards helping individuals overcome their needle phobia and improve their quality of life.

Conclusion

Novel pharmacological treatments, such as beta-blockers and anxiolytics, offer additional options for individuals struggling with trypanophobia. These medications, when used appropriately and under the guidance of a healthcare professional, can help reduce anxiety and make needle-related procedures more manageable.

Furthermore, the emergence of technologies like virtual reality therapy showcases the potential for innovative approaches to desensitize individuals to needle phobia. By creating immersive and controlled environments, individuals can confront their fears in a safe setting, leading to reduced anxiety and increased tolerance in real-life situations.

However, it is important to approach trypanophobia treatment holistically, considering a range of therapeutic modalities and addressing the underlying psychological factors. Medications should be seen as part of a comprehensive treatment plan rather than a standalone solution.

By developing a deeper understanding of novel pharmacological treatments and their integration with other therapeutic approaches, healthcare professionals can better support individuals with trypanophobia, helping them on their journey towards overcoming their fear of needles.

Cultural Perspectives on Needle Phobia

Understanding the cultural perspectives on needle phobia is crucial in addressing the complexities of this condition. Cultural factors play a significant role in shaping individuals' beliefs, attitudes, and behaviors towards needles and medical procedures. By examining the cultural lens through which needle phobia is viewed, we can gain valuable insights into the unique challenges faced by different communities and develop more effective interventions. In this section, we explore the cultural perspectives on needle phobia and their implications for understanding and supporting individuals with trypanophobia.

Cultural Beliefs and Superstitions

Cultural beliefs and superstitions surrounding needles and medical procedures greatly influence the perception of trypanophobia. In certain cultures, needles are associated with pain, suffering, and even death. These beliefs may stem from historical experiences or cultural narratives that have been passed down through generations. Understanding these cultural beliefs is essential for healthcare providers to provide culturally-sensitive care and develop trust with individuals who hold such perspectives.

For example, in some cultures, needles are believed to carry negative energy or evil spirits, leading to a heightened fear of medical procedures. To address these beliefs, healthcare professionals can work collaboratively with patients and their families to provide education and information about the benefits and safety of medical interventions.

Social Taboos and Stigmatization

In some cultures, discussing mental health or fears openly is considered taboo or a sign of weakness. This can make it challenging for individuals with needle phobia to seek help or disclose their condition. The fear of judgment and stigma prevents them from accessing necessary support and treatment.

To address this issue, it is essential to raise awareness about needle phobia and reduce the associated stigma. Community-based education campaigns and culturally sensitive communication strategies can help normalize discussions around mental health and create safe spaces for individuals to seek help.

Traditional Healing Practices

In many cultures, traditional healing practices coexist with modern medicine. These practices often involve alternative therapies and remedies for various ailments. Some individuals with needle phobia may turn to traditional healing practices as an alternative to invasive medical procedures. Understanding the role of traditional healing practices in managing needle phobia is crucial for healthcare providers to adapt their treatment approaches accordingly.

Collaboration between traditional healers and modern healthcare providers can create a holistic approach to address needle phobia. By respecting cultural beliefs and incorporating traditional healing practices into treatment plans, it is possible to provide more comprehensive care that is acceptable and effective for individuals with trypanophobia.

Cultural Differences in Healthcare Systems

Different cultural contexts result in variations in healthcare systems, including access to healthcare, medical practices, and patient-provider relationships. These cultural differences can significantly impact the experiences of individuals with needle phobia.

For example, in some cultures, healthcare providers may have a more authoritarian approach, which can further exacerbate the fear and anxiety experienced by individuals with needle phobia. Understanding these cultural differences allows healthcare professionals to tailor their approaches, provide more compassionate care, and build trust with patients who have trypanophobia.

Cultural Competence in Care Delivery

Cultural competence is the ability to provide healthcare that respects and is responsive to the cultural beliefs, practices, and needs of diverse populations. It is essential for healthcare providers to develop cultural competence to effectively support individuals with needle phobia from diverse cultural backgrounds.

Healthcare professionals can enhance their cultural competence by increasing their knowledge and understanding of different cultural beliefs and practices related to needle phobia. This can be achieved through cultural sensitivity training, engaging with community leaders, and partnering with interpreters to ensure effective communication.

Ultimately, by considering the cultural perspectives on needle phobia, we can develop more comprehensive and inclusive interventions that take into account the unique experiences and needs of individuals from different cultural backgrounds. This approach promotes cultural competence and facilitates positive outcomes for those seeking support and treatment for trypanophobia.

Societal Implications and Policy Changes

Addressing the societal implications of trypanophobia and implementing policy changes is crucial for supporting individuals with this phobia and promoting a fear-free healthcare environment. By recognizing the unique challenges faced by trypanophobics and taking proactive steps, societies can foster empathy, inclusivity, and efficient healthcare systems. In this section, we will explore various implications and propose policy changes to better accommodate those with trypanophobia.

Recognizing Trypanophobia as a Valid Medical Condition

One of the primary societal implications of trypanophobia is the need for widespread recognition of this phobia as a valid medical condition. Despite its prevalence, trypanophobia often goes unrecognized and stigmatized, leading to a lack of adequate support and understanding. By promoting education and awareness campaigns, societies can ensure that trypanophobia is recognized as a legitimate fear that deserves attention and empathy.

Policy Change: Integrate trypanophobia into diagnostic manuals and healthcare systems. This will increase the visibility of the phobia and facilitate appropriate interventions and accommodations for those affected.

Improving Healthcare Provider Training

Another crucial aspect of societal implications and policy changes involves enhancing the training of healthcare providers to better understand and address the needs of individuals with trypanophobia. By equipping healthcare professionals with the knowledge, skills, and empathy required to support patients with this phobia, we can ensure a more compassionate and effective healthcare experience.

Policy Change: Incorporate comprehensive education and training on trypanophobia into medical and nursing school curricula. This should cover the psychological underpinnings of the phobia, effective communication strategies, and techniques for creating a fear-free environment during medical procedures.

Creating Fear-Free Environments

Creating fear-free environments in healthcare settings is essential to support individuals with trypanophobia. By implementing specific measures and accommodations, societies can help alleviate the anxiety and distress experienced by those with this phobia.

Policy Change: Develop guidelines for healthcare facilities to create fear-free environments. This may include designating separate waiting areas for individuals with trypanophobia, implementing calming decor, providing distractions and relaxation techniques, and training staff on how to communicate effectively and empathetically with trypanophobics.

Standardizing Needle Procedure Protocols

Standardized needle procedure protocols can play a pivotal role in minimizing the distress experienced by trypanophobics. By implementing consistent practices across healthcare settings, societies can ensure that everyone involved in medical procedures understands and follows the most effective methods for minimizing pain and anxiety.

Policy Change: Establish standardized needle procedure protocols that prioritize patient comfort and minimize pain. This should include the use of smaller gauge needles, the application of numbing agents when appropriate, and employing distraction techniques during needle insertion.

Insurance Coverage and Accessibility

The financial burden of seeking treatment for trypanophobia can also pose significant challenges for individuals. Adequate insurance coverage for therapy sessions, medications, and other necessary interventions is crucial in ensuring accessibility and affordability.

Policy Change: Advocate for insurance providers to include coverage for trypanophobia treatments, such as cognitive-behavioral therapy, virtual reality therapy, and pharmacological interventions. Additionally, promote government funding initiatives to support research on trypanophobia and the development of innovative treatment approaches.

Reducing Stigma and Fostering Supportive Communities

Reducing stigma surrounding trypanophobia is vital for fostering supportive communities and encouraging individuals to seek help and support. By promoting open dialogue, challenging misconceptions, and providing platforms for sharing experiences, societies can create a safe space for trypanophobics to connect and find solace.

Policy Change: Implement stigma-reduction campaigns to raise awareness about trypanophobia and challenge stereotypes. Foster supportive communities through the establishment of online forums, support groups, and public events where individuals with trypanophobia can come together and share their experiences.

Advocacy for Improved Needle Safety

Needle safety is a critical aspect of addressing trypanophobia. By advocating for improved needle safety measures, societies can instill confidence in individuals with trypanophobia and encourage them to engage in necessary medical procedures.

Policy Change: Work with healthcare organizations and regulatory bodies to enhance needle safety standards. This may include promoting the use of safety-engineered needles, providing training on safe needle handling techniques, and encouraging the development of alternative needle-free medical technologies.

In conclusion, societal implications and policy changes play a significant role in supporting individuals with trypanophobia. By recognizing the phobia as a valid medical condition, improving healthcare provider training, creating fear-free environments, standardizing needle procedure protocols, ensuring insurance coverage and accessibility, reducing stigma, and advocating for improved needle safety, societies can make significant strides in addressing this phobia. These policy changes will not only benefit trypanophobics but also contribute to creating a more empathetic and inclusive healthcare system for all.

Collaborative Efforts between Researchers and Practitioners

Collaboration between researchers and practitioners is essential in advancing the understanding and treatment of trypanophobia. By combining their expertise and resources, researchers and practitioners can work together to create more effective interventions and improve the overall quality of care for individuals with needle phobia. In this section, we will explore the different ways in which researchers and practitioners can collaborate and the potential benefits of such collaboration.

One important aspect of collaboration is the exchange of knowledge and information between researchers and practitioners. Researchers can provide practitioners with the latest research findings and evidence-based practices in the field of trypanophobia. This information can help practitioners stay up-to-date with the most effective treatment approaches and techniques. Conversely, practitioners can provide researchers with valuable insights from their clinical experience, such as real-world challenges faced by trypanophobic patients and their caregivers. This exchange of knowledge can be facilitated through conferences, workshops, and collaborative research projects.

Collaborative research projects are an excellent way for researchers and practitioners to work together towards a common goal. These projects can involve conducting clinical trials to test the effectiveness of new interventions, evaluating the impact of existing treatment approaches, or identifying gaps in current knowledge. Such projects can benefit from the complementary expertise of both researchers and practitioners. Researchers can contribute their scientific rigor and analytical skills, while practitioners can provide their clinical insights and firsthand experience with trypanophobic patients. By pooling their resources and expertise, researchers and practitioners can develop more impactful interventions and address the specific needs of individuals with trypanophobia.

In addition to conducting collaborative research, researchers and practitioners can also collaborate in the development of training programs for healthcare professionals. Training programs can help healthcare providers better understand trypanophobia and provide them with the skills and knowledge necessary to address the needs of trypanophobic patients. Researchers can contribute by developing evidence-based curricula and training materials, while practitioners can provide their insights and expertise in delivering effective interventions. By working together, researchers and practitioners can ensure that healthcare professionals are equipped with the necessary tools to provide high-quality care for individuals with needle phobia.

Collaboration can also extend beyond the research and clinical realms. Researchers and practitioners can work together to advocate for better policies and support systems for individuals with trypanophobia. By joining forces, they can raise awareness about the challenges faced by trypanophobics and advocate for the development of more accessible and patient-centered healthcare practices. They can also seek funding and resources to support research and interventions related to needle phobia. By working together, researchers and practitioners can amplify their voices and drive positive changes in the healthcare system.

An unconventional yet relevant approach to collaboration between researchers and practitioners is the use of art and creative expressions. Researchers and practitioners can collaborate with artists to develop innovative interventions that leverage the power of art in helping individuals cope with their needle phobia. Art therapy can provide a non-threatening and expressive outlet for trypanophobics to explore their fears and emotions in a safe and supportive environment. Through collaboration with artists, researchers and practitioners can develop creative interventions that combine therapeutic techniques with visual arts, music, dance, or other art forms. This interdisciplinary approach can not only enhance treatment outcomes but also enrich the overall experience of individuals with trypanophobia.

In summary, collaboration between researchers and practitioners is crucial for advancing the understanding and treatment of trypanophobia. By exchanging knowledge, conducting collaborative research, developing training programs, advocating for policy changes, and exploring unconventional approaches, researchers and practitioners can work together to improve the lives of individuals with needle phobia. These collaborative efforts have the potential to shape the future of trypanophobia research and transform the way we approach and address this debilitating phobia.

Funding and Resources for Trypanophobia Research

Funding and resources are critical factors in advancing research on trypanophobia, as they facilitate necessary investigations and the development of innovative approaches to address this prevalent phobia. In this section, we will explore the current state of funding for trypanophobia research, discuss available resources, and highlight potential avenues for obtaining financial support.

Current State of Funding

Although trypanophobia is a widespread and debilitating condition, funding for research specifically targeted towards this phobia remains limited. This scarcity of resources contributes to a lack of comprehensive understanding and effective treatment options for individuals who suffer from trypanophobia. However, various funding sources can still provide potential support for researchers in this field.

Government Grants: National institutes of health, such as the National Institutes of Mental Health (NIMH), the National Institute of General Medical Sciences (NIGMS), and the National Institute of Child Health and Human Development (NICHD), offer grants to support research on mental health disorders, phobias, and anxiety-related conditions. Researchers focusing on trypanophobia can apply for grants through these agencies, which provide a significant avenue for financial assistance.

Private Foundations: Numerous private foundations also prioritize mental health research and may provide funding opportunities for trypanophobia studies. Foundations such as the Anxiety and Depression Association of America, the American Psychological Association Foundation, and the Brain & Behavior Research Foundation can offer financial support, scholarships, or grants to researchers working on understanding and treating phobias.

Academic Institutions: Universities and research institutions often have internal funding mechanisms to support faculty and student-led research initiatives. Academic researchers studying trypanophobia can explore their institution's research grants, internal funding programs, or seek collaborations with other departments or institutions that have available resources.

Resources for Trypanophobia Research

In addition to funding, access to resources is vital for conducting thorough research on trypanophobia. Researchers need various tools and platforms to collect data, analyze findings, collaborate, and disseminate knowledge. This subsection discusses some key resources available to trypanophobia researchers:

Laboratory Facilities: Well-equipped laboratories are essential for conducting experimental research, especially in understanding the neurobiological mechanisms underlying trypanophobia. Resources such as fMRI machines, EEG devices, and laboratory animals enable researchers to study the brain's response to needle-related stimuli, investigate genetic factors, and explore potential treatment interventions.

Collaborative Networks: Collaboration is paramount in research, and trypanophobia researchers can benefit from joining existing collaborative networks or establishing their own. These networks facilitate knowledge exchange, resource sharing, and collaboration on multi-center studies. By fostering collaborative efforts, researchers can pool resources, share data, and collectively advance the understanding and treatment of trypanophobia.

Data Repositories: Open-access data repositories play a crucial role in scientific research. Trypanophobia researchers can contribute their data to existing repositories, such as the National Database for Clinical Trials Related to Mental Illness (NDCT), to ensure data availability for subsequent analysis, replication, and meta-analyses. Access to data repositories also enables researchers to explore existing datasets, generating new hypotheses, and maximizing research output.

Scientific Journals and Conferences: Publications and conferences provide platforms for researchers to disseminate their findings, exchange ideas, and establish collaborations. Submitting research articles to relevant journals that focus on anxiety disorders, phobias, and mental health contributes to the existing knowledge base. Presenting research findings at conferences allows researchers to receive feedback, network with peers, and gain visibility within the scientific community.

Online Research Tools: Rapid advancements in technology have led to the development of various online research tools to aid researchers in their investigations. Online survey platforms, statistical analysis software, and virtual reality programs offer cost-effective and efficient means to collect data, analyze results, and create immersive environments for exposure therapy.

Obtaining Financial Support

Securing financial support for trypanophobia research can be challenging but not impossible. Researchers should explore multiple avenues and adopt a proactive approach to obtain the necessary funding. Here are some strategies and tips for obtaining financial support:

1. Grant Writing Skills: Developing effective grant writing skills is essential for researchers seeking external funding. Learning how to craft compelling research proposals, clearly outlining the objectives, methodology, and expected outcomes, increases the chances of securing grants.
2. Collaboration and Partnerships: Partnering with other researchers or institutions that have already secured funding for phobia-related studies can provide access to shared resources and increase the likelihood of obtaining additional financial support. Collaborative efforts also demonstrate a commitment to knowledge exchange and interdisciplinary research.
3. Crowdfunding: Researchers can explore crowdfunding platforms to raise funds for trypanophobia research. Utilizing social media, researchers can reach out to individuals who may be interested in supporting mental health studies, creating a sense of community involvement and increasing awareness of trypanophobia.
4. Philanthropic Donations: Reaching out to philanthropic organizations or individuals passionate about mental health can yield financial support. By presenting a compelling case for the impact and significance of trypanophobia research, researchers may attract donors interested in contributing to this cause.
5. Industry Partnerships: Collaborating with pharmaceutical or medical device companies that have a vested interest in needle-related interventions can provide both financial support and valuable expertise. Industry partnerships can offer access to specialized resources, clinical trial funding, or in-kind support, thereby facilitating research progress.
6. Government Initiatives: Staying updated on government initiatives related to mental health research, phobia treatment, or anxiety disorders can highlight potential funding opportunities. Researchers should regularly monitor grant announcements, policy changes, and research priorities outlined by governmental bodies.
7. International Collaboration: Seeking international collaboration can open doors to funding opportunities provided by foreign institutions, governments, or organizations. International collaborations also enhance the research's global perspective, introducing different cultural contexts and approaches to trypanophobia research.

By employing these strategies and actively seeking funding opportunities, researchers can maximize their chances of securing financial support for trypanophobia research. Persistent efforts and a proactive mindset are crucial in this process.

In conclusion, funding and resources are vital components of trypanophobia research. Despite the current limitations, researchers can explore various funding sources, leverage existing resources, and adopt proactive strategies to secure financial support. Additionally, collaboration, data sharing, and utilization of online tools can optimize research output and contribute to the advancement of knowledge in the field of trypanophobia. Through a multidimensional approach, researchers can work towards a future where effective treatments and support systems are available for individuals living with trypanophobia.

Bridging the Gap: Transdisciplinary Approaches

In order to fully understand and address trypanophobia, it is essential to adopt a transdisciplinary approach that brings together various disciplines and perspectives. By combining knowledge from fields such as neuroscience, psychology, medicine, and sociology, we can gain a comprehensive understanding of trypanophobia and develop more effective strategies for treating and supporting individuals with this phobia.

Integrating Neuroscience and Psychology

One key aspect of bridging the gap between disciplines is integrating the findings of neuroscience and psychology. Neuroscience provides valuable insights into the brain mechanisms underlying fear and anxiety, while psychology offers a deeper understanding of cognitive processes and behavioral responses. By combining these disciplines, researchers and practitioners can develop targeted interventions that address both the physiological and psychological aspects of trypanophobia.

For example, neuroimaging techniques such as functional magnetic resonance imaging (fMRI) can help identify specific brain regions involved in fear response and pinpoint any abnormalities in trypanophobics. This information can then be used to design cognitive behavioral therapy (CBT) interventions that target these regions and modify fear conditioning.

Collaborating with Medical Professionals

The collaboration between researchers and medical professionals is crucial in developing effective treatments and support systems for trypanophobia. Medical professionals, such as doctors and nurses, possess valuable firsthand knowledge and experience in dealing with trypanophobic patients. Their insights can inform the development of better tools and techniques for pain management during medical procedures involving needles.

For example, by collaborating with anesthesiologists, researchers can explore the use of alternative pain management techniques, such as local anesthesia or non-pharmacological methods like distraction, relaxation, or virtual reality therapy. These approaches can significantly reduce the distress experienced by trypanophobics during medical procedures and enhance their overall healthcare experience.

Accounting for Societal and Cultural Factors

Understanding the societal and cultural factors that contribute to trypanophobia is essential for providing effective support to individuals with this phobia. Societal attitudes and norms surrounding medical procedures, fears of contamination or disease transmission, and past experiences with healthcare providers can all impact the development and severity of trypanophobia.

By incorporating sociological perspectives, researchers can gain a deeper understanding of the unique challenges faced by individuals with trypanophobia. This understanding can inform the development of culturally sensitive interventions and support systems that address the specific needs and concerns of different populations.

Leveraging Technology and Innovation

Advances in technology offer exciting opportunities for bridging the gap between disciplines when addressing trypanophobia. Virtual reality therapy, for example, can provide a safe and controlled environment for exposure therapy, allowing trypanophobics to gradually confront their fears at their own pace. This technology can be integrated with biofeedback devices to monitor physiological responses and further enhance the effectiveness of the therapy.

In addition, mobile applications and online platforms can play a vital role in supporting individuals with trypanophobia. These platforms can provide information, educational resources, meditation exercises, and virtual support groups, connecting individuals with shared experiences and fostering a sense of community.

Training and Education

A transdisciplinary approach also calls for interdisciplinary training and education to bridge the gap between different professions. Medical professionals, psychologists, and researchers can benefit greatly from gaining insights into each other's fields and collaborating more effectively. Creating opportunities for interdisciplinary conferences, workshops, and training programs can encourage exchange and promote collaboration.

By fostering a shared understanding and language across disciplines, professionals can work together to develop innovative solutions and interventions that address the multidimensional nature of trypanophobia.

Case Study: The Needle Phobia Clinic

An innovative example of the transdisciplinary approach is the establishment of the Needle Phobia Clinic. This clinic brings together medical professionals, psychologists, and researchers to provide comprehensive support and treatment for individuals with trypanophobia.

At the Needle Phobia Clinic, individuals undergo a thorough assessment that includes both physiological and psychological evaluations. The team collaborates to develop personalized treatment plans that integrate exposure therapy, cognitive behavioral techniques, and technological interventions.

The clinic also provides educational resources for healthcare providers to enhance their understanding and sensitivity towards trypanophobia. This ensures that patients receive compassionate care from professionals who are knowledgeable about the specific challenges of needle phobia.

Conclusion

A transdisciplinary approach is essential in understanding, addressing, and supporting individuals with trypanophobia. By integrating knowledge from different disciplines such as neuroscience, psychology, medicine, and sociology, we can develop more effective strategies for treating trypanophobia and improving the overall well-being of individuals living with this phobia.

Collaboration between professionals, leveraging technology and innovation, and considering societal and cultural factors are key components of this transdisciplinary approach. By working together, we can bridge the gap between disciplines and create a more holistic and empathetic understanding of trypanophobia.

Index

-up, 82, 170

ability, 4, 5, 30, 50, 57, 72, 84, 106, 141, 149, 152, 184, 185, 195
absorption, 31
abuse, 37, 117, 183
acceptance, 25, 74, 79, 141, 144
access, 12, 14, 16, 38, 40, 41, 45, 46, 83, 126, 127, 137, 146, 185, 186, 195, 200, 202
accessibility, 45, 145, 165, 167, 197, 198
accommodation, 145, 153
accomplishment, 84, 85
accordance, 22
account, 12, 82, 119, 166, 183, 186, 193, 195
accountability, 40
accuracy, 22, 34
act, 6, 26, 75, 179
action, 49, 118, 177, 190
activation, 9, 48–50, 52
activity, 50, 52, 53, 182
acuity, 48
acupoint, 29
acupuncture, 6, 22, 24, 27–29, 32, 121
adaptation, 184
addiction, 43, 61, 117
addition, 3, 36, 37, 48, 80, 113, 115, 121, 173, 182, 199, 200, 204
address, 13, 16–18, 28, 40–42, 46, 61, 72, 75, 78, 83, 86, 105, 115, 118–120, 122, 127, 133, 136, 137, 143, 146, 148, 156, 163, 177, 178, 182, 185, 194, 196, 198–200, 203–205
addressing, 4, 6–8, 10, 14, 16–20, 41, 44, 46, 49, 55, 57, 59, 61, 62, 64, 69, 77, 80, 81, 83, 88, 106, 116, 122, 127, 131–134, 138, 143–145, 147, 150, 160, 171, 183–187, 190, 193, 197, 198, 204, 205
adjustment, 117
administration, 6, 24, 31, 37, 67
adoption, 43
adrenaline, 47, 48, 118, 190
adult, 133
adulthood, 13
advance, 7, 32, 40, 201
advancement, 6, 16, 34, 203

advice, 73, 132, 142, 145, 152, 167, 173, 178
advocacy, 19, 82, 83, 144–147, 149
advocate, 83, 87, 143, 145, 160, 199
affirmation, 142
affordability, 197
age, 4, 71, 82, 84
agility, 47
aid, 142, 201
aim, 7, 20, 22, 28, 42, 45, 74, 78, 80, 144
airflow, 48
alarm, 49
alcohol, 60
Alexander Wood, 30
alliance, 114
allocation, 146
almond, 1, 49
alternative, 7, 24, 32, 33, 37, 39, 44–46, 80, 119, 121, 132, 143, 145, 153, 164, 166–168, 194, 198, 203
ambiance, 161
amygdala, 1, 18, 49, 50, 52, 68, 125
analysis, 201
anatomy, 18
anchor, 139
anesthesia, 36, 67, 166, 203
animal, 32
anticipation, 1, 9, 60, 62, 125
anxiety, 1–5, 7–10, 12, 14–16, 33, 35, 37, 39, 48, 50, 55–60, 62, 63, 67–76, 78, 79, 84, 85, 88, 89, 93–95, 97, 99, 101, 102, 105, 106, 109, 110, 113, 114, 116–122, 125, 127, 130, 131, 134–136, 139, 141, 143, 148, 152, 155, 158, 159, 161, 163–166, 168, 169, 171, 181, 184, 187, 190–193, 195–197, 201–203
application, 28, 140, 197
appraisal, 50
appreciation, 179
apprehension, 44, 63, 134
approach, 2–4, 12, 13, 16, 17, 19, 20, 24, 28, 29, 41, 45, 57, 58, 61, 63, 64, 74, 75, 78, 80, 83, 84, 88, 94, 96, 105, 108, 114–116, 118, 119, 121, 122, 131–134, 136, 138, 141, 150, 164–168, 170–172, 184–186, 192–195, 199, 201, 203–205
area, 27, 55, 171
aromatherapy, 102, 121
arousal, 72, 73
array, 24
art, 19, 25, 26, 58, 75, 80, 113–116, 120, 122, 123, 132, 133, 185, 199
arthritis, 24
artwork, 114–116, 167
ask, 43
aspect, 8, 9, 28, 35, 37, 61, 76, 125, 134, 140, 142, 155, 165, 169, 175, 196–198, 203
aspiration, 36
assessment, 94, 205
assistance, 8, 111
association, 6, 7, 9, 26, 102, 125
assurance, 141
asthma, 118
atmosphere, 145, 161
attack, 60

attention, 8, 12, 31, 62, 106, 120, 131, 151, 155, 156, 166, 196
attitude, 70
audience, 144, 145
auditory, 49
automation, 8
autonomy, 38, 39, 45, 46
availability, 167
aversion, 58, 63
avoidance, 1–3, 9, 10, 12–14, 16, 39, 50, 58, 60, 62–64, 68, 70, 76, 78, 117, 126, 136, 184
awareness, 3, 5, 12, 13, 16, 17, 19, 74, 79, 82, 83, 106, 109, 131, 136, 137, 140, 144, 146, 147, 149, 155, 194, 196, 197, 199, 202

bacteria, 34
balance, 6, 22, 25, 27–29, 38, 39, 52, 53, 74
bamboo, 21, 30
barrier, 14, 15
base, 201
basis, 183
beach, 101
beauty, 25
bee, 23, 24
behavior, 2, 60, 70, 71, 117, 140, 155
behavioral, 8, 10, 19, 49, 52, 78, 97, 100, 105, 120, 122, 123, 133, 190, 192, 197, 203, 205
being, 2–4, 12, 16, 24, 25, 27–29, 33, 37, 38, 43, 48, 59, 61, 62, 65, 68, 72, 74, 77, 81–83, 85–88, 95, 99, 101, 106, 109, 113, 114, 121, 125, 128, 131, 133, 142, 146, 148–150, 153, 154, 156, 157, 168, 171, 177–179, 185, 205
belief, 11, 24, 27, 79, 84, 141, 142
benefit, 96, 121, 140, 145, 198, 201, 204
beta, 2, 118, 120, 190, 191, 193
bias, 8
bile, 22
biofeedback, 204
birth, 25
blocker, 118, 191
blood, 1–3, 7, 9, 14–16, 22, 29, 32, 36, 44, 47, 48, 56, 67, 85, 88, 118, 127, 139
bloodborne, 7, 38, 40, 43
bloodletting, 22, 24, 29, 32
bloodstream, 36, 48
body, 1, 5, 6, 22, 25–30, 33, 38, 47–49, 55, 74, 79, 80, 99, 125, 131, 190, 191
bone, 25, 30
book, 17, 20
boundary, 154
boy, 90
brain, 1, 19, 49, 50, 52, 55, 68, 78, 114, 125, 141, 181, 201, 203
branch, 47
bravery, 38, 64
break, 58, 106, 113, 178
breakdown, 94, 182
breath, 48, 60, 64, 74, 120, 131
breathing, 1, 48, 67, 69, 72, 74, 76, 79, 84, 94, 95, 101, 102, 113, 120, 127, 129, 131, 136, 142, 157, 166, 178
bride, 25

bridge, 204, 205
bronze, 21
building, 2, 71, 83–85, 149, 174, 177
burden, 16, 197
burnout, 19, 176–179
burst, 48

cactus, 25
calm, 70, 73, 79, 99, 101, 106, 118, 120, 121, 131, 139, 142, 168, 190
calmness, 94, 100–102, 139
cancer, 36
capacity, 39, 114
care, 3, 4, 13, 14, 17, 19, 24, 35, 44, 57, 59, 61, 64, 65, 77, 83, 92, 105, 108, 116, 119, 121, 126, 127, 129, 130, 145, 147–149, 156, 161, 165, 167, 169, 170, 176–179, 194, 195, 198, 199, 205
career, 15, 16
caregiver, 19, 56, 176–179
caregiving, 178, 179
cascade, 47, 49, 106
case, 1, 8, 20, 69, 88, 89, 91, 92, 100, 105, 113, 122, 127, 155, 202
catalyst, 7
cataract, 22
catheter, 8
cause, 3, 16, 24, 26, 28, 32, 44, 60, 63, 64, 117, 155, 191, 202
caution, 24, 117, 118, 121, 138, 191
center, 201
century, 23, 30, 31, 36
ceremony, 25
chair, 121
challenge, 11, 13, 14, 17, 37, 68, 72, 78, 94, 97, 122, 136, 141, 145, 197
challenging, 2–4, 39, 57, 62, 64, 72, 79, 85, 89, 93, 97, 105, 115, 131, 136, 156, 176, 177, 194, 197, 201
chance, 146
change, 25, 43, 144, 145, 182
chapter, 5, 17–19, 44, 63, 119, 130, 133
character, 62
characteristic, 9
charge, 148, 150
check, 1, 4, 119, 143, 148
chemistry, 44
child, 56, 59, 70, 71, 75, 76, 81–84, 183–185
childhood, 4, 13, 18, 56, 59, 67, 69, 129, 139, 143, 185
China, 24, 25, 27, 29, 30
choice, 11, 28, 33, 46, 114, 186
circle, 156, 179
circuitry, 50
claim, 24
clarity, 143
class, 118, 190, 191
classroom, 86, 88
cleaning, 23
cleanliness, 23
client, 94, 96
clinic, 205
closing, 22
clothing, 5
coach, 105
coating, 34
collaborate, 18, 19, 88, 96, 144, 146, 168, 198, 199, 201

collaboration, 61, 74, 81–83, 89, 164, 167–169, 171, 186, 198, 199, 201–204
collage, 115
collection, 183
college, 4
combination, 6, 92, 97, 118, 130, 136, 144
comfort, 7, 23, 34, 42, 44, 45, 78, 80, 82, 85, 115, 149, 153, 154, 165, 192, 197
commitment, 5, 17, 25, 96, 144, 153, 154, 202
communication, 17, 19, 43, 44, 50, 59, 70, 71, 81, 83, 86, 114, 119, 145, 151, 154, 157, 159, 162, 163, 171, 194–196
community, 37, 41, 43, 82, 113, 127, 132, 136, 142, 144, 145, 149, 185, 195, 201, 202, 204
compassion, 14, 63, 123, 141, 149, 152
compatibility, 33
competence, 186, 195
complex, 5, 8, 36, 38, 45, 47, 50, 55, 56, 59, 62, 70, 122, 182
complexity, 4, 11, 12, 26, 64
component, 50, 58, 75, 131, 136, 172, 179, 181, 192
compound, 179
computer, 35
concept, 18, 27, 187
concern, 5, 32, 36, 38, 39
conclusion, 8, 10, 17, 32, 38, 48, 55, 59, 64, 83, 105, 140, 142, 147, 150, 154, 167, 177, 183, 186, 198, 202
condition, 8, 62–64, 86, 155, 169, 193, 194, 196, 198, 200
conditioning, 9, 10, 12, 18, 49, 50, 52, 53
confidence, 84, 85, 94, 95, 102, 105, 106, 128, 133, 136, 139–142, 167, 197
confidentiality, 114, 172
confirmation, 8
confrontation, 47
conjunction, 59, 112, 118, 121, 122
connection, 25, 99, 115, 152
consent, 37–41
consideration, 37, 61, 76
consolidation, 68
construction, 5
consultation, 171
contact, 4, 10, 187
containment, 36
contamination, 23, 24, 37, 204
content, 20, 145
context, 3, 5, 11, 20, 24–26, 48–50, 72, 75, 76, 78, 102, 110, 114, 118, 141, 187
continuity, 77
contracting, 8, 125
contrast, 52
control, 2, 4, 6, 10, 32, 35, 36, 48, 49, 56, 59, 69, 71, 77, 85, 96–98, 101, 102, 105, 106, 109, 118, 125, 133, 139–143, 155, 167
controversy, 32
conversion, 60
coordination, 50, 117, 186
copper, 21
core, 13
corrosion, 33
cortex, 49, 50, 52

corticotropin, 55
cortisol, 68
cost, 43, 45, 201
counseling, 88, 149, 178
counselor, 88
courage, 142, 146
coverage, 197, 198
cowardice, 11
craftsmanship, 23
creation, 45, 80
creativity, 114
cross, 23, 24
crowdfunding, 202
culture, 25, 26, 44, 56
cure, 118
curiosity, 108
curricula, 196, 199
cutting, 19, 20, 34, 35, 190
cycle, 1, 9, 15, 58, 68, 106

damage, 31, 34, 41, 44, 45
dance, 199
danger, 47–49, 64
date, 198
death, 6, 41, 194
decade, 127
decision, 39, 50, 169
decor, 196
decrease, 34, 136
dedication, 77
defense, 58
delay, 2, 3, 68, 126
delivery, 7, 31, 32, 36, 44, 45, 164, 166–168, 186
dentist, 127
depression, 2, 3
depth, 18, 19
desensitization, 71, 78, 84, 93–96, 99–102, 119, 141
design, 7, 30, 44
destigmatization, 5, 16
detail, 19
detection, 36, 49
determination, 2, 5, 144, 146
development, 3, 6–10, 13, 18, 21, 23, 24, 31–33, 35–37, 40, 41, 43, 44, 48, 50, 53, 55–59, 64, 67, 68, 70, 71, 77, 82, 145, 148, 172, 181–184, 186, 187, 197–201, 203, 204
device, 43, 202
diagnose, 36
diagnosis, 28, 39, 60, 68
diagnostic, 28, 31, 36, 196
dialogue, 13, 83, 115, 156, 197
diameter, 34
diet, 121, 148, 179
difficulty, 85, 132
digestion, 48
dilemma, 39, 40
direction, 141
disability, 41
discomfort, 6, 8, 9, 26, 28, 31, 32, 34, 39, 44, 46, 56, 62, 63, 67, 70, 96, 125, 131, 164, 166
discovery, 23, 25, 132, 140, 150
discrimination, 40
discussion, 94, 115
disease, 36, 38, 48, 204
disgust, 72
disorder, 59, 60, 134, 136
disposal, 32, 36, 37, 40, 42
distortion, 8
distraction, 39, 71, 127, 133, 166, 197, 203
distress, 1, 4, 5, 9, 10, 32, 39, 56, 58, 60, 63, 64, 67–70, 72–74,

79, 85, 86, 92, 105, 127, 129, 142, 152, 161, 187, 191, 192, 196, 204
distressing, 2, 78, 157, 191
distribution, 40
dive, 18
diversity, 5, 64
divination, 30
dizziness, 1, 60, 117
doctor, 76, 77
domain, 145
donor, 139
doom, 64
door, 29
dopamine, 182
dosage, 117
dose, 117
dosing, 191
doubt, 130
drawing, 33, 34, 115, 120, 122, 132
dread, 63, 155
drowsiness, 117
drug, 7, 31, 32, 38, 40, 43–45, 117, 118
durability, 33
dysfunction, 48, 117
dysregulation, 55

ease, 30, 74, 95, 152, 162
edge, 19, 20, 35, 190
educating, 17, 71, 82–85, 129, 140, 147, 154–157, 169
education, 5, 16, 118, 142, 146, 154, 156, 157, 165, 167, 185, 186, 194, 196, 204
effect, 3, 117, 183
effectiveness, 28, 29, 33, 44, 45, 69, 76, 88, 103, 106, 119, 121, 122, 167, 186, 198, 204
efficacy, 35, 83–85, 94, 117
efficiency, 8
effort, 14, 83, 161
Egypt, 5, 23, 25
elevation, 48
embarrassment, 2, 3
emergence, 193
Emma, 76, 77, 88, 89
emotion, 50, 52, 61
empathy, 5, 11–14, 16, 17, 19, 61, 63, 64, 82, 86, 114, 119, 127, 144, 151, 152, 154–158, 160, 161, 168, 171, 173, 174, 177, 195, 196
emphasis, 28
empowerment, 2, 19, 61, 114, 130, 136, 140–142, 186
encapsulation, 42
encounter, 4, 14, 58, 63, 71
encourage, 13, 43, 58, 71, 81, 116, 197, 204
encouragement, 2, 71, 73, 96, 110, 120, 122, 132, 142, 144, 171
end, 40, 63, 64, 150, 170
ending, 95
energy, 6, 25–29, 48, 178, 194
engagement, 48
enjoyment, 133
enlightenment, 25
environment, 2, 5, 10, 11, 13, 17, 19, 37, 40, 43, 49, 58, 59, 64, 68–70, 74–78, 80, 84–86, 88, 89, 92–95, 105, 109, 114, 119, 131, 132, 141, 151, 154, 158–162, 165, 167, 168, 173, 174, 183,

184, 192, 195, 196, 199, 204
epigenome, 182
equipment, 39, 59
equipping, 88, 155, 196
error, 8
establishment, 197, 205
esteem, 16, 61, 141
Ethan, 90
evaluation, 41, 117
event, 26, 50, 56, 68, 78, 118
evidence, 10, 24, 29, 55, 59, 97, 121, 130, 131, 135, 136, 146, 198, 199
evil, 6, 26, 194
evolution, 18, 24, 29, 30, 32, 38
exam, 48
examination, 127
example, 6, 25, 30, 38, 39, 44, 57, 70, 75, 76, 79, 94, 95, 97, 101, 115, 118, 121, 127, 131, 143, 182, 194, 195, 203–205
exception, 190
exchange, 40, 43, 48, 132, 167, 198, 201, 202, 204
exemption, 145
exercise, 115, 118, 121, 148, 178
exertion, 48
exhaustion, 177
exhibit, 49, 63
expectancy, 9
expectation, 9
experience, 1, 4, 5, 9, 11, 12, 14, 16, 39, 46, 48–50, 56, 59, 60, 62–64, 67, 69, 70, 72, 75, 76, 86, 89, 100, 102, 110, 111, 115–117, 119, 120, 122, 139, 143, 149, 155, 157, 160, 161, 164, 166, 167, 171, 177, 179, 191, 192, 196, 198, 199, 203, 204
experiment, 100
expert, 145
expertise, 76, 80, 89, 111, 171, 184, 198, 199, 202
exploration, 7, 19, 20, 52, 58, 75, 115, 116, 132
explore, 5, 8, 11, 17–19, 24, 27, 33, 35, 38, 41, 44, 50, 55, 70, 72, 74–77, 80, 83, 86, 89, 99, 106, 109, 113, 114, 116, 119, 120, 125, 128, 130, 132, 134, 136, 140, 143, 148, 151, 158, 161, 165, 168, 171, 174, 177, 181, 184, 190, 193, 195, 198–203
exposure, 3, 5, 10, 12, 18, 19, 48, 64, 68, 69, 74, 76–78, 80, 82, 84, 93–96, 101, 102, 104, 105, 115, 119, 122, 126, 127, 129, 131, 132, 136, 141, 166, 167, 183, 184, 187, 190, 192, 201, 204, 205
expression, 56, 58, 70, 73, 76, 80, 114, 116, 132, 182
extension, 186
extent, 64, 94
extinction, 52
extract, 5

fabric, 26
fabrication, 35
face, 15, 47, 49, 71, 85, 101, 102, 106, 112, 113, 133, 143,

149, 173, 192
facilitator, 75
facility, 136, 167
factor, 9, 62
faculty, 200
fainting, 1, 8, 64, 67
family, 14, 15, 19, 23, 39, 59, 73, 129, 154–157, 171, 172, 178, 179, 185, 186
fascination, 5
fate, 30
fear, 1–20, 33, 35, 37, 39, 44, 45, 48–50, 52, 53, 55–64, 67–70, 72–85, 88–90, 92–102, 105–107, 109–111, 113–117, 119, 120, 122, 123, 125–134, 136, 137, 139–144, 146–150, 155–161, 165–168, 170, 171, 173, 181, 183, 187, 191–196, 198, 203
fearfulness, 181
feedback, 44, 142, 201
feel, 5, 63, 70, 80, 83, 85, 114, 118, 119, 121, 146, 152, 160–162, 166, 167, 172
feeling, 15, 95, 117, 170
fertility, 15
field, 6, 32, 33, 35, 36, 44, 53, 167, 190, 198, 200, 203
fight, 1, 18, 47–49, 58, 67, 190
file, 22
finding, 48, 122, 144, 149, 175
fit, 171
flaw, 11
flight, 1, 18, 47–49, 58, 67, 190
flow, 6, 25, 27, 28, 47
flu, 2
fluid, 45
focus, 8, 18, 19, 71, 79, 88, 101, 120, 131, 133, 145, 149, 188, 201
follow, 82, 170
following, 3, 82, 98, 100, 161, 175
footprint, 37
force, 27, 34
form, 21, 26, 62, 90, 116, 133, 184
formation, 41, 68
fortune, 26
forum, 167
Foster, 197
foster, 5, 56, 64, 85, 86, 113, 114, 116, 136, 167, 171, 174, 195
foundation, 55, 109, 131, 140, 154
framework, 75, 156, 187
freedom, 148, 150
friction, 34
fulfillment, 149
function, 44
functionality, 33
functioning, 52, 55, 184
funding, 20, 146, 197, 199–202
future, 7, 18–20, 32, 33, 35, 38, 44–46, 85, 92, 123, 130, 140, 150, 187, 188, 199, 203

gap, 203–205
garden, 101
gauge, 197
gene, 55, 56, 181, 182
generation, 56, 146
genetic, 2, 18, 19, 55–57, 181–183, 201
germ, 23
girl, 76, 89

glimpse, 4
glucose, 48
glutamate, 52
goal, 95, 133, 166, 198
goddess, 30
gold, 21, 25, 28
government, 146, 197, 202
grant, 202
Grant Writing Skills, 202
gratitude, 179
Greece, 22, 24, 25
grief, 149
grinding, 33
groom, 25
group, 80, 88, 96, 110–113, 115, 120, 122, 132, 133, 136, 156, 157, 182
growth, 15, 19, 25, 34, 83, 140–142, 148, 150, 172
guidance, 2, 12, 19, 24, 62, 69, 77, 78, 80, 82, 101, 102, 105, 109, 111–113, 120–122, 127, 130, 131, 138, 142–144, 172, 173, 191–193
guide, 3, 41, 77, 79, 83, 115, 183
guilt, 82

habit, 191
hammer, 22
hand, 22, 26, 47, 102
handling, 42, 76–78, 84, 113, 198
harm, 6, 8, 17, 40, 43, 115
harmony, 25, 28
head, 47, 112
headset, 132, 192
healing, 24–30, 37, 59, 61, 80, 83, 84, 113, 114, 116, 132, 137, 140, 148, 149, 170, 173, 187, 194
health, 1–4, 6, 14–16, 22, 25, 27, 29, 33, 36, 40, 43, 48, 59, 61, 63, 64, 68, 71, 79, 88, 95, 105, 108, 109, 112, 126, 127, 143, 144, 146, 148–150, 164–166, 171, 177, 179, 184, 186, 190, 192, 194, 201, 202
healthcare, 2–4, 6–8, 12, 14, 16–19, 24, 29–33, 35–44, 46, 57, 59, 61, 64, 71, 72, 74, 77, 80–86, 88–90, 92, 96, 108, 117–119, 121, 122, 126, 127, 133, 136, 144, 145, 147, 149, 157, 160–165, 167–172, 179, 183, 184, 191, 193–199, 204, 205
heart, 1, 9, 47, 48, 63, 67, 72, 101, 118, 155, 190
heartbeat, 1, 60, 64, 118, 121
help, 2, 4, 5, 8, 10, 13, 16, 17, 19, 37, 39–41, 48, 50, 55, 57, 59, 62–64, 69–85, 87–89, 91, 96–102, 106–108, 112, 115, 117, 118, 120–122, 126–131, 137, 139–144, 146, 152, 155, 159, 160, 164–169, 171–173, 178, 179, 181, 183, 186, 190, 193, 194, 196–199
helplessness, 72
hepatitis, 7, 31, 38
hernia, 22
hesitation, 148
hierarchy, 76, 77, 94, 95, 102, 115, 136
hippocampus, 49

histone, 182
history, 3, 5, 6, 8, 17, 18, 21, 24–27, 29, 30, 32, 33, 35, 47, 58, 114, 117, 119
home, 18, 77, 81, 82, 116
hope, 4, 5, 55, 144, 146, 166
hopelessness, 61
hormone, 55, 190
hospital, 143
hospitalization, 4
human, 8, 11, 26, 33, 38, 114
humor, 22
hyperactivity, 49
hyperarousal, 185
hypertension, 48
hypervigilance, 78
hypnosis, 137, 139
hypnotherapist, 139, 143
hypnotherapy, 19, 137–140, 143
hypoarousal, 185
hypothalamus, 50

idea, 6, 9, 100
identification, 64
illness, 4, 26
image, 115
imagery, 79, 84, 101, 102, 115, 120, 136, 166
imagination, 121
imaging, 18, 19, 55
imbalance, 22, 28
immune, 24, 48
immunization, 3
impact, 1–5, 8, 11–19, 35–38, 40, 41, 45, 48, 49, 52, 55, 56, 61–64, 67, 68, 71, 72, 74, 78, 86, 94, 113, 126, 130, 134, 136, 144, 146, 153, 155–158, 160, 161, 171, 182–184, 186, 195, 198, 202, 204
impairment, 64, 191
imperfection, 25
implement, 36, 72, 86, 88, 167, 183
implementation, 43, 145
importance, 16–20, 28, 41, 43, 53, 64, 69–72, 91, 109, 144, 148, 165, 171, 174
improvement, 139
in, 1–12, 14–50, 52, 53, 55–65, 68–89, 92–97, 100–109, 111–122, 125–127, 129, 131–149, 152–155, 157–159, 161, 162, 164–175, 177, 178, 181–187, 189–205
incidence, 35, 37
incident, 4, 143
inclusion, 86, 186
inclusivity, 195
income, 40, 185, 186
incorporating, 41, 42, 58, 105, 106, 120, 121, 133, 164, 194, 204
increase, 7, 47, 48, 83, 132, 196, 202
India, 22, 25, 29
individual, 1–3, 6, 12, 13, 15, 25, 40, 49, 50, 55–58, 61–64, 67, 68, 76, 78, 80, 84, 88, 93–96, 99–101, 108, 114, 115, 117, 119, 121, 122, 130–134, 137, 144, 148, 150–156, 166–168, 171–175, 178, 181, 185, 192
individuality, 12
industry, 40
infection, 22–24, 34, 38, 44

influence, 3, 18, 20, 40, 50, 55–57, 67, 70, 71, 85, 97, 181, 194
information, 8, 49, 71, 81, 84, 85, 127, 145, 167, 169, 185, 194, 198, 204
infrastructure, 40
inhibition, 52, 114
initiative, 153
injection, 31, 32, 38, 40, 41, 43, 67, 68, 76, 95, 122, 132, 143
ink, 38
innovation, 40, 41, 167, 168, 205
ins, 119
insertion, 6, 8, 25, 27, 28, 30, 31, 34, 37, 39, 44, 45, 197
insight, 4, 83, 115, 116, 132
inspection, 35
inspiration, 4, 19, 120, 142, 143, 146
instance, 3, 26, 36, 38, 45, 47, 48, 126
institution, 200
insulin, 31
insurance, 197, 198
integration, 8, 35, 76, 77, 123, 185, 193
intelligence, 46
intensity, 9, 12, 67, 98, 120, 130, 141, 192
interaction, 50, 57, 183
interconnectedness, 28
interest, 28, 40, 110, 181, 202
interplay, 47, 50, 56, 57, 60, 61, 183
intervention, 17, 19, 63, 64, 69, 115, 170, 183–187
interview, 171
introduction, 23, 30, 31, 34
introspection, 26, 115, 120, 140
Invalidating, 62
invasiveness, 36
invention, 36
involvement, 39, 202
irrationality, 2, 61
isolation, 3, 14, 80, 120, 132, 145, 167, 179
issue, 32, 40, 42, 194

Japan, 28
jewelry, 26
journal, 116
journaling, 80, 113, 140, 178
journey, 2, 5, 12, 26, 59, 70, 78, 80, 84, 99, 105, 108, 109, 113, 116, 121, 122, 129, 130, 132, 133, 136, 139–142, 144, 146, 148–150, 157, 170, 171, 173, 175, 177, 193
joy, 121, 149, 150, 178
judgment, 106, 131, 142, 151, 157, 194

Kampo, 28
kind, 99, 202
kit, 76
knowledge, 20, 23, 29, 71, 131, 146, 152, 156, 183, 195, 196, 198, 199, 201–203, 205

labeling, 32
labor, 22
laboratory, 3, 201
lack, 11, 12, 17, 39, 56, 196, 200
lacquer, 25
landscape, 39, 46
language, 140, 205
laser, 34
lavender, 121
layer, 31
laziness, 155

learning, 10, 14, 35, 56, 84, 92, 96, 99, 105, 112, 113, 141
length, 27, 31
lens, 193
level, 3, 16, 57, 67, 76, 78, 82, 85, 94, 115, 132, 137, 140, 143, 166, 192
leverage, 199, 202
life, 1–5, 10, 12, 15, 17, 20, 25–27, 38, 55, 61, 63, 64, 68–70, 74, 77, 80, 89, 90, 94, 95, 102, 105–109, 113, 123, 129, 130, 134, 136, 142, 144, 145, 148–150, 155, 156, 166, 171, 177, 182, 184, 187, 192, 193
lifespan, 13
lifestyle, 121, 148
light, 4, 5, 17, 18, 20, 27, 53, 55, 61
likelihood, 55, 64, 202
limit, 15
link, 182
listening, 5, 81, 83, 119, 127, 151, 152, 154
literature, 26
liver, 48
lobe, 49
location, 186
look, 17, 61
loop, 142
lorazepam, 117
loss, 4, 125
luck, 26
luxury, 178

machine, 35
machinery, 23
machining, 34
maintenance, 8–10, 95, 148
makeup, 57
making, 3, 4, 14, 15, 23, 31, 34, 36, 39, 44, 45, 50, 58, 59, 64, 68, 89, 114–116, 120, 158, 162, 169, 182, 191
man, 4, 127, 143
management, 17, 37, 39, 41, 45, 88, 89, 113, 168, 203
Manaka, 28
manifestation, 3, 181
manipulation, 6
manner, 20, 61, 71, 72, 75, 78, 85, 106, 115, 122, 166, 187
manufacturing, 22–24, 31–35, 37, 38, 42
Mark, 4, 5, 143, 144
mark, 8, 25
marking, 26
Marma, 28
marriage, 25
master, 99
mastery, 84
material, 28, 33, 34
meaning, 6, 182
means, 6, 80, 85, 114, 132, 148, 201
measles, 36
mechanism, 9, 47, 48, 58
media, 12, 56, 115, 145, 146, 202
medication, 2, 31, 36, 45, 61, 116–119, 122, 133, 136, 192, 193
medicine, 6, 18, 21, 24, 25, 27–30, 32, 36, 194, 203, 205
meditation, 19, 74, 79, 102, 106, 108, 109, 120, 131, 142, 146, 148, 178, 204
medium, 76, 114
meeting, 35, 156
meltdown, 4

member, 19
memory, 8, 55, 68
mention, 23, 72
mentorship, 85, 142
meridian, 27, 28
metabolism, 48
metal, 22, 29, 30
method, 29, 84, 97
methodology, 202
methyl, 182
methylation, 182
Michael, 127
microfabrication, 34, 45
microneedle, 32
microtechnology, 44, 46
middle, 64
milestone, 84
mind, 80, 99, 122, 137, 139, 140, 143
mindfulness, 19, 79, 80, 88, 102, 106–109, 120, 122, 123, 131, 133, 136, 142, 149, 166, 178
mindset, 98, 141, 168, 202
miniaturization, 44
minimization, 39
misconception, 11–13
misfortune, 26
misunderstanding, 12, 14
misuse, 37
mobile, 146, 204
model, 70, 97
modeling, 56, 57, 71
modification, 26
modulation, 53
molecule, 182
moment, 79, 106, 120, 141
monitoring, 36, 95, 117
mood, 55, 181
morale, 113
mortality, 16
motivation, 19
mouth, 131
movement, 131
mummification, 5
muscle, 69, 79, 84, 94, 95, 101, 102, 120, 129, 166
music, 13, 26, 71, 122, 127, 167, 199
mythology, 30

nanoneedles, 44
nanotechnology, 44, 46
nature, 7, 17, 23, 24, 70, 78, 84, 97, 105, 122, 131, 148, 165, 182, 183, 205
nausea, 1
necessity, 13, 19, 39, 71, 178
need, 5, 20, 39, 43–45, 62, 70, 71, 119, 126, 127, 169, 170, 186, 196, 200
needle, 1, 2, 4–10, 14, 17–19, 22–26, 29–46, 48, 49, 55, 56, 58, 59, 62–64, 67, 70–79, 82–85, 93, 94, 101–106, 114, 115, 117, 118, 120, 121, 125, 127, 133, 134, 136, 139, 144–147, 149, 155, 166–168, 170, 171, 173, 181–183, 188, 190–199, 201, 202, 205
Needlestick, 38
needlestick, 7, 31, 36, 42, 43
needlework, 26
neglect, 90, 183
nerve, 31, 41
network, 2, 83, 85, 120, 129, 142, 157, 171, 173, 201

neurobiology, 55
neuroimaging, 49
neuroscience, 203, 205
neurotransmission, 52
neurotransmitter, 52, 53, 55, 181
normalcy, 179
nose, 131
note, 24, 48, 56, 62, 67, 76, 78, 88, 95, 99, 101, 112, 117, 118, 121, 133, 144, 182, 191
number, 12, 47
nurse, 127
nursing, 196
nurture, 157, 183
nutrition, 186

object, 1, 75
obstinacy, 155
offer, 4, 5, 31, 33, 45, 55, 73, 77, 79, 82, 105, 109, 111, 112, 140, 142, 144, 152, 157, 164, 167, 172, 179, 186, 193, 201, 202, 204
offering, 5, 32, 43, 71, 120, 144, 153, 160, 167
on, 1, 3–5, 8, 11, 12, 16–20, 25–30, 32–38, 44, 45, 47–49, 52, 53, 55, 56, 60–64, 67, 70, 71, 74, 78, 79, 86, 88, 94, 97, 101, 102, 112–114, 116, 118, 120, 129, 131–134, 136, 137, 139, 140, 142, 145, 146, 148, 150, 152, 155, 157, 158, 170–172, 177, 179, 181–186, 188, 192, 193, 195–198, 200–202
one, 4, 13, 26, 38, 43, 56, 61, 63, 72, 78, 79, 105, 106, 108–110, 113, 119, 122, 148, 166, 177–179
online, 2, 132, 143–146, 173, 197, 201, 203, 204
onset, 55
opening, 25
openness, 108
opportunity, 83, 115, 167, 172
option, 24, 31, 105, 116, 117, 166
order, 17, 29, 53, 119, 134, 177, 203
organization, 20
origin, 8, 9
other, 12, 24–26, 28, 29, 36, 39, 40, 47, 48, 50, 58–62, 64, 73, 75, 88, 102, 109, 116, 118, 133, 134, 157, 166, 173, 178, 184, 188, 191, 193, 197, 199, 200, 202, 204
outlet, 58, 73, 114, 120, 199
output, 203
outreach, 144
overuse, 37
overview, 86
oxygen, 48

pace, 76, 96, 204
pain, 6–8, 26, 27, 30, 32, 39, 41, 42, 44–46, 56, 58, 62, 63, 67, 68, 70, 79, 115, 125, 194, 197, 203
painting, 73, 115, 120, 122, 132
pairing, 100, 102
palpation, 28
panic, 1, 4, 12, 14, 48, 60, 63, 64, 72, 76, 134, 143, 155, 157, 184
paralysis, 60
parent, 56, 70
parenting, 185

part, 11, 49, 116, 118, 121, 127, 133, 141, 178, 193
participation, 40, 112
passage, 6, 25, 26
past, 2, 3, 8, 12, 62, 83, 125, 204
path, 2, 61, 83, 144, 148, 150
patience, 2, 80, 82, 102, 123, 127, 133, 151, 177
patient, 7, 17, 23, 24, 29, 31–37, 39, 41, 42, 44–46, 85, 99, 108, 161, 165, 167–170, 188, 195, 197, 199
peer, 19, 85, 88, 96, 109, 111–113, 122, 132, 133, 149, 167, 168
penetration, 34
people, 26, 109, 155, 173
perception, 38, 67, 184, 194
performance, 34
period, 23
perpetuation, 8
perseverance, 96, 123, 133
persistence, 8, 9, 52, 177
person, 2, 5, 26, 39, 56, 57, 61, 64, 72, 108, 109, 119, 121, 130, 131, 133, 134, 151, 152, 154, 155, 158, 173, 174, 177
personnel, 146
perspective, 16, 79, 94, 111, 114, 132, 179, 202
pharmacology, 190
phenomenon, 58, 177
philanthropic, 146, 202
phlegm, 22
phobia, 1–10, 14–20, 31, 33, 39, 46, 55, 57–59, 61, 64, 68, 70, 72, 74, 78, 82, 83, 86–88, 101, 103–106, 114, 115, 117, 118, 122, 134, 136, 139, 140, 144–147, 149, 154, 155, 157, 158, 161, 166–168, 170, 171, 173, 181–183, 190–196, 198–200, 202–205
physiology, 18
picture, 56
place, 29, 32, 47
placement, 8
plan, 82, 94, 118, 119, 121–123, 133, 192, 193
planning, 15, 60, 76, 169
platform, 80, 110
play, 7–9, 21, 25, 34, 43, 53, 55–59, 70, 71, 74–77, 80–82, 85, 86, 88, 89, 99, 109, 111, 116, 120, 132, 136, 147, 171, 181–183, 185, 193, 196, 198, 204
playing, 71, 85
playroom, 75, 77
poetry, 26
point, 36, 105, 115, 143
policy, 145, 147, 195, 196, 198, 199, 202
polio, 36
polyethylene, 33
polypropylene, 33
popularity, 32, 38
population, 37
portal, 25
portion, 37
potential, 5, 7, 8, 13, 17–19, 23, 28–31, 34, 35, 37, 39, 40, 44–46, 48, 49, 52, 55, 72, 86, 115, 117, 118, 125, 166, 181, 182, 188, 190, 193, 198–202

pottery, 25
power, 27, 29, 49, 113, 130, 140, 141, 143, 145, 146, 199
powerlessness, 58
practice, 5, 22, 23, 27–29, 36–38, 76, 85, 94, 99, 102, 106, 108, 109, 131, 132, 172, 178, 181
Prana, 25
precision, 8, 31, 35, 36, 44
predisposition, 2, 58, 181, 183
presence, 58, 59, 64, 86, 94, 149, 167
present, 74, 79, 95, 106, 120, 141, 151
preservation, 6
pressure, 1, 25, 28, 47, 118
pretend, 75–77, 85
prevalence, 3, 4, 16, 18, 43, 144, 186, 196
prevention, 16, 36, 38, 95
principle, 39, 187
priority, 45, 121
privacy, 172
procedure, 4, 39, 71, 74, 75, 88, 121, 122, 127, 132, 143, 166, 196–198
process, 2, 10, 22, 25, 33, 34, 49, 50, 58, 59, 61, 62, 71, 73–75, 77, 79–82, 84, 85, 94–97, 99–102, 111, 114–116, 120, 133, 141, 142, 148, 149, 157, 167, 171–173, 175, 185, 202
processing, 1, 49, 50, 55, 68, 76, 114, 125, 149, 185
production, 21, 31, 33, 34, 42
professional, 2, 12, 16, 19, 69, 74, 77, 80, 105, 108, 112, 121, 122, 127, 130, 133, 138, 171, 173, 178, 191, 193
program, 185–187
programming, 19
progress, 5, 7, 8, 14, 24, 76, 78, 82, 84, 95, 96, 102, 113, 116, 119, 131, 133, 136, 141, 142, 187, 202
progressing, 64, 77, 130
proliferation, 37
prominence, 34
promise, 8, 33, 131, 135, 183, 189
proportion, 64
propranolol, 191
prospect, 48
protection, 6
provide, 4, 11, 12, 17–20, 29, 39, 43, 44, 46, 48, 55, 57–59, 61, 63, 64, 68, 69, 71, 73–75, 78–80, 83–88, 96, 101, 105, 106, 109–111, 113–115, 117, 119, 120, 122, 127, 131–134, 140, 145, 146, 149, 153, 158, 160, 164–167, 173, 177–179, 181, 185, 194, 195, 198–202, 204, 205
provider, 2, 7, 84, 85, 171, 172, 195, 198
provision, 146, 154
psyche, 67
psychoeducation, 64, 75, 94, 131
psychologist, 127
psychology, 20, 203, 205
public, 17, 36, 37, 40, 48, 144, 147, 197
pulse, 28
puncture, 22
punishment, 32
puppet, 185

purpose, 70, 71, 75, 84, 116, 141, 150
pursuit, 24, 149, 150

quality, 2–4, 10, 12, 15, 23, 28, 32, 33, 35, 37, 38, 42, 61, 63, 64, 68, 90, 130, 177, 193, 198, 199
question, 15, 79
questioning, 97

Rachel, 4, 5
Rachel vividly, 4
range, 13, 41, 64, 67, 71, 72, 149, 166, 183, 185, 186, 193
rapport, 80, 94, 119
rate, 1, 9, 47, 48, 63, 67, 72, 101, 118, 129, 155, 190
rationale, 81, 94
reach, 3, 117, 144, 145, 202
reaction, 47
readiness, 76, 185
reality, 17, 19, 102–105, 133, 166, 167, 193, 197, 201, 203, 204
realm, 25, 169
reassurance, 57, 71, 82, 84, 114, 122, 171
Rebecca, 139
receptor, 52, 55
recognition, 29, 30, 38, 196
recovery, 2, 5, 15, 59, 61, 81, 82, 132, 143, 144, 146, 149
recycling, 40
reduction, 40, 43, 131, 143, 178, 197
reflection, 62, 114–116, 120, 140, 142, 179
region, 68, 125
regulation, 18, 50, 52, 53, 55, 57, 72–74, 114, 149, 181, 182, 184, 185
reinforcement, 8, 9
relapse, 95
relationship, 38, 99, 134, 163, 184
relaxation, 48, 69, 73, 79, 80, 84, 88, 94, 95, 99–102, 105, 120, 121, 129, 131–133, 136, 137, 139, 141, 143, 149, 157, 166, 167, 178, 191, 196, 203
release, 32, 45, 47, 48, 52, 68, 73
relevance, 23
reliance, 32
relief, 9, 36, 116, 117, 133, 148, 149, 178
reluctance, 14
removal, 22, 42
repair, 22, 25
representation, 115
research, 12, 17, 19, 20, 28, 29, 32, 33, 35, 40, 41, 44, 53, 55, 83, 91, 129, 146, 147, 167, 168, 181–183, 197–203
resilience, 2, 5, 15, 38, 70, 71, 76, 77, 80, 83–85, 89, 94, 101, 102, 109, 120, 121, 132, 136, 140, 142, 146, 149, 150, 166, 178, 179, 183, 184, 187
resistance, 33, 43
resource, 38, 45, 201
respect, 46, 154, 172
respiration, 48
respite, 178, 179
response, 1, 9, 11, 12, 18, 47–50, 52, 55–60, 62–64, 67, 68, 74–79, 94, 96, 98–102,

118, 120, 125, 131, 132, 136, 141, 166, 190, 191, 201
responsibility, 38, 43, 168
rest, 1
restoration, 24
restructuring, 10, 19, 48, 68, 78–80, 97–99, 131, 136
result, 3, 14, 16, 41, 48, 68, 78, 88, 143, 144, 157, 182, 195
reuptake, 55
reuse, 23, 32, 38
revelation, 7
right, 2, 39, 43, 59, 70, 130, 143, 144, 171, 173
rigor, 198
risk, 1, 3, 7, 8, 22–24, 31–34, 36–38, 40, 42–44, 68, 118, 126, 143, 146, 181–183, 186
ritual, 26
role, 6–10, 17–19, 21, 22, 25, 27, 29, 33–36, 43, 49, 50, 53, 55–57, 59, 68, 70–73, 76, 80–82, 84–89, 93, 99, 105, 109, 111, 116, 120, 132, 136, 137, 142, 146, 147, 152, 158, 162, 171, 174, 179, 181–183, 185, 186, 190, 193, 194, 196, 198, 204
Rome, 22, 24
root, 28, 62, 137
routine, 1, 3, 4, 64, 72, 74, 85, 89, 100, 120, 121, 148, 178

sadness, 61
safety, 7, 18, 23, 24, 31–33, 35–38, 40–44, 49, 71, 74, 82, 84, 114, 131, 167, 191, 194, 197, 198
salt, 6
sampling, 7, 32, 45
sanctuary, 116
sandplay, 185
Sarah, 4, 5, 69, 95, 105, 122, 127, 129, 130, 136, 143, 144, 156, 157
satisfaction, 161
scale, 182
scan, 131
scarcity, 200
scenario, 132, 156
scene, 101
schedule, 171
scheduling, 82
school, 16, 18, 77, 85, 86, 88, 89, 185, 196
science, 6, 30, 33
sclerosis, 24
sculpture, 115, 133
seating, 88
section, 8, 11, 16, 24, 27, 33, 35, 38, 41, 50, 55, 57, 61, 70, 72, 74, 77, 83, 86, 89, 99, 102, 106, 109, 116, 128, 134, 140, 143, 144, 148, 151, 154, 158, 161, 168, 171, 173, 177, 181, 184, 190, 193, 195, 198, 200
security, 57
sedation, 39, 166, 167, 191
seeking, 2–5, 12, 14, 19, 24, 62, 63, 65, 80, 105, 109, 125, 127, 129, 130, 142, 143, 146, 155, 156, 171, 173, 195, 197, 202
Sekhmet, 30

selection, 33, 76
self, 6, 15, 16, 19, 25, 27, 58, 61, 73, 74, 76, 77, 83–85, 94, 95, 114–116, 120, 121, 132, 140–142, 146, 149, 150, 156, 176–179, 184, 185
sense, 2, 57, 63, 64, 71, 73, 74, 79–82, 84, 85, 96, 98, 105, 106, 108, 109, 113–116, 120, 127, 131, 132, 136, 139, 141–143, 149, 150, 152, 167, 179, 185, 202, 204
sensitivity, 167, 195, 205
sequence, 182
series, 4, 47, 97, 115, 139
Serotonin, 181
serotonin, 55, 57, 181
service, 186
session, 76, 105, 143, 157, 192
set, 109
setting, 40, 85, 95, 115, 132, 142, 149, 161, 193
severity, 5, 13, 14, 55, 204
sewing, 5, 21, 25
shame, 2, 3, 14, 15, 19, 82, 128, 130, 145
shape, 10, 38, 56, 71, 187, 199
share, 18, 80, 85, 88, 109, 110, 113, 120, 132, 142, 145, 152, 167, 178, 197, 201
sharing, 43, 82, 83, 110, 113, 115, 136, 142, 143, 147, 166, 167, 172, 173, 197, 201, 203
sharp, 7, 23, 36, 42, 44, 115
sharpening, 33
shielding, 42
shift, 46, 179
shortness, 48, 60, 64
shot, 2
shoulder, 139
show, 151, 189
side, 117–119, 157, 166
sight, 1, 4, 60, 62, 64, 72, 95
sign, 2, 11, 61, 64, 194
signal, 98
significance, 12, 16, 26, 27, 29, 30, 37, 102, 202
silver, 21, 25, 28, 34
site, 28, 41
situation, 1, 39, 49, 64, 75, 85, 101
size, 13, 34, 67, 122
sketchbook, 116
skill, 23, 108, 151
skin, 6, 25, 31, 38, 45, 62
sleep, 121, 148, 179
smell, 121
society, 8, 12, 14, 16–18, 26, 35–38, 144, 147, 149, 150
sociology, 203, 205
software, 201
solace, 85, 136, 197
solution, 13, 43, 108, 122, 191–193
sorcery, 6
sound, 122
source, 5, 6, 48, 141, 146, 148, 187
space, 63, 73, 75, 78, 80, 81, 83, 113, 114, 116, 119, 132, 142, 145, 154, 157, 158, 168, 173, 174, 177, 197
spectrum, 18, 63, 64
spread, 7, 16, 31, 36, 40
staff, 86, 163, 164, 167, 196
standard, 36
starting, 77, 115, 117, 129, 136, 141, 166

state, 4, 47, 94, 99, 101, 102, 121, 122, 137, 200
status, 186
steel, 23, 27, 28, 33, 44
step, 2, 13, 26, 34, 76, 77, 94, 115, 119, 131, 144, 148, 155, 166, 170, 173, 178
stereotype, 11, 12
sterilization, 7, 22, 23, 32
stigma, 4, 13, 15, 40, 144, 194, 197, 198
stigmatization, 14, 15, 17
stimulation, 29, 79
stimulus, 50, 94, 100
sting, 24
stone, 21, 29, 30
stopping, 97–99
story, 130, 143, 144
storytelling, 84
strain, 4, 179
strand, 25
strategy, 43, 58, 122
strength, 15, 38, 47, 62, 142, 149
stress, 1, 16, 48, 55, 68, 72, 79, 99, 106, 109, 118, 121, 131, 148, 149, 163, 178, 179, 182
structure, 1, 49
struggle, 4, 80, 83, 141, 149
student, 4, 88, 200
study, 69, 88, 201
subject, 5, 32, 152
subsection, 201
substance, 61
success, 80, 86, 95, 129, 130, 141, 143, 144, 146, 147, 166
suffering, 151, 194
suggestion, 139
summary, 50, 199
superstition, 6
support, 2, 4, 5, 12–14, 16–20, 39, 43, 55, 57, 59, 61, 63, 64, 69–71, 73–75, 77, 78, 80–86, 88, 89, 92, 96, 99, 101, 105, 109–113, 115–118, 120–123, 127, 129, 130, 132, 133, 136, 142–147, 149, 151, 154–158, 160, 161, 165, 167, 168, 170–173, 177–179, 184–186, 188, 192–197, 199–205
suppression, 48
surface, 34
surge, 7
surrounding, 7, 11, 18, 38, 39, 41, 56, 71, 84, 109, 120, 122, 144, 155, 194, 197, 204
survey, 201
survival, 47, 48
sweating, 1, 9, 48, 72, 118, 121, 155
sweaty, 63
symbolism, 18, 24–26, 30, 38, 115
syringe, 77
system, 4, 9, 25, 36, 47–49, 55, 57, 59, 88, 165, 182, 198, 199

taboo, 194
tailor, 78, 94, 96, 171, 195
talk, 74, 76, 77, 141
tape, 29
task, 22, 128
tattoo, 26
tattooing, 26
team, 172, 205
technique, 25, 28, 29, 67, 93, 97, 98, 100, 119, 131, 133, 137, 141

technology, 7, 24, 30, 32, 33, 38, 43–46, 132, 164, 201, 204, 205
tension, 80
term, 3, 19, 41, 61, 95, 117, 183, 184, 191
terror, 4
test, 127, 198
testament, 130
testing, 36
thalamus, 49
the United States, 185
theory, 9, 10, 22, 23
therapist, 2, 69, 74–78, 80, 94–96, 101, 102, 105, 114–116, 129–132, 136, 143, 144, 192
therapy, 5, 10, 12, 15, 18, 19, 23–25, 28, 29, 58, 62, 64, 68, 69, 74–80, 82, 84, 85, 88, 95, 96, 100, 102–105, 113–116, 118, 120–123, 129–133, 136, 141–144, 149, 166, 167, 172, 178, 185, 187, 190–193, 197, 199, 201, 204, 205
thinking, 8, 106
thought, 1, 63, 64, 72, 78, 93, 98, 99, 141, 143
thread, 25
threat, 47–49, 68
threshold, 67
time, 6, 9, 21, 22, 24, 29, 30, 44, 47, 55, 63, 64, 68, 69, 75, 77, 78, 80, 95, 96, 98, 99, 102, 108, 113, 127, 129, 131, 136, 141, 143, 148, 149, 166, 178
tip, 30, 33, 44
tissue, 31, 34, 42, 44, 45
today, 6, 26, 29, 33
tolerance, 76, 82, 84, 141, 192, 193
tool, 5, 45, 116, 121, 146, 149, 192
touch, 139
toy, 75–77
tracking, 55
trade, 23
trail, 26
training, 43, 86, 88, 163, 164, 186, 195, 196, 198, 199, 204
trait, 182
transformation, 25, 26, 137, 140, 148
transmission, 7, 31, 36, 38, 40, 41, 43, 56, 204
transparency, 40
transporter, 55
trauma, 12, 19, 42, 58, 59, 75, 77–80, 149, 183–187
treatment, 2, 3, 10, 12, 14, 17, 19, 24, 28, 55–63, 68, 70, 74–77, 81–83, 102, 104, 105, 116–119, 121–123, 126, 129, 130, 133, 134, 136, 141, 143, 144, 146, 161, 164–169, 171, 175, 177, 181, 182, 188, 189, 191–195, 197–202, 205
trepidation, 6
trial, 202
trigger, 14, 15, 64, 67, 168
trust, 17, 59, 81, 83, 94, 114, 119, 151, 152, 154, 159, 173–175, 177, 194, 195
trusting, 70
truth, 61
trypanophobia, 1–5, 7–14, 16, 17, 37, 45, 48–50, 55–57,

59–64, 67–86, 88–93, 95, 96, 98–102, 105, 106, 108–123, 125–158, 160, 161, 163–177, 179, 181–184, 186–205
trypanophobic, 8, 15, 17, 19, 86–89, 92, 101, 119, 151–154, 156, 161–165, 167, 174, 198, 199, 203
turning, 36, 143

understanding, 2–5, 8, 10–14, 16–20, 23, 28, 29, 50, 53, 56, 57, 62–64, 71, 74, 75, 77, 80–83, 85, 86, 92, 109, 115, 119, 120, 122, 129, 130, 134, 136, 140, 144, 145, 147–149, 151, 154–158, 160, 161, 163, 167, 168, 171–174, 177, 179, 182, 183, 193, 195, 196, 198–201, 203–205
uneasiness, 63
union, 25
unit, 172
unity, 116
up, 40, 63, 76, 82, 95, 148, 170, 182, 198
urgency, 39
usability, 34
usage, 24, 37, 43
use, 5–7, 13, 19, 23, 24, 26–33, 35, 36, 38–40, 42–45, 60, 61, 75, 101, 114, 116, 127, 133, 139, 166, 197, 199, 203
utilization, 203

vaccination, 4, 15, 16, 36, 40, 69, 89
validation, 73, 96, 113, 115, 142, 149, 152
validity, 12, 79, 97
variety, 62, 75, 105, 157
velocity, 45
venom, 23, 24
view, 95
violence, 183
visibility, 196, 201
vision, 25, 35
visit, 143, 170
visual, 26, 48, 49, 75, 84, 115, 133, 167, 199
visualization, 113, 129, 139, 140, 143, 166
volunteer, 113
vulnerability, 26, 55, 57, 58, 126

wait, 163
waiting, 163, 167, 196
warning, 72
waste, 37, 40
water, 40
way, 5, 17, 24, 25, 33, 36, 43, 63, 75, 76, 78, 80, 85, 92, 102, 112, 114, 141, 145, 149, 162, 182, 183, 198, 199
weakness, 2, 11, 61, 62, 64, 194
wedding, 25
welfare, 32
well, 2–4, 8, 12, 16, 24, 25, 27–29, 33, 38–41, 48, 58, 61, 62, 65, 68, 70, 72, 74, 77, 81–83, 85–88, 95, 99, 106, 109, 110, 113, 114, 117, 118, 121, 122, 128, 133, 142, 146, 148–150, 153, 154, 156, 157, 168, 171, 177–179, 182, 185, 205

whole, 16, 148
willingness, 40
willpower, 62
wire, 33, 34
wisdom, 29
witchcraft, 6
woman, 4, 69, 95, 105, 127, 129, 136, 139, 143
work, 4, 5, 16, 37, 71, 82, 88, 95, 99, 101, 108, 116, 118, 119, 122, 123, 130, 133, 144–146, 165, 166, 190, 193, 194, 198, 199, 203, 205
worker, 38
world, 5, 28, 41, 42, 75, 95, 148, 192, 198
worry, 134
writing, 202

year, 4, 76, 88–90, 95, 105, 127, 129, 136, 139, 143
yoga, 121, 148

zone, 85

Printed by
Libri Plureos GmbH · Friedensallee 273
22763 Hamburg · Germany

9 781998 557752